Advances in Spatial Science

The Regional Science Series

This series contains scientific studies focusing on spatial phenomena, utilising theoretical frameworks, analytical methods, and empirical procedures specifically designed for spatial analysis. Advances in Spatial Science brings together innovative spatial research utilising concepts, perspectives, and methods relevant to both basic science and policy making. The aim is to present advances in spatial science to an informed readership in universities, research organisations, and policy-making institutions throughout the world. The type of material considered for publication in the series includes: Monographs of theoretical and applied research in spatial science; state-of-the-art volumes in areas of basic research; reports of innovative theories and methods in spatial science; tightly edited reports from specially organised research seminars.

The series and the volumes published in it are indexed by Scopus.

For further information on the series and to submit a proposal for consideration, please contact Johannes Glaeser (Senior Editor Economics) Johannes.glaeser@springer.com.

More information about this series at https://link.springer.com/bookseries/3302

Elisa Panzera

Cultural Heritage and Territorial Identity

Synergies and Development Impact on European Regions

Springer

Elisa Panzera
Politecnico di Milano
Milan, Italy

ISSN 1430-9602 ISSN 2197-9375 (electronic)
Advances in Spatial Science
ISBN 978-3-030-94467-4 ISBN 978-3-030-94468-1 (eBook)
https://doi.org/10.1007/978-3-030-94468-1

This Springer imprint is published by the registered company Springer Nature Switzerland AG
The registered company address is: Gewerbestrasse 11, 6330 Cham, Switzerland

Foreword

Culture is widely recognized as a fundamental component of the identity of nations, countries and places. Cultural heritage therefore—considered as the set of all legacies of an artistic or cultural, material or immaterial nature that have survived up to the present day, a storage of collective memories—represents a crucial specificity and a factor of diversity and distinction in all countries, especially those with a long and rich historical evolution, and became a source of pride for the populations that hosted it and a source of interest and passion (sometimes excessive!) for foreigners. Interestingly enough, the ESDP—the *European Spatial Development Perspective* produced in 1999 after a long political and cultural interaction among the Ministries of the Union's countries involved—begins and ends with a reference to the European cultural heritage: its typical "variety", its link with "regional identities", its role in "enriching the citizens' quality of life".

And this cultural variety is supposed to be "potentially one of the most significant development factors for the EU", in line with the new dimension of European policy launched by the ESDP, namely "the Territory". This crucial message has been widely shared by the subsequent policy debate, the cultural, research and scientific elaboration and the consequent policy actions, at the European and at the national level, not just in Europe. But it has been largely interpreted in a single main sense, economically important but conceptually poor: a development factor working through the activation of tourism, understood as a comprehensive *filière*, encompassing international demand, direct services supply and a plethora of investment processes, from transport infrastructure to real estate and construction.

The novelty of the message was understood much later, when the multiple dimensions of the role of cultural heritage were explored in depth by scholars and international institutions—the Council of Europe, the European Commission, the OECD and UNESCO—and comprehensively presented in terms of benefits and impacts by the *Cultural Heritage Counts for Europe*, 2015 Report, co-funded by the Culture Programme of the European Commission. The link with the creation of a sense of awareness of national and place identities was justified by a host of ad hoc case studies.

Yet, the impact of cultural heritage on society—outside the effects through tourism—was restricted to the cultural, the social and the psychological dimensions: notable results were achieved in the direction of the creation of a sense of belonging to the wider human community and consequently of the nurturing of a higher social cohesion spirit. But the economic effects—outside tourism—were always left unaddressed.

This work by Elisa Panzera—*Cultural Heritage and Territorial Identity: Synergies and Development Impacts on European regions*—represents a first step in the direction of filling this gap. It is part of a long-term scientific program launched by the Research Group on Regional and Urban Economics of the Politecnico di Milano devoted to the inspection of the economic role played by intangible forms of territorial capital in spatial development. Cognitive capital, social capital, identitarian capital, creativity and innovativeness are supposed to lift the effectiveness and productivity of more traditional, material forms of capital, creating what we call a "territorial relational surplus", conceptually similar to the surplus generated by technical progress in a time dimension. The studies concerning the role of cultural heritage face a further complication: elements like local identity, local cohesion or local creativity may not just enhance the economic role of cultural heritage but are at the same time an effect of the presence of cultural heritage.

This work has a double aim. The first aim is to critically analyze and compare the results of existing traditional works on the economic impact of cultural heritage through the action of tourism, and to fill the void left by some uninspected empirical and econometric issues such as the attractiveness of tourism destinations and their inclusion, together with the presence of cultural heritage, in a structural model of regional growth for the EU.

The second aim, more relevant in a scientific perspective, is to explore the cultural heritage / local identity nexus and its impact on economic growth in the EU regions. The exercise is based on the belief that such abstract, immaterial and mainly psychological aspects of the regional realm are possibly liable to be measured and can be included in a formalized quantitative model. In fact, the availability of a sound regional data base on values and perceptions of people collected by the Euro-Barometer provides sufficient security and a guarantee of credible results.

As shown before, the theme is culturally fascinating, but presents a political interest too, widely underlined by the European Commission in recent years. The pace of European integration, its internal cohesion and the sentiment of trust itself toward the European institutions are put at risk in many cases by growing feelings of uncertainty, discontent, request for individual recognition, consequent localistic closure and egoism, which seem to hold a relative persistence and to drive local identities in a worrisome direction.

This undertaking looks difficult but worthwhile, and the results reward the effort and the courage involved. In fact, (local) identity is a multidimensional and multilayered concept referring to a collective psychological condition; dealing in a quantitative way with such a complex concept is a complicated matter, as identity cannot be measured through a one-dimensional, continuous metric. The methodological choice made by the author can be condensed in two words: selection—among the relevant dimensions—and classification—among the European regions.

In the present times—characterized by identity politics, widespread social concerns for jobs and remunerations but also by a multiplication and expanding geographical reach of interpersonal networks—and considering the new challenges for the European Union, the relevant parameters with which to consider alternative modes of expression of territorial identities are rightly selected in the following way. On the one side, the co-presence of two founding elements of collective identity, namely similarity (alone) and similarity *and* solidarity; on the other the spatial reach of main interpersonal networks, distinguishing a local reach and a local *and* European reach (in a multi-level interpretation of identities). The consequent classification of four "patterns" of regional identity—"individualistic localism", "parochial localism", "place-less cosmopolitanism" and "inclusive cosmopolitanism"—is built utilizing the regional answers to the appropriate questions present in the Euro-Barometer in the last decade. The moving picture of European regions that emerges from this classification represents in itself a brilliant and persuasive result (or by-product) of this work, showing at the same time the regional differences inside countries, the different psychological attitudes tied to geographical (urban/rural, accessibility) or economic conditions (wealth, innovativeness), the relative stability of the classification and the main typologies of the recent shifts toward a decreasing sense of solidarity.

The different patterns of local identity are included in complex econometric models, looking for the presence of a "territorial surplus" which could be attributed, *ceteris paribus*, to the single typologies in a differential way, synergically reinforcing the effects of the local presence of cultural heritage. Positive and statistically significant results are attained, with very interesting economic—but also "political"—interpretations.

For sure, a renovated attention to the preservation and valorization of European cultural heritage, a support to its non-trivial fruition and the effort to underline and communicate its deep symbolic meaning are actions likely to reinforce a diffused sense of belonging to the Union, with notable potential results in terms of both social cohesion and wealth. We should thank the author for this careful, competent, skilful and original work, shading new light on a complex but crucial issue for Europe and European citizens.

Roberto Camagni
Emeritus Professor of Urban and
Regional Economics
Politecnico di Milano
Milan, Italy

Acknowledgments

I would like to express my sincere gratitude to some special persons that have been of essential importance for the accomplishment of this book.

I am deeply grateful to professor Roberta Capello for being an inspiring, tireless, energetic and careful guide.

I would like to offer my special thanks to professor Roberto Camagni for his invaluable and precious support, for his kindness and his always insightful suggestions.

I would like to extend my sincere gratitude to the urban and regional economics research group and to the Department of Architecture, Built Environment and Construction Engineering at Politecnico di Milano. The multidisciplinary approach that permeates the Department is extremely useful to expanding views and adopting different perspectives.

A special mention goes to professors Valeria Pracchi, Leïla Kebir, Thomas de Graaff and Henri de Groot.

Finally, I am deeply grateful to Jacopo for being my main and affectionate supporter and for always encouraging me to face and overcome challenges, and to my family for being a constant, stable and respectful light in all the stages of my career.

Acknowledgments

Contents

Chapter 1
The Socio-Economic Impact of Cultural Heritage: Setting the Scene

1.1 Introduction and Motivation

It is widely recognized that cultural heritage represents a fundamental resource for individuals, communities, countries and different generations. In general terms, it can be argued that cultural heritage is an essential and integral element of the human condition: intellectual, psychological and moral. National and international institutions, non-governmental organizations and local communities believe that cultural heritage carries an intrinsic and significant value that needs to be safeguarded and promoted. According to the European Commission "*Europe's cultural heritage is much more than a repository of knowledge; it is also a shared resource, and a common good. Heritage makes a major contribution to defining the identity of European citizens and it is a resource for social cohesion and economic development*" (European Commission, 2014, p. 5). ICOMOS[1] states that cultural heritage holds spiritual, cultural, social and economic value and UNESCO[2] acknowledges it as of outstanding universal interest and value.

Cultural heritage can be considered jointly as a source of socio-economic development, societal cohesion, and individual well-being, facilitator of international relations, identity creator, cultural diversity supporter, locational factor and symbolic element, among others. The well-known and well-accepted major importance of cultural heritage notwithstanding, public administrations often neglect to adequately protect their heritage because of lack of money, scarce interest and different priorities. Even though cultural heritage is universally recognized as a potential and powerful generator of positive change, many issues still threaten its appropriate safeguarding and enhancing such as bad management, lack of resources or expertise and inadequate planning.

Recognizing, analyzing and trying to prove the powerful role that cultural heritage plays in many aspects of our societies is a challenge which is worth accepting. By

---

[1] International Council of Monuments and Sites.

[2] The United Nations Educational, Scientific and Cultural Organization.

E. Panzera, *Cultural Heritage and Territorial Identity*, Advances in Spatial Science,
https://doi.org/10.1007/978-3-030-94468-1_1

expanding the discussion on the role of heritage as a valuable resource for local communities, nations or supranational entities, a shift in the public and individual attitude toward cultural heritage can take place. Conservation and valorization activities, rather than representing a mere moral duty, become a forward-looking and effective strategy for development in its broader sense. Once the beneficial outcomes stemming from the presence of heritage are fully recognized, the chance for heritage preservation to concentrate on political priorities turns into concreteness.

In this sense, given the still marginal consideration saved for cultural heritage mainly in terms of political preferences and, consequently, of dedicated financial resources, much space for research aimed at detecting, substantiating and validating the multifaceted potentialities of heritage is still available.

Furthermore, the global health crisis that the world is nowadays facing due to the COVID-19 pandemic spread is affecting people's health but also economic and relational systems involving traditional productive processes and use of goods and services including the cultural ones. Within this critical context, there is an actual risk that less care, consideration and financial support will be dedicated to cultural heritage. To face this emergency, what instead is needed is a strategic and systemic approach to culture able to propose sustainable solutions in the long run based on reinforced predictive capacity and substantial evidence. Cultural heritage needs to be considered and activated as a relevant stimulus for helping to overcome this global challenge. By studying and validating different ways in which the presence of the cultural heritage can be beneficial for local communities, a more precise understanding of the relevant role of heritage as an engine for improving and enhancing local conditions can be reached.

Therefore, within this context, this book aims at exploring and delving into the realm of cultural heritage and, more specifically, at taking a step forward in the direction of thoroughly investigating some of the mechanisms through which the cultural heritage, interpreted as a shared resource, contributes to enhancing local conditions.

It must be noted that dealing with cultural heritage presents a first challenge related to its definition and characterization. The founding element of cultural heritage is represented by *culture* which is an extremely complicated concept to be detailed and delineated. In fact, there are multiple interpretations and meanings of culture, which vary over time, over space and over societies and systems of thought. What is more, the concept of *heritage* is not univocal; it can be referred to individuals, societies and nations, it is in constant evolution and, when associated with *culture*, it assumes all the same complexities and facets. Furthermore, cultural heritage stimulates the interest of many disciplines such as, just to mention a few, philosophy, history, sociology or anthropology that certainly adopt different perspectives and angles.

A second challenge undertaken with this book refers to the adoption of an economic perspective. Analyzing cultural heritage through the lens of the economist adds further elements of complexity. Cultural heritage is imbued with several values that seem to be rather far from the sphere of economy such as aesthetic, spiritual or historical values. Besides, when economics is associated with cultural heritage a perceived risk related to the potential treatment of heritage as a regular economic commodity causes concern among cultural professionals or academics. Certainly, one of the main challenges when an economic perspective is adopted—a challenge for economists, firstly—regards the attempt to associate measures, evaluations or estimations with a multifaceted element such as cultural heritage and its multiple effects without neglecting its peculiar nature and its characterizing socio-cultural values. However, since cultural heritage is a common public resource, it is extremely important to deal with it in economic terms to prevent negligence and market failure issues from causing deterioration and decline. Cultural heritage should be preserved and valorized as a shared resource embedding the accumulation of common experiences and common values that end up forming our collective capital. Besides recognizing that cultural heritage owns specific values, several spillovers or impacts are generated by the presence of heritage, which is often associated with, among others, increased societal cohesion, individual well-being and also economic development.

In this sense, a third challenge of this book is related to identifying and exploring different channels through which the endowment of cultural heritage is beneficial in economic terms to local society. More specifically, two main channels will be taken into consideration: through tourism and through territorial identity enhancement. When the economic literature deals with the role that heritage plays in economic development, the most studied and investigated channel is tourism. In fact, cultural heritage, through its symbolic power, contributes to creating a context specificity and a pleasant atmosphere which attract tourists curious to appreciate different experiences, cultures and ways of living. This tourist attractiveness, in turn, is beneficial for local economic dynamics. Since this mechanism is the most traditional and the one most examined by the economic literature it is certainly relevant to include it within a work that explores the role of heritage in influencing economic dynamics. Even though this channel has been already researched by the economic literature, some innovative perspectives and elements will be proposed, namely, the use of different typologies and measures of cultural heritage and a joint discussion on the relationships between cultural heritage, tourism and economic development.

A second and more innovative channel is explored within the context of this book: it is related to the role that the presence of cultural heritage plays in shaping or enhancing territorial identities and to the subsequent economic consequences. The idea is to relate cultural heritage to local socio-cultural and psychological characteristics and to find out which are the benefits and spillovers in terms of economic development. An intangible, soft and socio-cultural channel which is related with local context and local atmosphere is taken into consideration. It goes without saying that a local context comprises many different elements such as, among others, social cohesion, community participation, creativity and innovation. The choice has been made to examine the domain of identity since it is an extremely relevant territorial and contextual element which is believed to show strong interrelations with cultural heritage on the one side, and which, on the other side, is able to influence economic development. The hypothesis, in this latter case, derives from the literature on socio-psychological attitudes conducive to interpersonal trust, cooperation capability and openness, leading in the economic sphere to reduction of transaction costs and—more interestingly, in a dynamic setting—to reduction of technological and economic uncertainty, and through this, to innovation. Such interrelations and synergies between cultural heritage, territorial identity and economic development have been hypothesized on an abstract theoretical basis but have never been studied from an economic perspective and, what counts more, have never been empirically tested.

As mentioned before, by acknowledging and recognizing the socio-economic benefits stemming from the presence of cultural heritage, a more careful and conscientious attitude could be adopted by policy makers and more targeted policies might be implemented guaranteeing the right balance between cultural heritage valorization and safeguarding. As Throsby (1999, p. 9) well explains, "*It is becoming clearer that cultural 'ecosystems' underpin the operations of the real economy, affecting the way people behave and the choices they make. [...] by allowing heritage to deteriorate, by failing to sustain the cultural values that provide people with a sense of identity, and by not undertaking the investment needed to maintain and increase our stock of intangible cultural capital, will likewise cause cultural systems to break down, cultural and social identity of local areas to deteriorate, with consequent loss of welfare and economic output*".

Therefore, within the context of this book, cultural heritage, as also discussed in Carta (2007), will be simultaneously considered as a founding element of territorial and community identity and as an engine for a development which is local as regards resources, global in relations and self-sustainable in its modalities. In this sense, cultural heritage will be acknowledged and examined in its tight and solid connection with the territory in which it is located. In other words, cultural heritage cannot be isolated and abstracted from the environment to which it belongs since it entertains substantial relations with the territorial elements and assets whether they are tangible or intangible, geographical or artificial, socio-cultural, cognitive or relational in nature.

In order to reflect on the discourse and the challenges previously proposed, the following sections of this chapter will be dedicated to clarifying and contextualizing the concept of cultural heritage as it has been defined both by the literature and by the international institutions (Sect. 1.2); providing some background literature on the economic works devoted to examining cultural heritage (Sect. 1.3); explaining in detail which are the identified literature gaps, illustrating the main reasons, hypotheses and novelties behind the two chosen channels (tourism and territorial identity enhancement); and proposing the conceptual framework and structure adopted throughout the book (Sects. 1.4, 1.5 and 1.6).

1.2 The Concept of Cultural Heritage and the Evolution of Its Definitions

Taking on the challenge of delving into the realm of cultural heritage and exploring it from the economic perspective, the first issue to be faced regards the definition, interpretation and characterization of cultural heritage itself. In fact, cultural heritage represents a complex, composite and multifaceted concept which escapes simple and simplistic definitions. Furthermore, it is not even a static notion as it changes over time, geographical areas and society beliefs. Many different disciplines study cultural heritage as their object of research and try to investigate the concept following different approaches and points of view. Anthropology, law, philosophy, history, sociology and economics, among others, discuss the cultural heritage using diverse methodologies and exploring different aspects of it (Lazzeretti & Cinti, 2001; Tosco, 2014). By analyzing the word, *cultural heritage* is composed of two main blocks, one related to *culture* and the other one related to *heritage*. In order to shed light on the comprehensive concept of cultural heritage, there is the need to clarify as much as possible which idea of culture it is considered in this work and what is the meaning of heritage.

In 1952, a book by Kroeber and Kluckhohn collected 167 different definitions of culture and grouped them according to different criteria and disciplines highlighting and proving the complexity of the term. As argued by Williams (1976, p. 87) "*culture*" is one of the two or three most complicated words in the English language mainly because "*it has now come to be used for important concepts in several distinct intellectual disciplines and in several distinct and incompatible systems of thought*". As Dalmas et al. (2015, p. 682) pointed out, culture is not just a multifaceted and dynamic concept but also "*lacks a common unit of account and may contain elements that cannot be easily expressed according to any quantitative or qualitative scale*".

Despite the difficulties in the attempt to define the concept of culture, many proposals have been made by the literature out of which Settis (2005)'s contribution will be considered hereinafter. Following his idea, it is possible to define culture according to three different approaches:

- anthropological and sociological: within this approach culture is intended as a collective ensemble of knowledge, habits and behaviors developed by a community, which can be considered as a mental collective programming that guides actions and determines forms of productions according to procedures, or functional or ritual behavior models, targeting specific shared aims. In this sense, culture is a dynamic concept: each culture changes over time also because of the influence of other cultures. This first definition is neutral and descriptive and does not carry any value judgment;
- historic, ethic, political: culture is here intended as the consequence of a structured society and of its rules targeting a common good. It involves a series of choices in accordance with values elaborated through its history and evaluated as positive, which guide the judgment and the behavior of the communities and are named as politics. Concepts and values such as citizenship, democracy, justice, equity, human dignity and, more generally, civil rights play a significant role;
- institutional: in this sense culture is oriented according to a system of values and is modeled inside institutions having the role of transmitting its cultural memory, exploring its potential and safeguarding it for future generations. Education in all its forms, university, research, institutions dealing with art and music, museums

and all the offices in charge of safeguarding landscapes, artistic heritage and environment are part of this type of culture.

All three approaches define culture and they sometimes overlap; one approach does not exclude the others and they might be subject to changes, evolutions and enlargements.

As characterized by these three approaches culture is both source and result of cultural outcomes that exist in both tangible and intangible forms. Signs, symbols, written works, languages, artifacts, written and oral traditions can all be considered as cultural outcomes that are simultaneously fruits and origin of culture. As argued by Throsby (2001) all these elements have the role of establishing a distinctive group identity. Therefore, talking about culture, the definitions are not limited to something artistic or creative but generalized to the totality of goods, objects, ideas and knowledge that a society or a group generates (Tosco, 2014). Moreover, some of them are public and common goods (e.g., language or traditions) while some others are private or mixed goods (e.g., artifacts or museums).

To introduce the concept of cultural heritage we need to highlight a fundamental feature related to the concept of *heritage* which is, as Dalmas et al. (2015) stated, its strong interrelation between contemporaneity and inheritance from the past. During Roman times, the properties transferred from generation to generation within a family were considered as heritage. Throughout the years the concept of heritage witnessed an expansion of its meaning in the sense that it can also refer to a group of people and not just to individuals or families. This aspect leads to the fact that the act of owning the heritage is no longer typically or exclusively physical but also moral. In other words, as per the individual or familiar type of heritage, the inheritance is mainly related to physical and tangible assets that remain in private hands across generations. If instead the concept of heritage is enlarged to encompass inheritance of groups or communities, the typology of inherited assets becomes completely different as it is not private anymore but common and it refers to shared assets and resources that can be both tangible (such as cultural landscapes) or intangible (such as traditions or values). The peculiar and essential characteristics of heritage can be identified in the memory which is embedded in it and the identity which is carried by it (Vecco, 2010).

Having understood that heritage could be perceived as a storage of a collective memory and a vehicle of identity, the question now regards what can be considered as cultural heritage. It goes without saying that not everything which is cultural in the sense that we previously explained can be recognized as cultural heritage. As Tosco (2014) pointed out, the past dimension is not enough for a cultural expression, of whichever typology, to become cultural heritage. It is the present society that elects, safeguards and promotes certain kinds of cultural expressions crowning them as legitimate parts of its cultural heritage. As highlighted by Gillman (2006), heritage is linked with the stories that a specific society tells about itself. These stories usually tend to prefer and glorify the achievements, therefore assigning the best role to that society, sometimes at the expenses of others. The understanding of the term *cultural heritage* passes through the analysis of its symbolic relationship with culture. As Blake (2000) pointed out, an active choice is the basis of what can be identified as heritage, out of the broader concept of culture, and what is consequently worth preserving and passing on to future generations. It is the process of designation, elevation and institutionalization carried on by the present society that creates heritage and that gives it an autonomous character with respect to culture. Citing from Williams (1981, p. 187) "*for tradition ("our cultural heritage") is self-evidently a process of deliberate continuity, yet any tradition can be shown, to be a selection and reselection of those significant received and recovered elements of the past which represent not a necessary but a desired continuity*". In fact, as argued by Peacock (1998), in most cases, what it is nowadays considered as cultural heritage was originally produced as a means for satisfying contemporary tastes and needs rather than deliberately conceived as heritage to be inherited by future generations (Vincente, 2010). A transformation process is therefore needed to convert the past expression of culture into the institutionalized entity of cultural heritage. By means of valuation of a specific cultural outcome, a decision is made to preserve some distinct objects, sites or places as they represent more than others something that belongs to the local community, that deserves to be handed down to future generations and that is precious, irreplaceable and essential to personal and collective identity (Avrami & Mason, 2000; Lowenthal, 2005; Peacock, 1995, 1978; Vincente, 2010).

Therefore, cultural heritage turns out to be a social construction (Vecco, 2010), a subjective concept (Throsby, 2001), a nomadic term (Hutter & Rizzo, 1997), a process and an experience (Ashworth, 2013). Cultural heritage, then, is not just old culture or, in other terms, culture accumulated in the past. It is rather a *selection* of old culture mainly based on the values carried by past cultural expressions and evaluated through the lens of contemporaneity. These values might assume different forms such as aesthetic value, historical value but also moral and ethical values. Hence, the distinction between past culture and cultural heritage lies in the *extraordinary* features of cultural heritage recognized by societies. If, on the one hand, culture is *ordinary*, as stated in the well-known definition of culture proposed by Raymond Williams, according to which culture includes all the expressions of the social life of a community, on the other hand, cultural heritage is *extraordinary*, because only what is considered (for any reason) exceptional deserves to be remembered and preserved. Consequently, what is recognized and designated as *extraordinary* is then institutionalized as cultural heritage.

This form of institutionalization of culture into cultural heritage is linked with an important and powerful political dimension. In fact, the decision regarding which cultural outcomes need to be considered and designated as cultural heritage is usually made by national State authorities or international intergovernmental organizations. This role can be considered of paramount relevance because cultural outcomes have an instrumental value that serves other intrinsic values such as aesthetic, knowledge or symbolic values and they can be associated with specific narratives related to the development of a certain society (Gillman, 2006). As well explained in Blake (2000), cultural heritage can be used to transmit a particular interpretation of the past and legitimize social and political ambitions. Beyond the political dimension, emotional impulses and intellectual perspectives matter in the discourse related to cultural heritage designation, preservation and valorization. In fact, it can be argued that cultural heritage is a sort of storage of identities, which is not so much linked with its material characteristics but rather to traditions, customs and historical or religious identification. As pointed out by Kamenka (1988), these aspects are essential for the human being and for individual and societal dignity, self-confidence and expression. A social function is attributed as well to cultural heritage, which is considered as an intellectual factor for the development of a community and as an identifier of historical and local societal identity (Canziani & Moioli, 2010; Pitruzzella, 2000).

Even though it seems nowadays clear that the concept of cultural heritage can be referred to many different cultural elements both in tangible and intangible forms and more or less related to exclusively and predominantly aesthetic or creative characteristics, the concept itself has experienced throughout the years a progressive evolution and enlargement. The interpretation and evolution of the concept of cultural heritage in its role in the restoration of the memory of places and in the creation of development and identification in its values cannot neglect the reading of Charters, Conventions and Documents dedicated to governing cultural heritage conservation, preservation and management (Carta, 2007). It can be argued that national legislation and international documentation represent the formal expression of the previously mentioned political decisions related to the institutionalization of cultural heritage, which is therefore worthy of protection and preservation (Blake, 2000).

As Vecco (2010) explains, the concept of artistic and archeological heritage was considered for the first time during the Athens Conference in 1931, without however providing a definition of it. The Hague Convention for the Protection of Cultural Property in the Event of Armed conflict (UNESCO, 1954) introduces in the disciplinary and normative language the term *cultural property* with a specific reference to the concept of property and defined as a list of characteristics. Any mention of the context, the territory and a cultural or relational system is missing here. It is the International Charter of Venice (ICOMOS, 1964, p. 1) which provides a first definition of heritage and a first clear reference to the context (even though treated as a mere background rather than an integral element entertaining relations and synergies with cultural heritage): "*Imbued with a message from the past, the historic monuments of generations of people remain to the present day as living witnesses of their age-old traditions. People are becoming more and more conscious of the unity of human values and regard ancient monuments as a common heritage. The common responsibility to safeguard them for future generations is recognized. It is our duty to hand them on in the full richness of their authenticity*". This first attempt to delineate a definition focused on "*the concept of historic monument*", following Article 1 of the same Charter, "*embraces not only the single architectural work but also the urban or rural setting in which is found the evidence of a particular civilization, a significant development or a historic event. This applies not only to great works of art but also to more modest works of the past which have acquired cultural significance with the passing of time*". Cultural heritage is here intended as a shared inheritance of traditions, values and knowledge and, therefore, a common responsibility should inspire conservative actions to preserve this heritage for future generations.

Following a series of other international recommendations, conventions and conferences (see for instance UNESCO Recommendation, 1968; UNESCO Convention, 1971), which gradually enlarged the typology of goods to be considered as heritage, it was the 1972 UNESCO Convention that introduced for the first time the expression "*cultural heritage*", a notion which, citing from Article 1 (p. 2) of the same Convention, consists of:

- *monuments: architectural works, works of monumental sculpture and painting, elements or structures of an archaeological nature, inscriptions, cave dwellings and combinations of features, which are of outstanding universal value from the point of view of history, art or science;*
- *groups of buildings: groups of separate or connected buildings which, because of their architecture, their homogeneity or their place in the landscape, are of outstanding universal value from the point of view of history, art or science;*
- *sites: works of man or the combined works of nature and man, and areas including archaeological sites which are of outstanding universal value from the historical, aesthetic, ethnological or anthropological point of view.*

This perspective goes in the direction of acknowledging and granting normative relevance to the fact that a definition of cultural heritage needs to include, together with historical and artistic characteristics, also relational, environmental and topographic elements. Territorial context is intended both as a physical space and a stratification of social, economic and institutional relations and cultural heritage becomes an integral and integrated element of the territorial context (Carta, 2007). The same 1972 UNESCO Convention is extremely relevant not just in definitory terms but also for the specific reference to the interactions between socio-economic aspects and cultural heritage and more specifically to the issues related to economic and financial sustainability of actions related to management and preservation of heritage. In fact, the Convention recognizes at page 1 that "*cultural heritage and the natural heritage are increasingly threatened with destruction not only by the traditional causes of decay, but also by changing social and economic conditions which aggravate the situation with even more formidable phenomena of damage and destruction; the deterioration or disappearance of any item of the cultural heritage constitutes a harmful impoverishment of the heritage of all the nations of the world; protection of this heritage at the national level often remains incomplete because of the scale of resources which it requires and of the insufficient economic, scientific and technological resources of the country where the property to be protected is situated*". This concept is further reinforced by the European Charter of the Architectural Heritage (Council of Europe, 1975) in which cultural heritage is explicitly recognized, among other characteristics, as an economic asset. Citing from the third principle of the Charter "*The architectural heritage is a capital of irreplaceable spiritual, cultural, social and economic value. Each generation places a different interpretation on the past and derives new inspiration from it. This capital has been built up over the centuries: the destruction of any part of it leaves us poorer, since nothing new that we create, however fine, will make good the loss. Our society now has to husband its resources. Far from being a luxury this heritage is an economic asset which can be used to save community resources*".

Even though an enlargement of the definition of cultural heritage, an inclusion of the territorial dimension and a recognition of economic relevance happened within the context of the previous mentioned documents, the classification proposed in these years dedicates attention to mainly material or tangible cultural heritage, keeping out all the cultural expressions not vehicled by a physical support. The crowning of intangible cultural heritage as legitimately to be safeguarded in the same way as tangible cultural heritage took place within the context of the 2003 UNESCO Convention. In Article 2, p. 5 of the same Convention "*oral traditions and expressions; performing arts; social practices, rituals and festive events; knowledge and practices concerning nature and the universe, traditional craftsmanship*" are defined as intangible cultural heritage. The international recognition of the relevance of both tangible and intangible cultural heritage gives the heritage itself the status of guarantor not only of artistic and historic values but also of moral, societal, ethical and political ones. The Council of Europe proposed in the Faro Convention in 2005 a definition of cultural heritage which encompasses all the aspects previously described: "*cultural heritage is a group of resources inherited from the past which people identify, independently of ownership, as a reflection and an expression of their constantly evolving values, beliefs, knowledge and traditions. It includes all aspects of the environment resulting from the interaction between people and places through time*" (Council of Europe, 2005, p. 2).

The Faro Convention is particularly important because for the first time the relationships and interactions between cultural heritage and people are recognized as having an essential and crucial role. Given the tight nexus and symbolic attachment between cultural heritage and local communities, local inhabitants should be involved as determinant actors in the process of selection of cultural heritage, in the reconstruction of its symbolic meanings and in its management. As highlighted in Canziani and Moioli (2010), if the involvement of local communities is ineffective or insufficient, or if the designation and valorization of heritage sites are limited to a top-down political/institutional process, no cultural heritage-related intervention will have implications on, or mirror in awareness, sense of belonging, re-interpretation processes and the historical appreciation or stimulation of new knowledge. As Zetti (2010) puts it, heritage is a full aspect of European citizens' way of life, an integral element of local identity. Therefore, citizens' participation in determining and defining what should be considered as heritage is of essential importance to assure the role and the respect for cultural heritage as a resource for self-sustainable development. In fact, a cultural outcome or object does not own a particular meaning or value per se, but rather when it is put in relationship with a specific society living in a certain territory. As Nadel and Rourke (1975) have argued, cultural heritage is not an absolute expertise field and there is no univocal or trivial way of defining heritage lists. It is however true that excluding the citizens' opinions and desires from the process results in misrepresenting the concept of cultural heritage itself. Since heritage is about a negotiation process on how the past should be used (see for instance Harvey, 2008; Olsson, 2010;

Smith, 2006; Storm, 2008), there is sometimes a divergence between what professionals, experts or politicians acknowledge as heritage and people's perspective. In other words, designation of heritage might aim at meeting various objectives such as cultural, social, economic or political objectives, put forward by different actors or stakeholders. The process of designation, definition, management and valorization or cultural heritage is complex and multi-scale, involving different actors and resulting in a more or less developed attachment of people to their heritage. As highlighted in Mälkki and Schmidt-Thomè (2010), several discourses related to cultural heritage need to be taken into consideration, for instance the role of diverse typologies of expertise in defining aims of conservation and preservation and the necessity to involve and empower citizens in decision-making processes related to heritage. There is a *systemic relationship* between cultural heritage and the visitors, citizens and all the other stakeholders (Canziani & Moioli, 2010). These aspects are related to the ways in which the different stakeholders are involved in the designation, management and preservation of cultural heritage and, even though they are worth mentioning here, they are much better discussed in the urban and regional planning literature (see for instance Oppio et al., 2015 and Stevenson, 2007).

Several main characterizing attributes and essences of cultural heritage are worth keeping in mind hereinafter. Cultural heritage represents a resource intended in the broader sense of the term for the territories and communities in which it is located. In fact, it is considered as a social, economic, environmental, relational and identitarian resource. Representing the expression of common values, beliefs and traditions, cultural heritage is a common and shared resource able to preserve memories and narratives of communities and places and to blend them with contemporaneity on condition that present community identifies with that heritage and recognizes it as such. The concept of cultural heritage is in constant evolution; it depends on spatial and temporal characteristics and it encompasses different degrees of materiality. Furthermore, it is not limited to a specific, distinct or individual cultural asset but it is most importantly related to a system of connections with the territory and environment in which it is located. The relationship between cultural heritage and its spatial, social, relational, economic and institutional context is of fundamental importance. This territorial perspective of cultural heritage will be maintained throughout the whole book.

Having clarified the complexity of defining and delineating the concept of heritage, the following section is dedicated to discussing cultural heritage according to an economic perspective describing the contributions that the economic literature has proposed so far to investigate this topic.

1.3 Cultural Heritage Through the Economic Perspective: Some Background Literature

1.3.1 Cultural Heritage as an Economic Resource: Peculiarities and Specificities

As evidenced in the previous section, it is nowadays widely recognized that cultural heritage is a valuable resource and asset for individuals, societies, countries and communities. Its economic relevance has been progressively acknowledged by both public institutions and academia to reach a full appreciation of its consequences for development. As argued in the European report "Getting Cultural Heritage to work for Europe" "*cultural heritage must be seen as a special, but integral component in the production of the European GDP and innovation, its growth process, competitiveness and in the welfare of European society*" (European Commission, 2015, p. 6). The essential role of cultural heritage has been very recently stressed in Europe, 2018 being designated "*European Year of Cultural Heritage*".

Within this context, opportunities and advantages for local communities and societies stemming from cultural heritage have been highlighted and a significant number of institutional bodies have been involved in the initiatives related to the program (i.e., the European Commission, the European Parliament, the Council of the European Union, the Committee of the Regions and the European Economic and Social Committee). As highlighted by Sciacchitano (2019), succeeding the European Year of Cultural Heritage, the European Commission developed for the first time a European Framework for Action on Cultural Heritage, revealing the need to recognize and make explicit the key role of heritage within European policies and programs. More specifically, cultural heritage is referred to as a *common good* and a *shared resource* able to generate social and economic improvements (European Commission, 2019, p. 4). According to the European Commission, together with culture, society and environment, economy is one of the four areas on which cultural heritage exerts its influence (CHCfE Consortium, 2015).

By adopting this comprehensive perspective, the risk of evoking criticism from the heritage sector claiming that the economic perspective could undermine the cultural and social reasoning for heritage management and preservation is avoided. Citing from the Cultural Heritage Counts for Europe, "*culture has the power to connect people and become a strategic tool for the safeguarding of the identity and authenticity of places and local communities. The pursuit of an inclusive society is an objective to which heritage can contribute. A closer integration of economic and social values of heritage for sustainable growth and social cohesion seems to be the goal*" (CHCfE Consortium, 2015, p. 47).

Even though cultural heritage is nowadays considered as an economic resource, it has to be highlighted that, as such, it shows specificities and peculiarities. As Towse (2003), Mossetto and Vecco (2002) and Leriche and Daviet (2010) state, it is legitimate to describe cultural heritage as a resource since it is a scarce productive factor which becomes a fundamental input aiming at utility in terms of investment or consumption. Plus, the production of cultural heritage "*utilizes resources of land, labor and capital and other inputs, particularly human ingenuity. These resources have other uses and therefore have an opportunity cost and price*" (Towse, 2003, p. 2). Moreover, the European report "Cultural Heritage Counts for Europe" clearly states that "*cultural heritage assets are economic goods – commodities or materials that satisfy people's (consumers') wants and needs to provide them with certain utility*" (CHCfE Consortium, 2015, p. 64). As an effective economic resource, it can be said that cultural heritage is part of the *capital* of the territory in which it is located. It is Bourdieu (1986) who first introduces the concept of *cultural capital* as a production factor. He describes the social world as *accumulated history* that can be fully connected with the concept of capital, its accumulation and its effects. More in detail, he recognizes the existence of three types of capital namely *economic, cultural* and *social.* All the typologies of capital are described as potentially able to be converted into economic capital and to be institutionalized. *Cultural capital*, as proposed by Bourdieu, exists in three forms: the embodied state, the objectified state and the institutionalized state. Bourdieu's *cultural capital* is very much related to individuals: the embodied state corresponds to personal dispositions of mind and body; the objectified state relates to cultural goods (produced and consumed in tight relationships with the embodied state); and the institutionalized state coincides with academic qualifications. The truly comprehensive inclusion of cultural heritage (intended as a societal, shared resource rather than individual culture) in the economic narrative and in the concept of cultural capital takes place thanks to David Throsby in 1999. Throsby refers to cultural capital as a distinct kind of capital which is added to the physical, human and natural capitals already recognized by the economic discipline and literature. The concept is defined as "*the stock of cultural value embodied in an asset*" and it relies upon the relationship between economic value and cultural value. Using Throsby's words, "*this stock may in turn give rise to a flow of goods and services over time, i.e., to commodities that themselves may have both cultural and economic value. The asset may exist in tangible or intangible form*" (Throsby, 1999, pp. 6–7). By considering cultural heritage as capital and, more specifically, as cultural capital, it can be noted that, as in the case of all the other capital assets and goods, it is accumulated over time and is subject to deterioration and decay dynamics. Besides, its maintenance involves costs, not just in terms of conservation activities but also in terms of opportunity cost related to giving up short-sighted strategies and opportunistic behaviors for its use. Furthermore, like other capital goods, cultural heritage provides services such as flows of utility, profit and land rents (Camagni et al., 2020).

One of the main peculiarities of cultural heritage when treated and analyzed as an economic asset lies in its use and consumption. In fact, some forms and expressions of cultural heritage can be considered as *public* or *collective* consumption goods which means that they are provided for each person to enjoy or not, according to their preferences. To cite from Samuelson (1954, p. 387), "*each individual's consumption of such a good leads no subtraction from any other individual's consumption of that good*". More specifically, two characteristics define the public nature of a good which are non-excludability and non-rivalry. Non-excludability deals with the fact that it is "*technically infeasible to keep users from enjoying the good. […] sightseeing in an historic area of an old city is typically not an excludible activity – it is impractical to try to charge admission to a living part of a city*" (Navrud & Ready, 2002, pp. 3–4). Non-rivalry concerns consumption and it refers to the fact that, if the good is public, more than one person can enjoy the same good simultaneously without obstructing others. Cultural landscapes or monuments, for instance, belong to the family of public goods. However, as highlighted in Buchanan (1965), a whole spectrum of ownership-consumption possibilities exists, ranging from purely private to purely collective or public assets. He therefore introduces the theory and concept of club goods which position themselves in between private and public classes, "*the consumption of which involves some 'publicness', where the optimal sharing group is more than one person or family but smaller than an infinitely large number*" (Buchanan, 1965, p. 2). Club goods can be referred to also as impure public goods and they involve, for instance, museums and galleries or historic urban centers which are made up by both public and private assets. It is important to notice that it is not easy to make a clear distinction between public, club or private goods and it is instead better to talk about a smooth continuum. The properties of non-excludability and non-rivalry that characterize public goods and impure public goods (at different levels of intensity and pureness) discourage private suppliers from providing those goods, resulting in an undersupply or no supply at all. Public goods are subject to market failure issues because of opportunistic behaviors or free riding problems. Even though the user gains certain benefits from the consumption of the good, it is not possible to capture the value of this benefit, leading to underproduction problems. Market failure is determined by two other main issues: information asymmetries and externalities. As far as information asymmetries are concerned, exchanging cultural heritage assets on the market is a very complicated task since it is very difficult to assess whether, for instance, a house or a building has a heritage value and, if so, whether the corresponding quality is high or low in comparison with other similar assets. As far as externalities are concerned, privately owning a heritage site and investing in its conservation may result in private benefits deriving from, for instance, charging for access to the place or the increased value of the property because of its characterization. However, other social and public positive externalities can be associated with the presence of cultural heritage such as the contribution to cultural identity, to create an enjoyable atmosphere or to attract tourists. If heritage sites are privately owned and managed, investments in preservation and conservation activities occur up to the point where private benefits from the investments can be realized with the risk of neglecting all the other common externalities (Thorpe, 2008). Therefore, as highlighted in Camagni et al. (2020, p. 38), the appropriate administration and management of these complex assets "*cannot refer only to strict regulations but at the same time has to resort to incentives, moral suasion, public–private agreements or, even more interestingly, to community actions […]*".

Given the peculiarities of heritage treated as an economic asset and given the problematic management of this kind of asset resulting from market failure issues, cultural heritage becomes an interesting unit of analysis to be studied from the economic perspective. It is in fact extremely necessary to try to detect and specify its economic potentialities to justify public attention toward its conservation, preservation and valorization (Benhamou, 1996). The costs related to heritage are easily measurable and represent an evident burden for governmental budgets. The benefits resulting from maintenance and enhancement activities are instead much more complex to capture (McLoughlin et al., 2006).

However, it seems to be evident that cultural heritage carries and embodies relevant and vital *values* that have always been the rationale for its conservation and preservation. Additionally, cultural heritage is nowadays recognized as having an *impact* on several areas of economic and regional development. Therefore, when analyzed from the economic perspective, two main concepts are of cardinal importance: *value* and *impact*. As Throsby (2001) argues, the concept of value can be considered as the starting point from which a conjoint analysis of economy and cultural heritage is possible. More specifically, two main research issues stemming from the relationship between cultural heritage and economy based on heritage values open up:

1. the clarification of the relationship between cultural and economic value, the identification of the characteristics and differences between the two types of value and the attempt of measuring these values;
2. the identification, both conceptually and empirically, of the contribution, if any, that cultural heritage may make toward economic output and growth in the economy because of its values.

This distinction reflects the ones between the value owned or carried by different forms of heritage and the value they are able to generate or, in other words, the distinction between value and impact of heritage. Borrowing from the Cultural Heritage Counts for Europe report, pp. 52–52 "*the value of heritage refers to what given sites mean to people, while the impact of heritage is their real influence on a region's economy and society. […] The relation between values and impacts of heritage is twofold; values can affect impacts which in turn can lead to an elevation of values, since an increase of heritage impact will evolve into higher valuation of heritage*". The concept of value is more related to an intrinsic characteristic of cultural heritage whereas the concept of impact deals with a cause-effect relationship.

Two main lines of research can be identified following this discourse: one that tries to measure the value of cultural heritage and another one that tries to quantify the impact of cultural heritage on economy and society.

The following two sections (Sects. 1.3.2 and 1.3.3) will, respectively, explore the literature dedicated to the two streams of research identified.

1.3.2 The Economic Value of Cultural Heritage

Recognition and evaluation of the values held by cultural heritage enter the discourse related to the attempt to quantify the benefits stemming from investments in protection and promotion of heritage. As highlighted in the previous section (Sect. 1.3.1) and as also pointed out by Mourato and Mazzanti (2002), given the fact that cultural heritage assets are not traded in the market, if their value is not properly captured, problems related to the undervaluing and underpricing of heritage might happen together with scarce public resources allocated to it.

Assessing and capturing the values of cultural heritage is not an easy task since it is characterized by a simultaneous combination of different and multiple typologies of values. In fact, inspired by the 1979 Charter for Places of Cultural Significance known as the Burra Charter (ICOMOS, 1979), Throsby (2001) and Mason (2002) started to recognize that a "*certain duality in the value of heritage allows an integration of an assessment of the economic value of heritage with the sort of criteria for judging cultural significance used by heritage professionals*" (Throsby, 2013, p. 456). In other words, cultural heritage simultaneously shows two typologies of values: socio-cultural values and economic values. These two categories can be further specified into subcategories as shown in the Fig. 1.1.

In his *Economics and culture* (2001, pp. 28–29), Throsby identifies and details the different socio-cultural values which cultural heritage carries:

- *aesthetic value*: heritage owns and expresses beauty, as recognized for instance by the architectural or artistic community of professionals, of certain fundamental significance;
- *spiritual value*: heritage can contribute to the formulation of the sense of identity of entire communities or individual members of communities;
- *social value*: cultural heritage contributes to the stability and coherence of a given community;
- *historical value*: contributes to the shaping of identity of a group, providing a link with the past and acting as a source in the present;
- *symbolic value*: heritage possesses a certain sense and content that help a community interpret its identity and define its cultural personality;

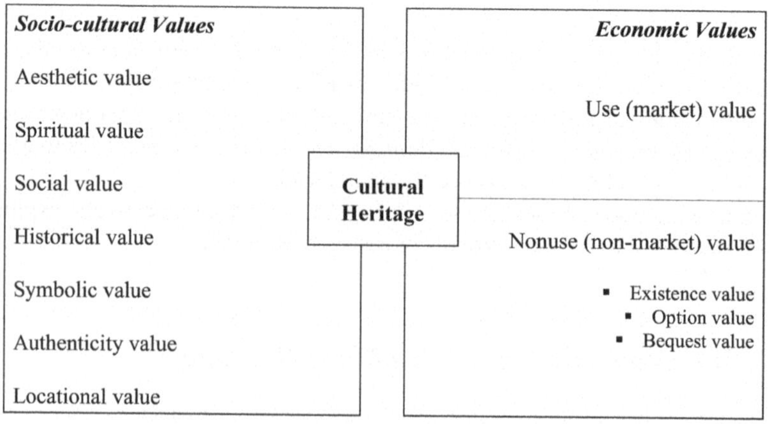

Fig. 1.1 Typologies of cultural heritage values (*Source* Author's elaboration from Throsby [2001] and Mason [2002])

- *authenticity value*: integrity and uniqueness characteristics that distinguish each and every heritage site from the others and form reproductions;
- *locational value*: heritage is able to provide a place with unique features contributing to create a certain image to that place.

As far as the economic values of heritage are concerned, de la Torre (2002, p. 13) argues that *use values* or *market values* of heritage refer to the goods and services that stem from cultural heritage and that are tradable and priceable in existing markets (e.g., admission fees, costs of land, wages of workers). As per the *non-use economic values* a difference is made between:

- *existence value*: a heritage item is valued because of its mere existence;
- *option value*: the option value of heritage refers to someone's desire to preserve the possibility (the option) that she might consume the heritage services at some future point in time;
- *bequest value*: wish to bequeath a heritage asset to future generations.

As evident from the previously presented classification of the different values held by cultural heritage, a quantification or evaluation of them is extremely complex especially because of the need to consider both use and non-use economic values. Different methods that try to evaluate the economic value of cultural heritage have been proposed so far by the literature. Navrud and Ready (2002), Seaman (2006), Vecco (2011) and Snowball (2013) among others summarize the techniques that have been used. Figure 1.2 summarizes the most frequently used methods.

As Mason (2002) well explains, market valuation methods regard financial calculations, audit of existing preservation, cost–benefit analysis or return on investment studies (see for instance Báez & Herrero, 2012; Limonov et al., 2020; Tuan & Navrud, 2008). These kinds of methods have some major drawbacks. Firstly, they do not consider the non-use values of cultural heritage leading to distorted evaluations and they do not encompass negative effects such as congestion. Furthermore, they do not

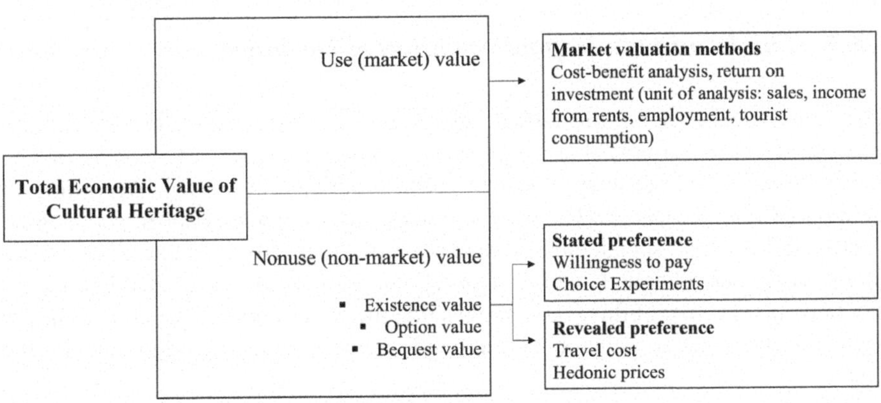

Fig. 1.2 Methods for measuring cultural heritage value (*Source* Author's elaboration from Snowball [2013])

take into account alternative investments in order to prove that investing in cultural heritage is advantageous and better than a different investment.

Non-market valuation methods are instead mainly focused on the measurement of non-use values of cultural heritage. These kinds of techniques, in the stated preference case, build their analysis on surveys about consumer preferences. The interviewees are asked to state the maximum price they are willing to pay, for instance, to enter a free cultural heritage site or for a re-vitalization intervention (see for instance Choi et al., 2010; Durán et al., 2015; Foster & Mourato, 2002; Jaffry & Apostolakis, 2011; Kinghorn & Willis, 2007; Mazzanti, 2003; Sælensminde, 2002; Santagata & Signorello, 2000). As per the revealed preference methods, since it is not possible to use market prices, travel costs or housing prices are used in the attempt to evaluate public goods (see for instance Bilbao-Terol et al., 2017; Del Hoyo et al., 2019; Lazrak et al., 2014; Listokin et al., 1998; Moro et al., 2013; Poor & Smith, 2004; Tourkulias et al., 2015).

Evaluating cultural heritage by quantifying its value, besides being a complex challenge, is also related to a defined and circumscribed object of analysis. In other terms, to grasp the economic value of cultural heritage the analysis needs to be performed on a specific site or *ensemble* of cultural sites resulting in the investigation of a specific case study. Furthermore, to encompass and properly taking into consideration all the different typologies of values held by cultural heritage including the socio-cultural ones, one may consider the consequences or impacts of this sophisticated system of determining values. Borrowing from Sable and Kling (2001, p. 78), "*many types of cultural assets or activities produce multidimensional non-market social benefits, particularly when they serve as communicators of social identity, forces for change, and evidence of cultural continuity*".

The following section (Sect. 1.3.3) will be dedicated to exploring the literature devoted to highlight and assess the impact of cultural heritage on socio-economic systems.

1.3.3 The Economic Impact of Cultural Heritage

As a consequence of the diversified system of values that characterizes cultural heritage, it can be argued that its presence generates a series of impacts on the society living in the territory in which cultural heritage is located. According to the report Cultural Heritage Counts for Europe, four main areas of impact can be identified: economic, social, environmental and cultural. These four areas of impact interact with each other and overlap creating intersections. As mentioned before, the economic perspective of this work implies that the area of impact which is of major interest in this context is the economic one together with its intersections with the others.

It seems nowadays to be widely recognized by the scientific literature that cultural heritage has an economic impact in the sense that it can be considered as an engine for socio-economic development (see, for instance, Ashworth & Larkham, 1994;

Capello & Perucca, 2017; Fusco Girard, 2014; Sacco et al., 2010; Storhammar & Tohmo, 2010; Throsby, 2001; Tubadji et al., 2015; Tufts & Milne, 1999; Vaughan & Booth, 1989). However, given the multiplicity of values held by cultural heritage and given the variety of ways in which the consequences and impacts stemming from the presence of heritage can be actualized, assessment and evaluation of economic impacts are challenging and complicated tasks.

In general terms, it can be argued that the economic literature devoted to exploring the impacts of heritage is attributable to the issue of understanding the relationship between cultural heritage and local socio-economic development. The main idea behind this literature is that heritage sites are embedded in local economic systems which both influence them and are influenced by them. As explained in Lyck (2013) cultural heritage can be considered as being both an expenditure and a production factor able to generate economic revenues. If in the past cultural heritage was seen as a good deserving to be safeguarded as a moral duty and to be enjoyed just by a wealthy and educated elitist class, "*the present view reverses this relationship between wealth generation and culture for, whereas once heritage was seen as a resultant and beneficiary of wealth, it is now expected to be a wealth generator being enlisted in the economic development process not for its own merit but to further a range of extrinsic objectives*" (Ashworth, 2013, p. 372). Following both the public debate and the economic literature, success stories demonstrating the role of cultural heritage as an economic resource capable of stimulating local economies do exist and the perception of heritage as an economic driver is in continuous expansion.

Many economic activities are related to and impacted by the presence of cultural heritage in a territory. Firstly, heritage institutions—whether private, mixed or public—can be considered as economic subjects directly employing a labor force and generating revenues from ticket sales (where an entrance fee is required). Furthermore, as explained in 2019 by the ESPON report titled *The Material Cultural Heritage as a Strategic Territorial Development Resource: Mapping Impacts through a Set of Common European Socio-economic indicators*, considering the value chain related to tangible forms of heritage, starting from the creation passing through management and dissemination and ending in consumption, various economic sectors are influenced and stimulated such as archaeology, architecture, museums, libraries, archives activities, tourism, construction and real estate but also ICT and insurance (ESPON, 2019). Following the reasoning of Greffe (2004), it is appropriate to consider the idea of a *heritage ecosystem* built on the interrelation and synergies between the endowment of material cultural heritage, the providers of heritage-related services (e.g., maintenance, conservation and renovation activities) and the consumers (local inhabitants or tourists). Once the sectors with which cultural heritage has economic interdependencies are identified, the consequences on local economies can be measured using, for instance, employment (see Greffe, 2004), value added (see ESPON, 2019) or expenditure (see Greffe, 2011) and applying input–output or Keynesian multiplier methodologies.

Other ways in which cultural heritage can play a role in local economic growth is through the typology of effects that Bowitz and Ibenholdt (2009, p. 4) call *gravitation effects* including the increased attractivity of a territory both for people and firms and the ability to feed entrepreneurship and innovation (see for instance Backman & Nilsson, 2018).

Furthermore, cultural heritage can be associated with socio-cultural and psychological effects that might be correlated with economic consequences. As argued by Wilson et al. (2016), cultural heritage and cultural engagement are sources of togetherness, cultural democracy and cultural freedom. Participation in culture increases possibilities of self-expression, learning transferrable skills and feeling part of a community (Wilson et al., 2016). As pointed out by Hand (2018), arts are associated with happiness and, as reported in Matarasso (1997), cultural heritage contributes to shaping a stable, confident and creative society. In other words, by supporting the enrichment of human beings' lives and contributing to the formation of cultural and social capital, cultural heritage influences local economic dynamics (see also McCarthy et al., 2004; Reilly et al., 2018).

Recently, cultural heritage has been also associated with the concept of sustainable development in terms of the humanistic and ecological paradigm. Multi-dimensional benefits that move in the direction of a sustainable way of development are linked with cultural heritage such as cultural, social and economic benefits (see for instance Axelsson et al., 2013; Birkeland, 2015; Dessein et al., 2015; Langhelle, 1999; Leach, 1998; Nocca & Fusco Girard, 2018; Nurse, 2006; Seghezzo, 2009).

In general terms, several studies apply impact analysis aimed at understanding the role of cultural heritage in stimulating economic development. Two main observations emerge from the analysis of the literature: the first is that many studies focus on specific heritage sites (see for instance Plaza and Haarich [2015] on the Guggenheim Museum of Bilbao; Srakar and Vecco [2017] on the European Cultural Capital project in the city of Maribor; Greffe [2011] on the Louvre; Viu et al. [2008] on the Alhambra in Granada) or specific countries (see for instance Greffe, 2004; Thompson et al., 1997); the second is that the most analyzed channel through which the relationship between the presence of cultural heritage and economic development happens is tourism (see for instance Cuccia & Cellini, 2007; Huang et al., 2012; Patuelli et al., 2013).

Some consequences and research gaps stem from these two observations. First of all, focalizing and circumscribing the field to a single case study does not allow for comparability and generalization of the results. In other words, even if it might be true that a specific heritage site contributes positively to the economic development of the defined area in which it is located, it is not necessarily the case that a general mechanism is at work according to which, in general terms, the presence of cultural heritage is able to act as an engine for development. Besides, by studying the functioning of a single case study it is not possible to identify common channels or mechanisms through which cultural heritage represents a catalyst for development. Secondly, even though tourism is the most common and extensively studied channel through which the endowment of cultural heritage shows economic impacts and consequences, the research field is still underdeveloped. In fact, a clear consensus on the role of heritage in enhancing tourist attractiveness has not yet been reached by the literature. Furthermore, the analysis of the topic is fragmented in the sense that when an analysis of the link between heritage and tourism is carried out, the economic development dimension is left out because it is taken for granted that if heritage stimulates tourism, this, in turn, stimulates economic growth. On the other hand, when tourism is analyzed in relationship with economic development, the role of cultural heritage in influencing tourism has not been examined. A third and relevant consideration stemming from the analysis of the existing literature is very much related to a peculiar characteristic of heritage which is its idiosyncratic nature. As Santagata (2004) argues, cultural goods are idiosyncratic, meaning that they have an essential connection with a given territory and a given time. Citing from Santagata (2004, p. 6) "*culture has two profound anthropological roots: time and space. The production of a culture is indissolubly linked to a place, or in a social sense, to a community and its history*". The endogenous nature of cultural heritage was already mentioned by Throsby (1999) and the European Spatial Development Perspective (ESPD, 1999, p. 7) defined cultural variety as "*... the characteristic territorial feature of the EU*", which must "*be retained in the face of integration*". This definition is particularly important since it emphasizes the place-based nature of cultural heritage; it is an endogenous territorial asset, like capital and labor, formed over years, rooted in the local society and fed by its history (Capello & Perucca, 2017). Like all locally embedded resources, cultural heritage requires a long time to be created. Its local anchorage and local accumulation are the characteristics that make this resource strategic and unique for socio-economic development (Mazzanti, 2002). Besides, Plaza and Haarich (2015, p. 1457) highlight the concept of "*regional embeddedness*" of cultural heritage able to generate positive effects on urban regeneration and regional development. As Scott (1997, p. 325) suggests, "*place, culture and economic order are highly symbiotic with one another. The more the specific cultural identities and economic order of these cities condense out on the landscape the more they come to enjoy monopoly powers of place that enhance their competitive advantages*".

Therefore, it can be argued that cultural heritage interacts and creates synergies with the territories (in terms of geographic attributes but also social, relational and institutional ones) in which it is located. When performing an analysis on the impact of the endowment of cultural heritage on local economic development, it is not possible to neglect the context in which cultural heritage is located. This consideration gives rise to the idea that different typologies of channels other than tourism or activities strictly related to the value chain fed by the presence of cultural heritage exist and need to be considered. These different channels are more related to the place-specific nature of cultural heritage and can be referred to as context effects or atmosphere effects being more sophisticated, soft and intangible in nature. The endowment of heritage exerts impacts on and shows synergies with non-economic aspects of territories and communities such as social capital, well-being, creativity or identity and sense of belonging. It is reasonable to assume that these elements might result in some spillovers for local economies (Cerisola & Panzera, 2020). Citing from Camagni et al., (2020, p. 39), "*the presence of cultural heritage is supposed to have an impact on many immaterial elements of the local context and atmosphere, in a mainly psychological and cultural dimension. Attitudes of open-mindedness, hospitality, curiosity, cosmopolitanism; diffused sense of belonging and pride in local cultural and social traditions; sensibility, (good) taste and love of beauty, artistic and scientific creativity, general education of people and knowledge; all these elements find a favourable environment for their flourishing in a heritage-rich local context and, in their turn, can become the drivers for new forms of (qualified) development*".

1.4 Research Gaps and Innovative Perspectives

As explained in the previous sections (Sects. 1.3.2 and 1.3.3) two main research streams attempting to assess and measure the economic relevance of cultural heritage can be identified. On the one hand, part of the economic literature tries to quantify the value carried by specific heritage sites, and on the other hand, the socio-economic impact derived from the presence of cultural heritage is explored. The main interest of the present research lies in investigating the role of the endowment of cultural heritage in acting as an engine for socio-economic development and, therefore, it is positioned within the second identified stream of research (described in Sect. 1.3.3). However, the socio-economic impact that derives from cultural heritage is strictly connected with its system of values. Cultural heritage is in fact able to play a role as a catalyst for development in a singular and peculiar way through its multiple and heterogeneous values. Interpreted as an economic resource, cultural heritage can clearly have consequences on local economies through its economic value in terms of, for instance, sales, tourist consumption or related investments, acting as an economic actor. Nonetheless, the socio-cultural values carried by cultural heritage influence its role in local development. Through, for instance, its historical, symbolic and aesthetic values, cultural heritage represents a significant engine for curiosity, capability to doubt, to learn and to innovate, resulting in a relevant driver of development in its broader sense involving cultural, social and economic domains (Della Torre, 2010). As highlighted before, these values strongly interact and build synergies with the territories in which cultural heritage is located. In fact, these values are both the result of the interpretation given by the present society and the source and inspiration of sentiments, behaviors and morals.

Without a doubt, the most studied channel of transmission between cultural heritage and economic development is tourism. The economic literature focuses on the role that cultural heritage has on tourist attractiveness through its aesthetic, historical, authenticity and locational values. This economic perspective is justified as the tourism sector is the most traditional, direct and strong channel that links the endowment of cultural heritage and local economic consequences. Therefore, in this work, considerable attention will be dedicated to the tourism sector in its connections with both cultural heritage and economic development. Even though this kind of analysis is long-established and traditional, there are research gaps that still need to be filled. In fact, there is no consensus yet on the positive effects stemming from the presence of cultural heritage on tourism attractiveness. This is partially due to the different aims of the contributions, the heterogeneity in the methods and the multiplicity of measures adopted. The focus on particular countries, the usage of a certain empirical methodology and the exploitation of a specific proxy for measuring cultural heritage rather than another lead to different results in terms of absence, presence or direction of the causality nexus between the endowment of heritage and tourism attractiveness as well as to scarce opportunity for generalization of the results. Furthermore, it has been taken for granted that, once the endowment of cultural heritage is able to engage more tourists, positive economic consequences are achieved. The triadic relationship between cultural heritage, tourism and economic dynamics has never been considered jointly by the literature so far. This book aims instead to jointly analyze these relationships closing a reasoning which has been left open by the literature trying to prove that cultural heritage represents a beneficial element for tourism attractiveness which, in turn, stimulates local economic development.

Even though undeniably relevant, tourism is not the only way in which cultural heritage plays a role as a catalyst for local development. If tourism can be considered and classified as a direct channel, other indirect channels do exist that are more intangible, soft and socio-cultural in nature. In this sense, the most relevant research gap identified in the literature regards the absence of the recognition that cultural heritage, because of its values, interacts with local communities shaping cultural, social and psychological attitudes of both individuals and communities, enhancing identitarian capital, creativity and, more generally, immaterial capital. All these aspects, in turn, influence and determine local potentialities for development and competitiveness. In other words, the relationship between cultural heritage and the place in which it is embedded gives rise to different schemes of development, all other factors being equal.

The scarce attention dedicated by the economic literature toward these aspects is demonstrated by a careful and detailed analysis presented in the Report *Cultural Heritage Counts for Europe*. Inside a comprehensive logical view, cultural heritage is assumed/hypothesized to exert its influence on four macro-areas of impact: economic, social, environmental and cultural. Within each of these, many potential sub-domains of impact are listed (for instance image and symbols creation, sense of place or regional attractiveness). Table 1.1 reproduces the one presented in the Report. The columns present the four macro-areas of impact and the rows the detailed impact sub-domains. Each "X" means that a specific sub-domain of impact in some way (theoretical, empirical or at least anecdotal) has been analyzed adopting the perspective captured by the corresponding macro-area of impact.

Focusing on the economic macro-area, several sub-domains of impact which have already been discussed and deepened in the literature are indicated. For instance, the role of cultural heritage in generating new knowledge and skills and consequently influencing economic dynamics has been discussed by Backman and Nilsson (2018); the economic dynamics influenced by regional attractiveness and place branding fostered by the presence of heritage and fed by tourism attractiveness are extensively discussed in the literature (see for instance Cuccia & Cellini, 2007; Di Lascio et al., 2011; Patuelli et al., 2013; Pompili et al., 2019). A rich branch of the literature examines the role of heritage in the real estate market (see for instance Franco & Macdonald, 2018; Franquesa, 2013; Lazrak et al., 2014) as well as its role in generating value added or return on investment (see for instance Bowitz & Ibenholdt,

Table 1.1 Potential areas of cultural heritage impact

	Economic	Social	Cultural	Environmental
Image and symbol creation			X	
Visual attractiveness			X	
Architectural language			X	
Creativity and innovation			X	
Sense of place		X	X	X
Cultural landscape			X	X
Reducing urban sprawl				X
Preserving embodied energy				X
Lifecycle prolongation				X
Education	X	X	X	
Skills	X	X	X	
Knowledge	X	X	X	
Creation of identity		X	X	
Regional attractiveness	X		X	X
Social cohesion		X		
Community participation		X		
Continuity of social life		X		
Place branding	X	X		
Labor market	X	X		
Regional competitiveness	X	X		X
Real Estate Market	X			
Gross Value Added	X			
Return on Investment	X			
Tax Income	X			
Housing Stock Management	X			X

Source Author's elaboration on Cultural Heritage Counts for Europe

2009). As evident from Table 1.1, the domains of impact related to the economic dimension are mainly linked to monetary flows such as return on investment, real estate market and gross value added. Non-monetary flows have also been considered in terms of, for instance, employment generated by cultural activities, place branding or regional competitiveness and attractiveness. It looks clear that all the analyses concerned refer—directly or indirectly—to the effects of tourism.

However, the main idea behind this book is that other sub-domains of impact that so far (and in the table) have been discussed exclusively from a socio-cultural perspective, involve an economic dimension as well. In other words, economic effects may indirectly derive from peculiarities and traits of societies such as community participation, social cohesion, creation of identity, creativity and innovation. These territorial elements are influenced, directly and notably, by the presence of cultural heritage and, in turn, the combination between these context socio-cultural elements and the endowment of cultural heritage affects local economic development.

As testified by the Table presented by the quoted Report, the economic literature has so far overlooked these aspects from a theoretical point of view, or implicitly implied the impossibility of any economic measurement. Two notable exceptions are Capello and Perucca (2017) and Cerisola (2019a, 2019b). In fact, Capello and Perucca (2017) analyzed the role of the local endowment of social, ethical and behavioral values of places in enhancing the impact of cultural heritage on economic growth. They proposed the idea that the economic impact of the endowment of cultural heritage is not place-neutral, and it is instead influenced by the presence of intangible assets such as individual cultural attitudes, social cultural values or institutional behavior supporting culture. Cerisola (2019a, 2019b) explored instead the role of an intangible local asset, i.e., creativity, as a mediator of the link between cultural heritage and economic development. More specifically, she empirically proved that the endowment of cultural heritage inspires creativity that in turn exerts positive effects on local development. Going back to Table 1.1, it can be said that, through the work of Capello and Perucca (2017), an X can be placed in the intersection between "Sense of place" and the economic macro-area of impact and, through the work of Cerisola (2019a, 2019b), another X can be placed in the intersection between "Creativity and Innovation" and economy.

Following this *fil rouge*, the main focus of this book lies in developing some other intangible territorial assets so far neglected by the economic literature namely territorial identity and social cohesion. These specific intangible territorial assets have been chosen for two main reasons. First, cultural heritage is very frequently associated with place identity. In fact, it is considered as a relevant source and vehicle of identitarian processes. Secondly, the discourse on territorial identity is becoming nowadays extremely interesting and relevant since a claim of identity recognition is at the heart of the rise of consensus for populist and nationalist parties led by (and leading to) a profound feeling of discontent and disappointment. On the other hand, the discourse related to identity is of fundamental importance for the foundation of a substantial European community. Therefore, deepening the relationship, interactions and synergies between cultural heritage, territorial identity and economic dynamics might prove an attractive, modern and innovative research topic. The same table presented by the *Cultural Heritage Counts for Europe* Report can be integrated showing the sub-domains of impact that, according to the perspective of this book, determine economic effects and can be analyzed from an economic perspective. Table 1.2 fills the gaps by indicating the names of the authors who analyze the previously neglected sub-domains of impact.

Summarizing, two main channels through which cultural heritage plays its role in local economic development will be examined within the context of this work. The first one, the most traditional, is represented by tourism attractiveness and demand. The second channel is instead more innovative and is related to context or atmosphere elements and, more specifically, to the role that territorial identity has in the link between the endowment of cultural heritage and socio-economic dynamics.

Table 1.2 Upgraded potential areas of cultural heritage impact

	Economic	Social	Cultural	Environmental
Image and symbol creation			X	
Visual attractiveness			X	
Architectural language			X	
Creativity and innovation	*Cerisola* (2019a, 2019b)		X	
Sense of place	*Capello and Perucca* (2017)	X	X	X
Cultural landscape			X	X
Reducing urban sprawl				X
Preserving embodied energy				X
Lifecycle prolongation				X
Education	X	X	X	
Skills	X	X	X	
Knowledge	X	X	X	
Creation of Identity	*Panzera*	X	X	
Regional attractiveness	X		X	X
Social cohesion	*Panzera*	X		
Community participation		X		
Continuity of social life		X		
Place branding	X	X		
Labor market	X	X		
Regional competitiveness	X	X		X
Real Estate market	X			
Gross Value Added	X			
Return on Investment	X			
Tax Income	X			
Housing Stock Management	X			X

Source Author's elaboration on Cultural Heritage Counts for Europe

The following section is dedicated to explaining in more detail the relevance and rationale of the two logic channels and the approach that will be adopted in the empirical test of these conceptual hypotheses.

1.5 The Link Between Cultural Heritage and Development: The Proposed Conceptual Framework

1.5.1 Cultural Heritage and Socio-Economic Development: The Traditional Channel

The relevance of analyzing the tourism sector in its connections with both cultural heritage and economic development is undeniable and widely recognized by institutions, scientific communities and citizens. The European Union, for instance, recognizes the importance of culture as a fundamental driver for tourism experiences and for the enhancement of the role of Europe as a global destination. The estimates affirm that 40% of all European tourism can be attributed to cultural tourism thanks to the endowment of outstanding historical sites, theaters, archaeological sites, museums as well as gastronomy, music and cultural events in general. As highlighted by the OECD, culture and tourism present many synergies that are a potential for growth. Cultural tourism is a fast-growing market and cultural and creative assets are progressively being used to grant visibility to destinations (OECD, 2008). As Timothy (2011) argues, cultural heritage, both in its tangible and intangible forms, is one of the most significant elements feeding the global tourism system. Using his words, "*many destinations rely almost entirely upon art, culture and built patrimony for their economic well-being, and even the most devout non-heritage destinations have some elements of culture that can be shared with visitors as part of the tourism product mix*" (Timothy, 2011, p. 8).

When the economic consequences of the presence of cultural heritage are taken into consideration the traditional and most mentioned channel is tourism. In fact, tourism contributes consistently to the formation of global GDP (representing its 10%), 7% of total world exports and 30% of world services exports are ascribed to tourism and, since 2009, international tourist arrivals have been showing a constant 4% or more annual increase (UNWTO, 2017).

Given the relevance of the topic especially in terms of economic outcomes, the academic literature has extensively discussed the relationship between cultural heritage and tourism and between tourism and economic development. Several studies have explored the determinants of tourism attractiveness and investigated the role of cultural heritage as an engaging element for tourists. By the same token, the role of the tourism sector as an engine for development has been widely investigated. However, three main aspects deserve additional attention and research:

- No clear consensus has been reached so far on the existence or direction of causality of a nexus between endowment of heritage and tourism attractiveness. More specifically, even though theoretically speaking heritage and tourism present synergies and interactions, conflicting evidence has been proposed when empirical analyses have been undertaken to prove these connections. It can be noted that this might be due to the differences in the aims of the research, the heterogeneity

of the methods adopted and the focus on specific countries or specific heritage sites (see Sect. 2.2 for further details).
- No agreement on the relevant role of tourism in influencing economic development can be found in the literature. Contrasting empirical outcomes ranging from confirmation of the validity of a causal relationship between tourism attractiveness and economic development, passing through bilateral causality and arriving to neutrality or even a negative relationship can be found in the literature. A great variety of methodologies has been applied and different geographical units have been taken into consideration leading to problems related to the comparability of the results (see Sect. 2.3 for further details).
- The research developed so far on the link between cultural heritage, tourism and economic development has been carried out using a fragmented approach. In fact, either the relationship between cultural heritage and tourism or that between tourism and economic growth have been deepened resulting in an incomplete analysis of the story. When the focus is on the link between heritage and tourism, the economic impact seems to be taken for granted and, on the other hand, when the relationship analyzed is the one between tourism and economic growth, the role of cultural heritage in tourism enhancement is unknown.

Therefore, within the context of this book, an effort in the direction of overcoming these research gaps will be made. More specifically, the relationship between cultural heritage and tourism will be considered jointly with the economic consequences stemming from the relationship itself. In this way, a comprehensive analysis of the role of tourism in the link between cultural heritage and local economic development will be proposed (see Chapter 3).

1.5.2 Cultural Heritage and Socio-Economic Development: The Role of Territorial Identity

There are two main reasons for the relevance of jointly studying cultural heritage, territorial identity and economic development, the first being more related to the links between heritage and identity and the second being linked to the importance that nowadays the discourse on identity is gaining.

The association between cultural heritage and identity is one of the most recurrent and frequent ones. In fact, cultural heritage is considered as a source of the sense of belonging and cultural identity, being a store of collective memory and values and a legacy for future generations. Citing from the report Cultural Heritage Counts for Europe, "*cultural heritage can lead to a greater national awareness, social cohesion, sense of place and identity*" (CHCfE Consortium, 2015, p. 148).

The same concept of identity is gaining an increasingly important role in the public arena because of the substantial challenges facing European citizens nowadays because of globalization and a new technological paradigm. Highly competitive environments, variations in territorial patterns of value chains together with threats deriving from automation and smart machines have contributed to perceived and actual inequality and uncertainty about economic and personal stability. In a context in which a severe discrepancy exists between expectations and opportunities, the question of identity becomes crucial. A claim for identity recognition is at the heart of the rise of consensus and support for populist and nationalist parties: identity is felt to be a psychological anchor holding a nostalgic attachment for a past, imagined, strong and cohesive national community without the risks and downsides of modern society. On the other hand, identity—perceived in a remarkably different way—is believed to be crucial for the process of European integration. As argued in the European Identity Study, to reach the legitimation of any political system it is necessary that a sentiment of sameness and some form of identification be perceived by the members of that system (Prutsch, 2017).

Both the relationship between cultural heritage and identity and the concept of identity itself are usually referred to and studied as socio-cultural in nature. However, economic consequences and spillovers are linked to these elements. As is true for social capital and relation capital, territorial identity represents a "*soft architecture*" and puts the emphasis on intangible assets such as, for instance, shared mindsets or common interests (Staber & Sautter, 2011, p. 1350). Social capital as theorized by Bourdieu (1986), Coleman (1988) and Putnam (2000) presents some overlapping characteristics with territorial identity in the sense that it involves more or less institutionalized connections and networks between and among individuals, the recognition of membership in a group, and it is associated with societal traits such as civic engagement or trust. Furthermore, as Coleman (1988) puts it, social capital is a resource that inspires and boosts behaviors targeted toward the achievement of mutually beneficial aims. These soft elements are very much related to the functioning of local economic dynamics and performances. A strong sense of territorial identity felt by the inhabitants of a place might in fact be associated with enhanced trust toward others, cooperation, civic engagement and civic responsibility.

The recognition of a certain convergence between private and public interests fed by place identity and manifested as cooperative and synergic conducts generates favorable effects on local productivity. A solid attachment to places facilitates interactions among territorial actors that don't necessarily speak the same language but are interested in the proper functioning of their economic systems and, therefore, identify the opportunity of making exchanges and trades establishing communication codes, conditions for reliability, alliances, partnerships and collaborations. These soft elements play a crucial role in the functioning of economic dynamics since they facilitate interactions and coordination, foster collective learning processes through the presence of networks and generate social proximity.

As highlighted in Malecki (2012), networks contribute to gaining faster access to information and knowledge at lower costs and help obtain a greater quantity and quality of information and knowledge. In a knowledge-based economic paradigm, the ways in which knowledge and information are exchanged and transformed into innovative processes and practices represent crucial territorial assets. As Jeannerat and Kebir (2016, p. 276) put it, "*innovation is not the by-product of an exogenous knowledge change but emerges from endogenous learning processes taking place within particular production systems organized in time and space*". A common identity gives a common purpose to the entity with which the members identify and sustains the awareness of mutual benefits stemming from reciprocal respect and transversal cooperation. As argued by Della Torre (2015), by being aware of and participating in the needs and vocations of the territory, as well as by acknowledging common interests, public and private actors activate strategic relationships able to generate processes of sustainable innovation. If individuals recognize a certain correspondence between private and public interests, the productivity of a community benefits from collective and cooperative behaviors and the absorptive capacity of new innovations might be faster (Iyer et al., 2005). Communities endowed with a strong territorial identity might also be better prepared to face external changes and crises showing resilience, cooperation and flexibility. It has to be noted that, even though the functioning of local production systems is crucial to understanding local development and competitiveness, the relationships between local territories and external entities are likewise essential. Regional innovation and development are not only triggered by endogenous dynamics, but they are instead fed by external knowledge flows (Jeannerat & Kebir, 2016). In a global and connected world in which knowledge, innovation and people continuously move, relocate and interact, the establishment of relationships between territories and external actors and entities is of essential importance. This aspect is again linked with the discourse related to social capital and, more specifically, to the concepts of bonding and bridging social capital put forward by Putnam (2000). On the one hand, bonding social capital is made up by tight bonds and deep trust but it is exclusive and might have illiberal effects in the sense that the inclusion of the members may depend on the exclusion of others. On the other hand, social capital becomes bridging when the networks' members forge ties with others and present inclusive rather than exclusive attitudes and wills. Bridging capital represents a necessary and unavoidable condition in order to move forward and to develop.

By the same token, a typology of territorial identity characterized by exclusive behaviors might be linked with support for populism or nationalism that endanger the very factors on which recent economic development has been grounded: open markets, migration, economic integration and globalization (Rodríguez-Pose, 2017). Exclusive and inclusive behaviors characterizing different typologies of territorial identity can be influenced by cultural heritage and, more specifically, by the associated narratives. The efforts of the European Union go in the direction of creating a narrative of shared and inclusive common heritage building and bridging sentiments. However, examples of bonding, exclusive and illiberal behaviors deriving from built and sometimes even distorted narratives on cultural heritage exist and need to be taken into consideration. The very recent storming of the US Capitol on January 6, 2021 represents a case in which cultural heritage is put forward as the basis and the reason for controversial acts of a very cohesive group of people. As highlighted in Castells (2000, p. 7), social structures continuously produce and reproduce meaning through symbolic interaction between actors and "*the consolidation of shared meaning through crystallization of practices in spatio-temporal configurations creates cultures, that is systems of values and beliefs informing codes of behavior*". By being a materialization of intangible forms of culture, cultural heritage embodies these aspects and influences territorial identities and the feeling of being part of a larger community of networks. As highlighted in Putnam (2000), the sense of self of the individuals participating in dense networks of interactions broadens up and develops from "I" to "we" and stimulates the awareness of and fondness for collective benefits.

So far, the literature has never examined the economic role of the ties between cultural heritage and territorial identity and therefore the present work tries to take a step further in this direction filling the identified research gap.

The first innovative contribution corresponds to the proposal of an original taxonomy of different typologies of territorial identity. It has to be noted that, as in the case of cultural heritage, finding a comprehensive definition of identity is a complicated task and many different perspectives can be adopted to analyze the concept. Identity can refer, for instance, to individuals, groups, communities or nations, it can be multiple, flexible, dynamic, inclusive or exclusive. Within the context of this book, identity is interpreted as the perception of sameness felt by the inhabitant of a territory. This feeling of sameness can be combined with diverse sentiments that, consequently, lead to different behaviors. More specifically, the perception of being similar to a certain group can be associated with a feeling of solidarity which takes place whenever a certain convergence between private and common interests is recognized by the participating individuals. Depending on the presence of this solidarity feeling, different behaviors can be put in place by the individuals. Furthermore, the perception of sameness can be on different spatial or geographical scales. In other words, individuals can feel they are similar to groups of people living in the same neighborhood, city, region, nation or supra-national entity. A perception of sameness can be felt toward a single spatial level or toward more than one spatial level simultaneously. Following this discourse, a classification of different typologies of identity is proposed starting from the basis of the perception of sameness as the founding element of identity. Different typologies of identity can be identified according to two main elements: the behaviors that follow this feeling of sameness and the different spatial levels toward which this sameness can be perceived. Four different typologies of identity have been identified according to these two main elements (a detailed explanation of this classification can be found in Chapter 4):

- *Individualistic localism* characterized by the absence of solidarity and the exclusively local feeling of sameness;
- *Parochial localism* characterized by the presence of solidarity and the exclusively local feeling of sameness;
- *Place-less cosmopolitanism* characterized by the absence of solidarity and the simultaneously local and supra-local feeling of sameness;
- *Inclusive cosmopolitanism* characterized by the presence of solidarity and the simultaneously local and supra-local feeling of sameness.

Once these four different typologies of identity have been determined, the role that cultural heritage plays in shaping, influencing and affecting them is considered. So far, both the institutional documents and the literature seem to take for granted that cultural heritage is able to carry, instill and inspire identity. This statement, however, has never been empirically tested. In this sense, a second innovative contribution of the book regards the attempt to both conceptually and empirically detect in which ways cultural heritage influences identity and which are the typologies of identity (as identified through the original taxonomy) that are more impacted by the endowment of cultural heritage.

A third innovative contribution has the aim of filling the gap left empty by the literature and related to the missing investigation of the economic consequences of the synergies and interactions between cultural heritage and identity. A main assumption, neglected by the literature, will be presented and tested: the role of the endowment of cultural heritage in influencing local economic dynamics is not place-neutral. It is instead strictly linked to intangible context or atmosphere effects (in this specific case territorial identity) that enhance or reduce the ability of heritage to have an impact on local economic development.

The following section summarizes the proposed logic and explains the conceptual framework of this part of the book.

1.5.3 The Proposed Conceptual Framework for the Link Between Cultural Heritage and Local Development

Having clarified the paramount importance of discussing, deepening and proving the positive economic spillovers that can be obtained thanks to the presence of cultural heritage, the present book concentrates on two main channels: tourism, the most traditional one studied by the economic literature, and identity, a more innovative, modern and intangible channel still unexplored by the literature especially using an economic perspective.

Figure 1.3 summarizes the two mechanisms analyzed.

Following this logic, the book will be divided into two parts: Part A, focused on the traditional channel, and Part B, dedicated to examining the innovative channel.

Both Part A and Part B will be devoted to answering the following research question: *Does the endowment of cultural heritage play an active role in influencing local economic dynamics?*

Part A will be specifically dedicated to answering the following research question: *Is tourism a relevant element in actualizing the positive role of cultural heritage in influencing local economic development?*

Part B will be instead specifically dedicated to answering the following research question: *Does territorial identity perceived as an intangible, soft and context element play a role in the influence of cultural heritage on local economic development?*

The proposed conceptual framework will serve an empirical analysis aimed at quantitatively assessing the proper functioning of the previously expressed mechanisms. The scope of the empirical investigation is the European Union and, more specifically, its NUTS2[3] regions as defined by Eurostat. The choice of the regional

[3] Nomenclature of Territorial Units for Statistics.

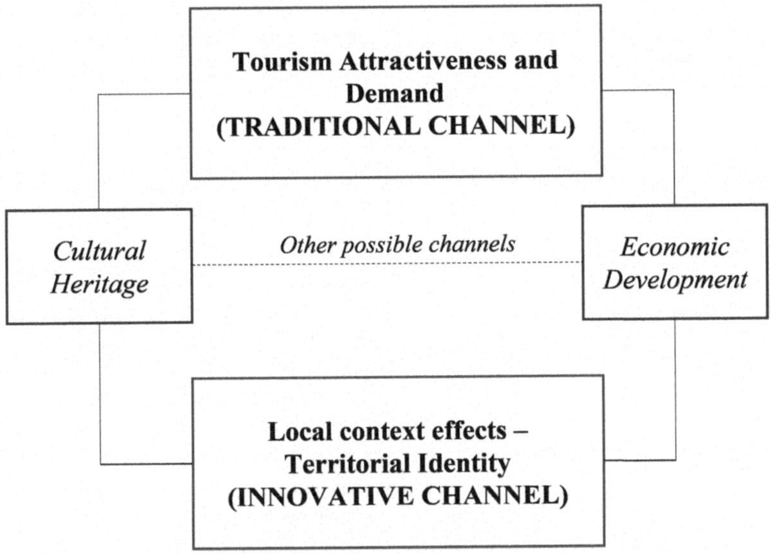

Fig. 1.3 Cultural heritage—Economic development link: the proposed conceptual framework

level has been made for two main reasons: the first one relates to the fact that the region can be considered a sufficiently disaggregated level to detect and consider the specific, peculiar and different characteristics of territories (including heritage, tourism and territorial identity) within the national boundaries; the second reason relates to data availability. Since the scope of the analysis is the whole European Union, the most disaggregated level for which the data related to cultural heritage and territorial identity are available is the regional (NUTS2) one.

By hypothesizing and trying to empirically prove the relationship between cultural heritage and local economic development through touristic activities and territorial identity formation, it is not implicitly asserted that those are the only mechanisms through which heritage might influence economic dynamics. The main idea here is to try to overcome the separate and independent analysis of economic and socio-cultural spillovers stemming from the presence of cultural heritage. In fact, the influence exerted by cultural heritage on socio-cultural domains of society does not cease there but brings along potentially positive economic consequences.

1.6 Structure of the Book

To analyze the two chosen mechanisms and to answer the previous mentioned research questions, the book will follow the structure indicated in Fig. 1.4.

Chapter 2*:* the chapter is aimed at exploring the literature related to cultural heritage and tourism attractiveness and the one related to tourism and economic

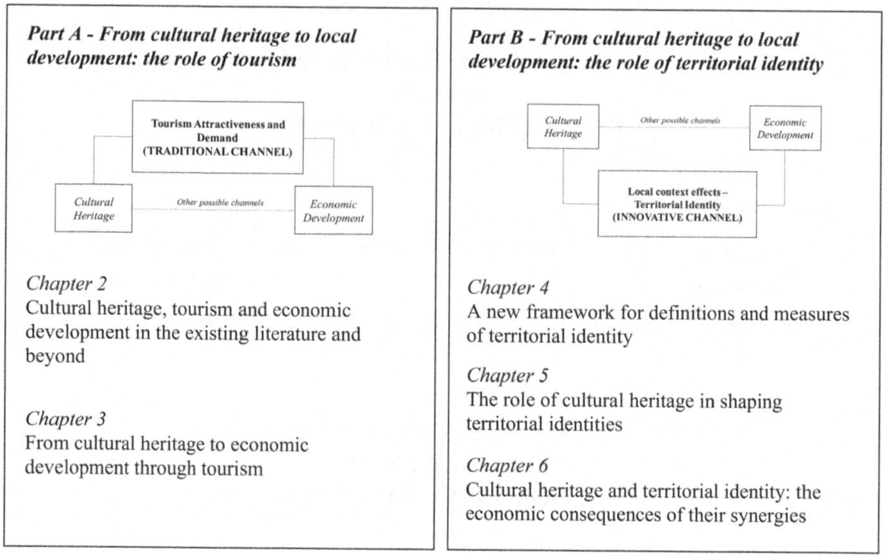

Fig. 1.4 Structure of the book

development. Furthermore, two main issues linked with tourism and cultural tourism will be discussed: the controversial phenomenon of overtourism and the current tourism crisis due to COVID-19 pandemic.

Chapter 3: the chapter aims at jointly exploring the relationship between material cultural heritage, tourism and economic development. Starting from the idea that tangible forms of cultural heritage represent critical resources potentially able to contribute to local economic growth through the mediation effect played by the tourism sector, a structural equation model is applied to European regions to figure out whether tourism represents a solid and substantial channel—out of potentially many others—for the functioning of this mechanism. In other words, an econometric model is used to quantitatively demonstrate the existence of an indirect impact of regional cultural heritage endowment on economic development *through* tourism. Testing the model with different heritage-related variables results in confirming the mediating role of tourism between tangible forms of cultural heritage and economic growth across European regions.

Chapter 4: the chapter introduces the concepts of identity and territorial identity focusing on the difficulties related to defining those concepts and on the attempts made so far by the literature. A new taxonomy of different typologies of territorial identity is presented together with the proposal of a way to measure these typologies and assign each European region a specific corresponding typology of identity.

Chapter 5: this chapter is aimed at exploring the role that cultural heritage has in shaping and influencing territorial identity and the four identified typologies. A first part of the chapter will be dedicated at conceptually deepening the mechanisms through which cultural heritage might affect territorial identity with the aid of the literature that already discussed these relationships. In a second part of the chapter, the nexus between tangible forms of cultural heritage and the four typologies of territorial identity will be empirically tested resulting in confirming the assumption that heritage does have a role in this relationship even though differentiated according to the typology.

Chapter 6: this chapter is aimed at discussing and empirically testing the role that synergies and interactions between tangible forms of heritage and territorial identity might have on local economic development. The main assumption here is that the endowment of cultural heritage does have a role in influencing local economic dynamics, but these influences are not place-neutral. In fact, the specific type of territorial identity which characterizes the place in which heritage is located might determine the effectiveness of cultural heritage as a valuable resource for economic development. The first part of the chapter will be dedicated at conceptually exploring the potential role of different typologies of territorial identity on local economic development. The second part of the chapter will be instead dedicated at empirically test the assumption that cultural heritage does have an influence on regional economic dynamics under certain specific conditions related to the typology of territorial identity.

Finally, Chapter 7 concludes summarizing the logic of the book and the main results obtained and proposing some subsequent policy recommendations related to conservation and valorization of cultural heritage also in relation with tourism and territorial identity.

References

Ashworth, G. J. (2013). Heritage and local development: A reluctant relationship. In I. Rizzo & A. Mignosa (Eds.), *Handbook on the economics of cultural heritage* (pp. 367–385). Edward Elgar.

Ashworth, G., & Larkham, P. (Eds.). (1994). *Building a new heritage. Tourism, culture and identity in the new Europe*. Routledge.

Avrami, E., & Mason, R. (Eds.). (2000). *Values and heritage conservation*. The Getty Conservation Institute.

Axelsson, R., Angelstam, P., Degerman, E., Teitelbaum, S., Andersson, K., Elbakidze, M., & Drotz, M. K. (2013). Social and cultural sustainability: Criteria, indicators, verifier variables for measurement and maps for visualization to support planning. *Ambio, 42*(2), 215–228.

Backman, M., & Nilsson, P. (2018). The role of cultural heritage in attracting skilled individuals. *Journal of Cultural Economics, 42*, 111–138.

Báez, A., & Herrero, L. C. (2012). Using contingent valuation and cost-benefit analysis to design a policy for restoring cultural heritage. *Journal of Cultural Heritage, 13*(3), 235–245.

Benhamou, F. (1996). Is increased public spending for the preservation of historic monuments inevitable? The French case. *Journal of Cultural Economics, 20*, 115–131.

Bilbao-Terol, C., Cañal-Fernández, V., Valdes, L., & Del Valle, E. (2017). Rural tourism accommodation prices by land use-based hedonic approach: First results from the case study of the self-catering cottages in Asturias. *Sustainability, 9*(10).

Birkeland, I. (2015). The potential space for cultural sustainability: Place narratives and place-heritage in Rjukan. In E. Auclair & G. Fairclough (Eds.), *Theory and practice in heritage and sustainability: Between past and future* (pp. 161–175). Routledge.

Blake, J. (2000). On defining the cultural heritage. *The international and comparative law quarterly, 1*, 61–85.

Bourdieu, P. (1986). The forms of capital. In I. Szeman & T. Kaposy (Eds.), *Cultural theory—An anthology* (pp. 81–94). Wiley.

Bowitz, E., & Ibenholdt, K. (2009). Economic impacts of cultural heritage—Research and perspectives. *Journal of Cultural Heritage, 10*, 1–8.

Buchanan, J. M. (1965). An economic theory of clubs. *Economica, 32*(125), 1–14.

Camagni, R., Capello, R., Cerisola, S., & Panzera, E. (2020). The cultural heritage—Territorial Capital nexus: Theory and empirics. *Il capital culturale,* Supplementi(11). https://doi.org/10.13138/2039-2362/2547

Canziani, A., & Moioli, R. (2010). The learning-based cultural district and the Monza and Brianza case. Learning from cultural heritage. In M. Mälkki & K. Schmidt-Thomé (Eds.), *Integrating aims—Built heritage in social economic development* (pp. 157–181). Aalto School of Science and Technology—Centre for Urban and Regional Studies (YTK).

Capello, R., & Perucca, G. (2017). Cultural capital and local development nexus: Does the local environment matter? In H. Shibusawa, K. Sakurai, T. Mizunoya, & S. Uchida (Eds.), *Socioeconomic environmental policies and evaluations in regional science—Essays in Honor of Yoshiro Higano* (pp. 103–124). Springer.

Carta, M. (Ed.). (2007). *L'armatura cultural del territorio*. Franco Angeli s.r.l.

Castells, M. (2000). Materials for an exploratory theory of the network society. *The British Journal of Sociology, 51*(1), 5–24.

Cerisola, S. (2019a). A new perspective on the cultural heritage-development nexus: The role of creativity. *Journal of Cultural Economics, 43*(1), 21–56.

Cerisola, S. (2019b). *Cultural heritage*. Edward Elgar.

Cerisola, S., & Panzera, E. (2020). Cultural and creative cities and regional economic efficiency: Context conditions as catalyzers of cultural vibrancy and creative economy. *Sustainability, 13*, 7150.

CHCfE Consortium. (2015). *Cultural heritage counts for Europe*. http://blogs.encatc.org/culturalheritagecountsforeurope//wp-content/uploads/2015/06/CHCfE_FULL-REPORT_v2.pdf, [29/10/2020].

Choi, A. S., Ritchie, B. W., Papandrea, F., & Bennett, J. (2010). Economic valuation of cultural heritage sites: A choice modeling approach. *Tourism Management, 31*(2), 213–220.

Coleman, J. S. (1988). Social capital in the creation of human capital. *American Journal of Sociology, 94*, S95–S120.

Council of Europe. (1975). *European charter of the architectural heritage*. https://www.icomos.org/en/charters-and-texts/179-articles-en-francais/ressources/charters-and-standards/170-european-charter-of-the-architectural-heritage, [29/10/2020].

Council of Europe. (2005). *Council of Europe framework convention on the value of cultural heritage for society (Faro Convention)*. https://rm.coe.int/CoERMPublicCommonSearchServices/DisplayDCTMContent?documentId=0900001680083746, [26/11/2020].

Cuccia, T., & Cellini, R. (2007). Is cultural heritage really important for tourists? A contingent rating study. *Applied Economics, 39*(2), 261–271.

Dalmas, L., Geromini, V., Noel, J. F., & Tsang, K. S. J. (2015). Economic evaluation of urban heritage: An inclusive approach under a sustainability perspective. *Journal of Cultural Heritage, 16*(5), 681–687.

de la Torre, M. (Ed.). (2002). *Assessing the values of cultural heritage*. Getty Conservation Institute.

Del Hoyo, J. J. G., Madariaga, C.J., & Espino, D. C. (2019). Approximation of the value of an asset inscribed on the list of intangible cultural heritage of UNESCO: Estimation of a hedonic price model for the fiesta of the patios in Cordoba. *Scientific Annals of Economics and Business, 66*, 5–23.

Della Torre, S. (2010). Conservazione programmata: i risvolti economici di un cambio di paradigma. *Il capitale culturale, I*, 47–55.

Della Torre, S. (2015). Lezioni imparate sul campo dei distretti culturali. *Il capitale culturale, S.O3*, 61–73.

Dessein, J., Soini, K., Fairclough, G., & Horlings, L. (2015). *Culture in, for and as sustainable development. Conclusions from the COST action IS1007 investigating cultural sustainability*. University of Jyväskylä.

Di Lascio, F. M. L., Giannerini, S., Scorcu, A. E., & Candela, G. (2011). Cultural tourism and temporary art exhibitions in Italy: A panel data analysis. *Statistical Methods & Applications, 20*(4), 519–542.

Durán, R., Begoña, A. F., & Vázquez, M. X. (2015). Conservation of maritime cultural heritage: A discrete choice experiment in a European Atlantic Region. *Marine Policy, 51*, 356–365.

ESPON. (2019). *HERITAGE—The material cultural heritage as a strategic territorial development resource: Mapping impacts through a set of common European socio-economic indicators*. https://www.espon.eu/cultural-heritage, [29/10/2020].

European Commission. (1999). *ESPD—European spatial development perspective: Towards balanced and sustainable development of the territory of the European Union*. Office for Official Publications of the European Communities.

European Commission. (2014). *Report from the commission to the European Parliament, the Council, the European Economic and Social Committee and the Committee of the regions—Report on the implementation and relevance of the Work Plan for Culture 2011–2014*. Brussels: COM (2014) 535 final. https://eur-lex.europa.eu/legal-content/EN/TXT/PDF/?uri=CELEX:52014DC0535&from=EN, [20/10/2021].

European Commission. (2015). *Getting cultural heritage to work for Europe*. https://op.europa.eu/en/publication-detail/-/publication/b01a0d0a-2a4f-4de0-88f7-85bf2dc6e004, [29/10/2020].

European Commission. (2019). *European framework for action on cultural heritage*. https://op.europa.eu/en/publication-detail/-/publication/5a9c3144-80f1-11e9-9f05-01aa75ed71a1, [29/10/2020].

Foster, V., & Mourato, S. (2002). Testing for consistency in contingent ranking experiments. *Journal of Environmental Economics and Management, 44*(2), 309–328.

Franco, S. F., & Macdonald, J. L. (2018). The effects of cultural heritage on residential property values: Evidence from Lisbon, Portugal. *Regional Science and Urban Economics, 70*, 35–56.

Franquesa, J. (2013). On keeping and selling: The political economy of heritage making in contemporary Spain. *Current Anthropology, 54*(3), 346–369.

Fusco Girard, L. (2014). *The role of cultural urban landscape towards a new urban economics: New structural assets for increasing economic productivity through hybrid processes*. In A. Maturo, B. Ferri, M. D'Incecco, F. Eugeni, R. Radoccia, & E. Sciarra, *Housing policies and urban economics—Hopui* (pp. 3–29). Fondazione Panta Rei Alta Scuola di Scienza e Formazione.

Gillman, D. (Ed.). (2006). *The idea of cultural heritage*. Cambridge University Press.

Greffe, X. (2004). Is heritage an asset or a liability? *Journal of Cultural Heritage, 5*(3), 301–309.

Greffe, X. (2011). The economic impact of the Louvre. *The Journal of Arts Management, Law and Society, 41*(2), 121–137.

Hand, C. (2018). Do the arts make you happy? A quantile regression approach. *Journal of Cultural Economics, 42*, 271–286.

Harvey, D. C. (2008). The history of heritage. In B. Graham & P. Howard (Eds.), *The Ashgate research companion to heritage and identity*. Ashgate.

Huang, C. H., Tsaur, J. R., & Yang, C. H. (2012). Does world heritage list really induce more tourists? Evidence from Macau. *Tourism Management, 33*(6), 1450–1457.

Hutter, M., & Rizzo, I. (Eds.). (1997). *Economic perspectives on cultural heritage*. Springer.

ICOMOS. (1964). *International charter for the conservation and restoration of monuments and sites (The Venice Charter 1964)*. https://www.icomos.org/charters/venice_e.pdf, [29/10/2020].

ICOMOS. (1979). *The Australia ICOMOS guidelines for the conservation of places of cultural significance ("Burra Charter")*. https://australia.icomos.org/wp-content/uploads/Burra-Charter_1979.pdf, [29/10/2020].

Iyer, S., Kitson, M., & Toh, B. (2005). Social capital, economic growth and regional development. *Regional Studies, 39*(8), 1015–1040.

Jaffry, S., & Apostolakis, A. (2011). Evaluating individual preferences for the British Museum. *Journal of Cultural Economics, 35*(1), 49–75.

Jeannerat, H., & Kebir, L. (2016). Kowledge, resources and markets: What economic system of valuation? *Regional Studies, 50*(2), 274–288.

Kamenka, E. (1988). Human rights, people's rights. In J. Crawford (Ed.), *The rights of peoples.* Clarendon Press.

Kinghorn, N., & Willis, K. (2007). Estimating visitor preferences for different art gallery layouts using a choice experiment. *Museum and Curatorship, 22*(1), 43–58.

Kroeber, A. L., & Kluckholn, C. (Eds.). (1952). *Culture: A critical review of concepts and definitions.* The Museum.

Langhelle, O. (1999). Sustainable development: Exploring the ethics of our common future. *International Political Science Review, 20*(2), 129–149.

Lazrak, F., Nijkamp, P., Rietveld, P., & Rouwendal, J. (2014). The market value of cultural heritage in urban areas: An application of spatial hedonic pricing. *Journal of Geographical Systems, 16*, 89–114.

Lazzeretti, L., & Cinti, T. (Eds.). (2001). *La valorizzazione economica del patrimonio artistico delle città d'arte.* Firenze University Press.

Leach, M. (1998). Culture and sustainability. In L. Emmerji & P. Streeton (Eds.), *World culture report* (pp. 93–104). United Nations Educational, Scientific and Cultural Organisation.

Leriche, F., & Daviet, S. (2010). Cultural economy: An opportunity to boost employment and regional development? *Regional Studies, 44*(7), 807–811.

Limonov, L. E., Nesena, M. V., & Semenov, A. A. (2020). Application of cost-benefit analysis to evaluate the efficiency of cultural heritage preservation projects in historic towns of Russia. *Regional Research of Russia, 10*(4), 530–537.

Listokin, D., Listokin, B., & Michael, L. (1998). The contributions of historic preservation to housing and economic development. *Housing Policy Debate, 9*(3), 431–478.

Lowenthal, D. (2005). Natural and cultural heritage. *International Journal of Heritage Studies, 11*(1), 81–92.

Lyck, L. (2013). Culture as a generator of regional development and economic growth. In L. Lindeborg & L. Lindkvist (Eds.), *The value of arts and culture for regional development—A Scandinavian perspective* (pp. 60–74). Routledge.

Mälkki, M., & Schmidt-Thomé, K. (Eds.). (2010). *Integrating aims—Built heritage in social economic development.* Aalto School of Science and Technology—Centre for Urban and Regional Studies (YTK).

Malecki, E. J. (2012). Regional social capital: Why it matters. *Regional Studies, 46*(8), 1023–1039.

Mason, R. (2002). *Assessing values in conservation planning: Methodological issues and choices.* In M. de la Torre (Ed.), *Assessing the values of cultural heritage* (pp. 5–31). Getty Conservation Institute.

Matarasso, F. (1997). *Use or ornament? The social impact of participation in the arts.* Comedia.

Mazzanti, M. (2002). Cultural heritage as multi-dimensional, multi-value and multi-attribute economic good: Toward a new framework for economic analysis and valuation. *Journal of Socio-Economics, 31*, 529–558.

Mazzanti, M. (2003). Discrete choice models and valuation experiments. *Journal of Economic Studies, 30*(3), 584–604.

McCarthy, K. F., Ondaatje, E. H., Zakaras, L., & Brooks, A. (2004). *Gifts of the Muse—Reframing the debate about the benefits of the arts.* Rand research in the arts. https://www.rand.org/content/dam/rand/pubs/monographs/2005/RAND_MG218.pdf, [25/02/2021].

McLoughlin, J., Sodogar, B., & Kaminski, J. (2006). Economic valuation methodologies and their application to cultural heritage. In J. McLoughlin, B. Sodogar, & J. Kaminski (Eds), (2005), *Heritage impacts 2005. Proceedings of the first international symposium on the socio-economic impact of cultural heritage* (pp. 8–27). Budapest: EPOCH.

Moro, M., Mayor, K., Lyons, S., & Tol, R. S. J. (2013). Does the housing market reflect cultural heritage? A case study of Greater Dublin. *Environment and Planning A, 45*(12), 2884–2903.
Mossetto, G., & Vecco, M. (Eds.). (2002). *Economia del patrimonio monumentale.* Franco Angeli.
Mourato, S., & Mazzanti, M. (Eds.). (2002). *Economic valuation of cultural heritage: Evidence and prospects.* In M. de la Torre (Ed.). *Assessing the values of cultural heritage* (pp. 51–77). Getty Conservation Institute.
Nadel, M. V., & Rourke, F. E. (1975). Bureaucracies. In F. Greenstein & N. Polsby (Eds.), *Handbook of political science.* Addison-Wesley.
Navrud, S., & Ready, R. C. (Eds.). (2002). *Valuing cultural heritage. applying environmental valuation techniques to historic buildings, monuments and artifacts.* Edward Elgar.
Nocca, F., & Fusco Girard, L. (2018). Towards an integrated evaluation approach for cultural urban landscape conservation/regeneration. *Region, 5*(1), 33–51.
Nurse, K. (2006). *Culture as the fourth pillar of sustainable development.* Institute of International Relations, University of the West Indies.
OECD. (2008). *The impact of culture on tourism.* https://www.oecd.org/industry/the-impact-of-culture-on-tourism-9789264040731-en.htm, [29/10/2020].
Olsson, K. (2010). *Cultural heritage as a resource in place marketing.* In M. Mälkki & K. Schmidt-Thomé (Eds.), *Integrating aims—Built heritage in social economic development* (pp. 251–269). Aalto School of Science and Technology—Centre for Urban and Regional Studies (YTK).
Oppio, A., Bottero, M., Ferretti, V., Fratesi, U., Ponzini, D., & Pracchi, V. (2015). Giving space to multicriteria analysis for complex cultural heritage systems: The case of the castles in Valle D'Aosta Region, Italy. *Journal of Cultural Heritage, 16*(6), 779–789.
Patuelli, R., Mussoni, M., & Candela, G. (2013). The effects of World Heritage Sites on domestic tourism: A spatial interaction model for Italy. *Journal of Geographical Systems, 15*(3), 369–402.
Peacock, A. (1978). Preserving the past: An international economic dilemma. *Journal of Cultural Economics, 2*(2), 1–11.
Peacock, A. (1995). A future for the past: The political economy of heritage. *Proceedings of the British Academy, 87*, 189–243.
Peacock, A. (1998). The economist and heritage policy: A review of the issue. In A. Peacock (Ed.), *Does the past have a future? The political economy of heritage.* Institute of Economic Affairs.
Plaza, B., & Haarich, S. N. (2015). The Guggenheim Museum Bilbao: Between regional embeddedness and global networking. *European Planning Studies, 23*(8), 1456–1475.
Pitruzzella, G. (2000). *La nozione di bene culturale.* In Aedon, 1/2000. http://www.aedon.mulino.it/archivio/2000/1/pit.htm, [24/02/2021].
Pompili, T., Pisati, M., & Lorenzini, E. (2019). Determinants of international tourist choices in Italian provinces: A joint demand–supply approach with spatial effects. *Papers in Regional Science, 98*(6), 2251–2273.
Poor, P. J., & Smith, J. M. (2004). Travel cost analysis of a cultural heritage site: The case of Historic St. Mary's City of Maryland. *Journal of Cultural Economics, 28*(3), 217–229.
Prutsch. (2017). *Research for CULT committee—European Identity, European Parliament, policy department for structural and cohesion policies.* Brussels. https://www.europarl.europa.eu/RegData/etudes/STUD/2017/585921/IPOL_STU(2017)585921_EN.pdf, [26/11/2020].
Putnam, R. D. (2000). Bowling alone: America's declining social capital. *Culture and Politics*, 223–234.
Reilly, S., Nolan, C., & Monckton, L. (2018). *Wellbeing and the historic environment.* Historic England. https://historicengland.org.uk/images-books/publications/wellbeing-and-the-historic-environment/wellbeing-and-historic-environment/, [25/02/2021].
Rodríguez-Pose, A. (2017). The revenge of the places that don't matter (and what to do about it). *Cambridge Journal of Regions, Economy and Society, 11*(1), 189–209.
Sable, A. S., & Kling, R. W. (2001). The double public good: A conceptual framework for "shared experience" values associated with heritage conservation. *Journal of Cultural Economics, 25*, 77–89.

Sacco, P. L., Tavano, B. G., & Nuccio, M. (2010). Cultural policies and local planning strategies: What is the role of culture in local sustainable development? *The Journal of Arts, Management, Law, and Society, 39*(1), 45–64.

Samuelson, P. A. (1954). The pure theory of public expenditure. *The Review of Economics and Statistics, 3*(4), 387–389.

Santagata, W., & Signorello, G. (2000). Contingent valuation of a cultural public good and policy design: The case of "Napoli Musei Aperti." *Journal of Cultural Economics, 24*, 181–204.

Santagata, W. (2004). *Cultural districts and economic development* (Working Paper No. 01/2004). Dipartimento di Economia "S. Cognetti de Martiis"—International Centre for Research on the Economics of Culture, Institutions, and Creativity (EBLA).

Sælensminde, K. (2002). The impact of choice inconsistencies in stated choice studies. *Environmental and Resource Economics, 23*(4), 403–420.

Sciacchitano, E. (2019). European year of cultural-heritage. A laboratory for heritage-based innovation. *Scientific Research and Information Technology, 9*(1), 1–14.

Scott, A. J. (1997). The cultural economy of cities. *International Journal of Urban and Regional Research, 2*, 323–329.

Seaman, A. B. (2006). *The relationship among regional economic impact models: contingent valuation versus economic impact in the case of cultural assets* (Working Paper 06/05). Georgia State University, Non-profit studies program.

Seghezzo, L. (2009). The five dimensions of sustainability. *Environmental Politics, 4*, 539–556.

Settis, S. (Ed.). (2005). *Battaglie senza eroi*. Mondadori Electa.

Smith, L. (2006). *Uses of heritage*. Routledge.

Snowball, J. D. (2013). The economic, social and cultural impact of cultural heritage: Methods and examples. In I. Rizzo & A. Mignosa (Eds.), *Handbook on the economics of cultural heritage* (pp. 438–456). Edward Elgar.

Srakar, A., & Vecco, M. (2017). Ex-ante versus ex-post: Comparison of the effects of the European Capital of Culture Maribor 2012 on tourism and employment. *Journal of Cultural Economics, 41*(2), 197–214.

Staber, U., & Sautter, B. (2011). Who are we, and do we need to change? Cluster identity and life cycle. *Regional Studies, 45*(10), 1349–1361.

Stevenson, D. (2007). "Civic Gold" Rush. *International Journal of Cultural Policy, 10*(1), 119–131.

Storhammar, E., & Tohmo, T. (2010). The Nexus between culture and economics—Culture as a contributory factor in the competitiveness of regions. In M. Mälkki & K. Schmidt-Thomé (Eds.), *Integrating aims—Built heritage in social economic development*, (pp. 43–59). Aalto School of Science and Technology—Centre for Urban and Regional Studies (YTK).

Storm, A. (2008). *Hope and rust. Reinterpreting the industrial place in the late 20th century*. KTH.

Thompson, E. C., Berger, M. C., & Allen, S. N. (1997). *Arts and the Kentucky Economy*. Report of the Center for Business and Economic Research, University of Kentucky, Gatton College of Business and Economics.

Thorpe J. (2008). *Assessing policy instruments, price waterhouse cooper, Department of the Environment, Water, Heritage and the Arts*. https://www.environment.gov.au/system/files/resources/da10a766-2ef7-4989-b202-edac0f5d6f3e/files/economics-assessing.pdf, [29/10/2020].

Throsby, T. (1999). Cultural capital. *Journal of Cultural Economics, 23*, 3–12.

Throsby, D. (Ed.). (2001). *Economics and culture*. Cambridge University Press.

Throsby, D. (2013). Assessment of value in heritage regulation. In I. Rizzo & A. Mignosa (Eds.), *Handbook on the economics of cultural heritage* (pp. 456–470). Edward Elgar.

Timothy, D. J. (Ed.). (2011). *Cultural heritage and tourism—An introduction*. Channel View Publications.

Tosco, C. (Ed.). (2014). *I beni culturali. Storia, tutela e valorizzazione*. Il Mulino.

Tourkulias, C., Skiada, T., Mirasgedis, S., & Diakoulaki, D. (2015). Application of the travel cost method for the valuation of the Poseidon temple in Sounio, Greece. *Journal of Cultural Heritage, 16*(4), 567–574.

Towse, R. (Ed.). (2003). *A handbook of cultural economics*. Edward Elgar.

Tuan, T. H., & Navrud, S. (2008). Capturing the benefits of preserving cultural heritage. *Journal of Cultural Heritage, 9*(3), 326–337.

Tubadji, A., Osoba, B. J., & Nijkamp, P. (2015). Culture-based development in the USA: Culture as a factor for economic welfare and social well-being at a county level. *Journal of Cultural Economics, 39*, 277–303.

Tufts, S., & Milne, S. (1999). Museums—A supply-side perspective. *Annals of Tourism Research, 26*(3), 613–631.

UNESCO. (1954). *Convention for the protection of cultural property in the event of armed conflict with regulations for the execution of the convention 1954.* http://portal.unesco.org/en/ev.php-URL_ID=13637&URL_DO=DO_TOPIC&URL_SECTION=201.html, [29/10/2020].

UNESCO. (1968). *Recommendation concerning the preservation of cultural property endangered by public or private works.* http://portal.unesco.org/en/ev.php-URL_ID=13085&URL_DO=DO_TOPIC&URL_SECTION=201.html, [29/10/2020].

UNESCO. (1971). *Universal Copyright Convention as revised at Paris on 24 July 1971, with Appendix Declaration relating to Article XVII and Resolution concerning Article XI 1971.* http://portal.unesco.org/en/ev.php-URL_ID=15241&URL_DO=DO_TOPIC&URL_SECTION=201.html, [29/10/2020].

UNESCO. (1972). *Convention concerning the protection of the world cultural and natural heritage*, https://whc.unesco.org/archive/convention-en.pdf, [29/10/2020].

UNWTO. (2017). *2017 International year of sustainable tourism for development.* http://www.tourism4development2017.org/why-tourism/, [29/10/2020].

Vaughan, D. R., & Booth, P. (1989). The economic importance of tourism and the arts in Merseyside. *Journal of Cultural Economics, 132*(2), 21–34.

Vecco, M. (2010). A definition of cultural heritage: From the tangible to the intangible. *Journal of Cultural Heritage, 11*, 321–324.

Vecco, M. (Ed.). (2011). *L'Evoluzione Del Concetto Di Patrimonio Culturale.* Franco Angeli.

Vincente, E. (2010). Economics of built cultural heritage. In M. Mälkki & K. Schmidt-Thomé (Eds.), *Integrating aims—Built heritage in social economic development* (pp. 17–43). Aalto School of Science and Technology—Centre for Urban and Regional Studies (YTK).

Viu, J. M., Fernandez, J. R., & Caralt, J. S. (2008). The impact of heritage tourism on an urban economy: The case of Granada and the Alhambra. *Tourism Economics, 14*(2), 361–376.

Williams, R. (Ed.). (1976). *Keywords. A vocabulary of culture and society.* Oxford University Press.

Williams, R. (Ed.). (1981). *The sociology of culture.* The University of Chicago Press, published by an arrangement with Shocken Books, Inc.

Wilson, N., Gross, J., & Bull, A. (Eds.). (2016). *Towards cultural democracy—Promoting cultural capabilities for everyone.* King's College.

Zetti, J. (2010). Built heritage, local communities and the production of territory. Citizen participation in heritage preservation and improvement. In M. Mälkki & K. Schmidt-Thomé (Eds.), *Integrating aims—Built heritage in social economic development* (pp. 231–251). Aalto School of Science and Technology—Centre for Urban and Regional Studies (YTK).

Part I
From Cultural Heritage to Local Development: The Role of Tourism

Chapter 2
Cultural Heritage, Tourism and Economic Development in the Existing Literature and Beyond

2.1 Tourism and Cultural Tourism

As cultural heritage is studied and discussed through the economist's lens, the first, most intuitive and straightforward association is the one with tourism. Millions of visitors from all over the world are attracted by the outstanding and differentiated European heritage and millions of travelers seek to experience the richness and the vibrancy of European cultural life. As highlighted in the *Cultural Heritage Counts for Europe* report "*Cultural heritage provides European countries and regions with a unique identity that creates compelling city narratives providing the basis for effective marketing strategies aimed at developing cultural tourism and attracting investment*" (CHCfE Consortium, 2015, p. 20). From this vast interest toward cultural heritage that moves people to travel and visit places, the economic development of touristic destinations is stimulated and enhanced.

Generally speaking, tourism plays an important role in the world economies. As De Micco et al. (2021) reported, international worldwide arrivals passed one billion in 2011 and, until 2020, this number was increasing by about 50 million each year. 2018 witnessed the 9th consecutive year of sustained growth of tourist arrivals and tourist receipts, demonstrating the sector's strength and resilience (UNWTO, 2019). As highlighted by UNWTO in the 2019 edition of *International Tourism Highlights*, p. 2, the stable expansion of tourism is driven and facilitated by "*a relatively strong global economy, a growing middle class in emerging economies, technological advances, new business models, affordable travel costs and visa facilitation*". In terms of export revenues, tourism is the world's third largest export category after fuels and chemicals, and ahead of automotive products and food (UNWTO, 2019). Tourism also contributes to generate millions of direct and indirect jobs with a definite prevalence of micro, small and medium sized enterprises (around 80%) that employ a high share of women, young people and people from a migrant background (World Tourism Organization, 2018a). In this context, Europe accounts for half of the world's international arrivals and represents almost 40% of international tourism receipts. These numbers emphasize the extremely important role that tourism

E. Panzera, *Cultural Heritage and Territorial Identity*, Advances in Spatial Science,
https://doi.org/10.1007/978-3-030-94468-1_2

plays in Europe, the world's most visited region. As reported in the 2018 *European Union Tourism Trends* report, tourism generates 10% of European GDP, it represents 9% of total employment and accounts for 6% of EU overall exports and 22% of services exports. Tourism is nowadays considered as one of the key pillars of the EU strategy dedicated to creating jobs and supporting inclusive growth (World Tourism Organization, 2018a).

Shifting the focus on cultural tourism, even though precise and detailed data accounting for the number of tourists traveling for cultural purposes is still scant, it is estimated that around 40% of European tourism is cultural as 4 out of 10 tourists select their destination based on its cultural offering (https://ec.europa.eu/growth/sectors/tourism/offer/cultural_en). The European Union recognizes the relevance of cultural tourism for its economy, society, culture and ways of living. As stated in the Treaty of Lisbon in article 195 of the TFEU, the Union shall complement the action of Member States promoting the competitiveness in the tourism sector and encouraging the creation of a favorable environment and a cooperative attitude between the Member States by exchanging good practices. As highlighted in the *European Tourism Manifesto* "[*Tourism*] *helps to sustain our cultural and natural heritage, provides revenue to find facilities and infrastructure enjoyed by visitors and residents, and promotes awareness of a common European identity and citizenship distinguished by its diversity*" (https://tourismmanifesto.eu/). In fact, tourism and culture are strictly interlinked, they evolve together, and they complement each other (European Commission and Council, 2020).

It is worth noticing that, as the concept of culture and cultural heritage are so complex to delineate, a straightforward definition of cultural tourism is similarly complicated. The seventeenth- and eighteenth-century "Grand Tour" of Europe created the basis for cultural tourism as it was pleasure travel driven by cultural and educational motivations. After that, the development and expansion of museums, exhibitions and cultural events contributed to the attraction of cultural tourists. As highlighted in the European Commission and Council 2020 report *Cultural tourism in the EU macro-regions* it is during the twentieth century that the concept of cultural tourism saw the light and it mainly concerned visits to historical buildings and famous sites. Following the enlargement of the concept of cultural heritage from tangible manifestation only to intangible, symbolic and folkloristic ones, nowadays tourists want to experience communities' local cultures, customs and beliefs as well as enogastronomic traditions. Heritage tourism is therefore complemented by cross-cultural tourism which involves "*active learning through interactions with people who can explain an activity from their perspective, and its meaning for them: passive observation is replaced by active experience*" (European Commission and Council, 2020, p. 7).

Following the UNWTO, cultural tourism can be defined as "*a type of tourism activity in which the visitor's essential motivation is to learn, discover, experience and consume the tangible and intangible cultural attractions/products in a tourism destination. These attractions/products relate to a set of distinctive material, intellectual, spiritual and emotional features of a society that encompasses arts and architecture, historical and cultural heritage, culinary heritage, literature, music, creative industries, and the living cultures with their lifestyles, value systems, beliefs and traditions*" (UNWTO Assembly, 22nd session, 2017—https://www.unwto.org/tourism-and-culture). Cultural heritage is an asset for tourism, and, in turn, tourism is an opportunity for cultural heritage. Citing from the 2018 report *Tourism and cultural synergies* (2018, p. 13) "*culture and tourism have a symbiotic relationship. Arts and crafts, dances, rituals, and legends which are at risk of being forgotten by the younger generation may be revitalized when tourists show a keen interest in them. Monuments and cultural relics may be preserved by using funds generated by tourism*" (World Tourism Organization, 2018b).

Following the increasing relevance of tourism for European and world economies and the growing importance and expansion of cultural tourism, the academic field of applied economics developed and is increasingly developing, a great amount of scientific literature related to both tourism and cultural tourism. More specifically, the empirical literature focuses on the role of culture and cultural heritage in attracting tourists and in parallel on the impact of tourism in general on economic growth. The following sections summarize the main findings of these two strands of research.

2.2 Cultural Heritage, Tourism and Economic Implications: The Existing Literature and the Novelties of the Book

2.2.1 From Cultural Heritage to Tourism: Some Literature Background

As cultural heritage and tourism show a symbiotic and intertwined relationship, the academic literature has widely explored this link focusing on different perspectives and with different aims of the analysis. Within the context of this book, the empirical literature in the field of applied economics is considered and discussed even though cultural heritage and tourism have been the objects of interest of many other scientific disciplines such as anthropology, history or management studies.

Overall, the main aim of the academic studies dealing with this topic lies in determining whether the presence of cultural heritage sites, museums, cultural events or cultural expressions in general do have a quantifiable impact on tourism attractiveness and tourism performance. The topic is particularly relevant for two main reasons: on the one hand, tourism has nowadays achieved such prominence in virtually all economic and social spheres that, if well planned and managed, it can be highly beneficial for conservation, preservation and acknowledgment of heritage; on the other hand, however, culture and history of places are developed totally outside the scope of tourism. Moreover, as argued in Crouch and Ritchie (1999), the risk of altering local cultures to meet touristic needs should be avoided and prevented: overtourism phenomena might have detrimental consequences for heritage care and protection.

As well explained by Fusco Girard and Nijkamp (2009), cultural heritage has a *love-hate* relationship with tourism. In fact, it plays a key role in attracting travelers from many different origins thus stimulating local socio-economic development together with a sense of local identity and pride. However, excessive and disproportionate volumes of tourists may threaten the ecologically benign development of places and negatively affect social cohesion generating controversial consequences. As Throsby (2009, p. 14) puts it "*tourism may be the only viable source of recurrent revenue to maintain certain heritage assets, but at the same time may threaten the very survival of those assets*".

Understanding whether cultural heritage and tourism are actually linked by an empirically proven relationship is therefore of fundamental importance to express some policy recommendations aimed at finding the right balance between heritage usage and conservation. By adopting the classification proposed by Crouch and Ritchie (1999, pp. 142–144), tourist destinations are characterized by *comparative advantages* and *competitive advantages.* The first category refers to factor endowment of places, both naturally occurring and created. Four broad areas usually enter this category of advantages (see Porter, 1990), namely human resources, knowledge resources, capital resources and infrastructure. When comparative advantages are considered within the tourism context, historical and cultural resources should be added to this typology of advantages. *Competitive advantages* are instead referred to the ability of a destination to effectively use its resources over the long term. As highlighted by Pompili et al. (2019) and Marrocu and Paci (2013), the tourism market is increasingly operating as a competitive industry, where destinations, also at different territorial levels, are horizontally differentiated, fitting with different personal and social tastes. Therefore, the identification and understanding of the determinants of competitiveness are of paramount importance to address tourism planning and destination management. In this sense, the endowment of cultural heritage is a strong endogenous territorial element contributing to the competitive advantage of an area.

A variety of perspectives have been proposed by the literature of tourism economics, tourism management, heritage economics, cultural management and cultural policy. Nevertheless, in spite of the great effort undertaken by the scientific literature, a clear consensus on the existence of an actual, quantitatively proven nexus between endowment of cultural heritage and tourism attractiveness is still to be reached. In fact, the heterogeneity of the methods adopted and the multiplicity of measures used to proxy the presence of cultural heritage or the success of tourism attractiveness, all contribute to the diversity of the results and to the difficulty in generalizing the main messages.

More specifically, multiple aims are sought for by the literature devoted to exploring the cultural heritage-tourism nexus. Several studies investigate the determinants of tourism demand taking into consideration the attributes of both tourist origins and destinations (see for instance Faber & Gaubert, 2019; Petit & Seetaram, 2018). The endowment of cultural heritage in tourist destinations is usually considered as a factor that potentially stimulates tourism movements toward that destination; however, measuring and assessing such a composite and multi-faceted element as cultural heritage inevitably introduce an issue related to results comparability.

In fact, given both the complex nature of cultural heritage and its place-based and idiosyncratic nature, various measures have been adopted to proxy destinations' cultural endowment in single countries or in specific case-studies. For instance, as also highlighted in Panzera et al. (2020), Cuccia and Cellini (2007) study the role of museums and monuments' attendance on tourism demand in Italian regions; Yang et al. (2010) include in their analysis the number of cultural areas as classified by the Chinese regulation to study tourism movements in China's provinces; Di Lascio et al. (2011) explore the role played by temporary art exhibitions; Pompili et al. (2019) adopt a proxy for cultural importance together with the number of museums. Overall, however, the most used proxy for tangible forms of cultural heritage is the presence of UNESCO World Heritage Sites (see Groizard & Santana-Gallego, 2018; Huang et al., 2012; Patuelli et al, 2013; Park & Jang, 2014; Ribaudo & Figini, 2016; Van Blarcom & Kayahan, 2011). As previously mentioned, the results are mixed. For instance, Cellini and Cuccia (2013) found a co-integrated link between tourism and museums and monuments attendance. In the long run, in particular, the causality relation goes from tourism arrivals to heritage attendance. Ribaudo and Figini (2016) did not find any empirically proven nexus between the presence of UNESCO World Heritage Sites and tourism attractiveness. Furthermore, they highlight the great difference between different destinations within the same country. The same result is obtained by Huang et al. (2012) who, focusing on the specific case study of the Chinese city of Macao, argue that the role of UNESCO World Heritage Sites is minor in the long run. On the other hand, Di Lascio et al. (2011), Massidda and Etzo (2012) and Pompili et al. (2019) find a positive relationship between, respectively, temporary art exhibitions, local government support for cultural activities and cultural relevance and museums on tourism attractiveness. By the same token, several studies empirically test and confirm a significant nexus between the presence of UNESCO World Heritage Sites and tourist movements (see for instance, Panzera et al., 2020; Park & Yang, 2014; Patuelli et al., 2013; Van Blarcom & Kayahan, 2011; Yang et al., 2010).

If the previously mentioned studies focused on destinations (and sometimes origins) macro-attributes, several other studies aim to explore the determinants of tourism choices based on micro-data (or both micro and macro data) such as the socio-economic conditions of tourists or their psychographic characteristics (see, for instance, Brida & Scuderi, 2013; Marrocu et al., 2015; Park et al., 2019). The main idea behind these studies refers to the fact that the presence of cultural heritage or cultural amenities consolidates the tourism competitiveness of a destination by improving tourists' satisfaction and increasing their utility and happiness (Bernini et al., 2020; Cracolici & Nijkamp, 2009). Besides, Bernini et al. (2017) blended the microeconomic research at the individual level and the tourist amenities at a local territorial level. In fact, the decision about where to travel for holidays is codetermined by planned tourist expenditures (dependent on income, education, gender, age) and both destination and origin characteristics and, among other factors, origin and destination endowment of cultural amenities.

Destination endowment of cultural heritage does also play a relevant role in the studies dedicated to detecting tourism efficiency and competitiveness in terms of increased overnight stays using both parametric and non-parametric methods (DEA). A virtual production function is the basis of this approach in which tourist destinations display the capacity to operate on their tourism resources to maximize their tourism output or impact (Gomez-Vega et al., 2021). More in detail, the presence of cultural heritage has (recently) been considered as a territorial asset that might support destination efficiency improvement. Gomez-Vega et al. (2021) and Guccio et al. (2017) agree on the positive role that cultural heritage, cultural participation and leisure have on the performance of a touristic destination. The presence of cultural sites and facilities contributes to maximizing the profitability of international tourism, given the flow of arrivals, the accommodation capacity and the importance attached to the tourism industry.

Overall, this strand of the literature aims at exploring the relationship between cultural heritage (in the broader sense of the term) and tourism attractiveness adopting quantitative methodologies. When this relationship holds, the consequent economic implications are given for granted, without necessarily empirically test them. A different and independent strand of the literature focuses on the economic impact driven by the tourism sector and aims at quantifying it. The following section describes this parallel research line.

2.2.2 *From Tourism to Economic Development: Some Literature Background*

As previously highlighted, tourism represents a relevant economic sector worldwide. The academic literature dedicated its interest to the topic and produced a great number of studies, articles and scientific material devoted to exploring the relationship between tourism and economic development. Many scientific journals in the field of applied economics are specifically specialized in deepening the role of tourism in the economies worldwide such as, among others, Annals of Tourism Research, The International Journal of Tourism Research and Tourism Management. As highlighted in Adie and Falk (2020), investigating the impact of tourism on localized economies and employment creation is not a new topic (see, for instance, English et al., 2000; Hohl & Tisdell, 1995; Kadiyali & Kosovà, 2013; Liu & Song, 2017; Paramati et al., 2017).

Multiple mechanisms underlie the relationship between tourism and economic development. As well explained by Liu and Song (2017) economies are influenced by tourism through three different types of effects. Tourists visiting places spend a certain amount of money generating direct revenues for tourist-related activities such as accommodation establishments, transportation enterprises, bars and restaurants or travel agencies inducing an unambiguous effect on the local economy increasing the level of domestic demand. In the second place, in order to provide their services to the travelers, these tourist-related activities need inputs from suppliers who therefore indirectly benefit from the tourism sector. Finally, a third order of effects occurs as soon as the beneficiaries of tourist expenditures consume their earnings either spending in consumption or investment goods, favoring local economy. As highlighted by Kadiyali and Kosovà (2013), tourism generates spillover effects deriving from the increased demand of local goods and services by the visitors, both in the form of direct spending or indirectly via multiplier effects. The impact of tourism flows on the local economies is not limited to the sectors that are strictly related with tourism, such as accommodation and establishment, and spills over to other sectors such as construction, retail, health care and professional and technical services.

Tourism can be considered as a form of trade in services (Morley et al., 2014), and it allows local economies to export non-tradable services since it implies tourist flows rather than good flows (Copeland, 1991; Faber & Gaubert, 2019). In other words, local services are consumed in the same place where they are produced. Tourist expenditures generate inflows of foreign currency contributing to the balance of payment through foreign exchange earnings (Seetanah, 2011; Soukiazis & Proença, 2008). Furthermore, other incentives for local economies stemming from tourism are related to production and employment. In fact, larger amount of import of capital goods (Seetanah, 2011), inter-industry connection upturn (Paci & Marrocu, 2014) and increased efficiency obtained through competition between local firms and analogous activities in different tourist destinations (Dritsakis, 2004) are able to induce higher production levels. Besides, being the tourism sector strongly reliant on labor, an expansion of the sector positively impacts local employment (Dritsakis, 2004). As argued by Naranpanawa et al. (2018, p. 1732), the tourism industry presents some unique characteristics as it is labor intensive, and it can absorb both high and low-skill labor; using their words "*tourism can be considered as an accessible and attractive option during times of economic transition and labor displacement*".

Other potential economic gains deriving from the development of the tourism sector concern gaining tax revenues (Seetanah, 2011); increasing investments in infrastructure or tourism-related services (Paci & Marrocu, 2014; Soukiazis & Proença, 2008); generation of positive economies of scale and scope related to hotel firms that tend to expand their size and to provide diversified facilities (Brida & Pulina, 2010). Finally, since tourism usually takes place in territories endowed with natural or cultural amenities, the rent and price of the houses appear to be higher being positively affected by both general higher demand for residential assets and by tourism activity (see for instance Biagi et al., 2015; Copeland, 1991).

As highlighted by Nunkoo et al. (2020), the economic implications of tourism have provided several research opportunities. One of them is the econometric and quantitative documentation of the tourism-growth relationship. This literature finds its basis in the so-called *tourism-led growth hypothesis* developed and analyzed by Balaguer and Cantavella-Jordà (2002). As explained in Brida and Pulina (2010), this hypothesis was directly derived from the export-led growth hypothesis according to which exports contribute to economic growth through the improvement of the efficiency in the allocation of the factors of production and through the expansion of their volumes. Furthermore, the level of investment is increased by exports. Similarly, the tourism-led growth hypothesis provides the theoretical foundations for this relationship, in the case of tourism econometrically proves the nexus. Following the pioneering effort of Balaguer and Cantavella-Jordà (2002) several studies tried to confirm this hypothesis and aimed at understanding whether tourism leads to economic expansions or, instead, economic growth boosts tourism growth or a bidirectional relationship exists, in a more macro-economic and macro-territorial approach. Building on standard growth models, the tourism-led growth hypothesis, has been econometrically investigated applying diverse econometric techniques to different countries, time spans, geographical disaggregation levels or development conditions. A great variety of methodologies has been applied ranging from vector autoregressive model for time-series data to generalized method of moments for panel data (for a comprehensive overview see Brida & Pulina, 2010). Apparently, no agreement on the tourism-led growth hypothesis has been reached so far by the literature (Zuo & Huang, 2017). Empirical outcomes range from the validity of the direct causality nexus (see for instance Arslanturk et al., 2011; Balaguer & Cantavella-Jordá, 2002; Bronzini et al., 2019; Cortés-Jiménez, 2008; Liu & Song, 2017; Salifou & ul Haq, 2017; Soukiazis & Proença, 2008), documentation of a bilateral causality (see for instance Dogru & Bulut, 2018; Dritsakis, 2004; Ridderstaat et al., 2014), finding of a reverse mechanism (Narayan, 2004; Oh, 2005), but also neutrality (Singh et al., 2010) and negative relationships (Capò et al., 2007). Overall, however, as highlighted by Nunkoo et al. (2020) that conducted a meta-analysis on more than 100 studies dedicated at exploring the tourism-led growth hypothesis, there is a general support for a causality nexus between tourism and economic development; the results are though sensitive to various factors.

2.2.3 *The Novelties of the Book in This Research Field*

As highlighted in the previous two sections two separate and independent strands of the literature study the link between cultural heritage and tourism and the role of tourism in economic development. However, in the first case, the economic implications stemming from the nexus heritage-tourism are implicit, without quantitatively testing them. In the second case, when tourism is proven beneficial for economic growth, the role of cultural heritage and cultural tourism in this mechanism remains unknown. Furthermore, most of the studies focus on specific countries or specific regions resulting in difficulties of generalization of the outcomes.

To try to fill these gaps, this book aims at jointly exploring the nexus between tangible forms of cultural heritage, tourism and economic development: Chapter 3 will be dedicated at quantitatively exploring this triadic relationship. Cultural heritage is hypothesized to play a role in local (regional) economic development through the touristic channel going beyond the fragmented analysis of the three elements. Furthermore, the scope of the analysis is the European Union and its regions in the attempt to give some generalizable messages.

More specifically, starting from the idea that material cultural heritage represents a critical resource potentially able to contribute to local economic growth through the mediation effect played by the tourism sector, a structural equation model is applied to European regions to figure out whether tourism represents a solid and substantial channel—out of many others—for the functioning of this mechanism. In other words, an econometric model is used to quantitatively demonstrate the existence of an indirect impact of regional cultural heritage endowment on economic development *through* tourism. Testing the model with different heritage-related variables, results confirm the mediating role of tourism between tangible forms of cultural heritage and economic growth.

Before presenting the analysis, some controversial aspects related to tourism should be mentioned. In fact, as tourism and cultural tourism grow in size, some issues arise concerning their environmental, social and cultural sustainability. These issues must be taken into consideration, even though (and especially because) the positive impact of cultural heritage through tourism will be proven true. Furthermore, by the time of writing (summer 2021), it is not possible to discuss about tourism without mentioning and debating the COVID-19 pandemic implications for tourism. The following section is dedicated at deepening the overtourism issue and the effects, consequences and future perspectives of tourism after the COVID-19 crisis.

2.3 Tourism and Economic Development: Some Controversial Facets

2.3.1 Tourism: Between Positive Economic Implications and Overtourism

The relevance of tourism as an economic sector and its continuous expansion over time are undeniably beneficial for the global and local economies in terms of income, job creation, infrastructure and services development. However, the very unstoppable and persistent multiplication of tourist flows generate concerns related to the medium and long-term sustainability of large floods of people that, in some cases, invade popular touristic destinations. Starting from the second half of the twentieth century, mass tourism began to flourish as a consequence of greater spending capabilities, development of public transportation and increasingly cheaper possibilities to travel, together with internationalization and globalization of modern communities (Bramwell, 2004). Therefore, concerns and complaints about the potentially negative implications of tourism started to grow resulting in coining new related terms such as overtourism and tourismophobia. These terms embrace the challenges experienced by touristic destinations derived from incoming vast flows of people that impact natural and built environment as well as residents' living conditions. As highlighted by the UNWTO report *Overtourism? Understanding and Managing Urban Tourism Growth beyond Perceptions*, a large number of tourists might determine the overexploitation of natural resources as well as exert socio-cultural pressure, overuse of infrastructure facilities and potential damage of heritage sites. In the same report overtourism is defined as "*the impact of tourism on a destination, or parts thereof, that excessively influences perceived quality of life of citizens and/or quality of visitors experiences in a negative way*" (World Tourism Organization et al., 2018, p. 4). It goes without saying that it is not possible to define a univocal threshold to declare an area as overtouristified. The UNWTO tries to delineate some limits through the introduction and definition of the concept *carrying capacity* which is "*the maximum number of people that may visit a tourist destination at the same time, without causing destruction of the physical, economic and socio-cultural environment and an unacceptable decrease in the quality of visitors' satisfaction*". However, the concept remains a subjective, idiosyncratic and controversial term as it might reflect the interest of some specific actors (such as real estate investors) at the expenses of others (e.g., the residents). In fact, an unequivocal definition of overtourism does not exist, and it is very much related to the interested context. As reported in Adie et al. (2020, p. 3), the Oxford Dictionary define overtourism as "*an excessive number of tourist visits to a popular destination or attraction, resulting in damage to the local environment and historical sites and in poorer quality of life for residents*". More specifically, Milano et al. (2019, p. 1858) associate overtourism to "*the excessive growth of visitors leading to overcrowding in areas where residents suffer the consequences of temporary and seasonal tourism peaks, which have caused permanent changes to their lifestyles, denied access to amenities and damaged their general well-being*". Salerno and Russo (2020, p. 2) propose an even more severe definition referring to overtourism not only as a "*strong and increasing tourism pressure on destination spaces, but most significantly the magnitude of its environmental and social effects, the most remarkable of which are possibly the unaffordability of housing for residents and for the very workers of the tourism industry*". As D'Eramo (2017) puts it, a threshold identifies a tourist city from a city that exploits tourism as one among other resources: the demarcation between a situation in which tourists enjoy services and facilities designed for residents and an opposite one in which the residents are the ones who become obliged to make use of services and facilities designed for tourists.

Even though the idea that tourism might cause issues in terms of, for instance, congestion or damage of the locals' well-being is not new, it is nowadays increasingly clear that anti-tourists movements are becoming more popular and determined. Cities like Barcelona, Amsterdam, Venice and Florence are experiencing a fast-growing development of conflicts between residents and policies aimed at supporting tourism (see for instance Amore et al., 2020; Milano et al., 2019; Salerno & Russo, 2020). The increase in visitor arrivals and the economic growth notwithstanding social movement activism has emerged to contrast the negative externalities linked with tourism flows. Several controversial and adverse consequences are usually associated with overtourism (see, for instance, Szromek et al., 2019). Increased congestion, crowding and overload of infrastructure generate unpleasant conditions for both residents and tourists themselves resulting also in higher maintenance costs for services and infrastructures, costs mainly paid by the local community (Albaladejo & Gonzalez-Martinez, 2019; Du Cros & Kong, 2020; Riganti & Nijkamp, 2008). Furthermore, excessive tourist flows cause problems to both the natural environment and cultural heritage in terms of physical deterioration and symbolic and emotional deprivation of these sites from the local community (Saeporsdottir & Hall, 2020). Issues related to environmental degradation such as water, land and air pollution, trash and waste management and removal are also to be considered when dealing with tourism planning strategies (Fang et al., 2018). An over-dependency on tourism—the so-called tourism monoculture—might also result in negative economic consequences (e.g., high risks of seasonality; great vulnerability linked to the exposure to external shock that might reduce tourist flows; neglecting investments in other sectors). As highlighted in Salerno and Russo (2020) destinations' space might change its original configuration to adapt to other uses and market forces resulting in the destruction of sense of place and territorial local identity felt by the local community. This is particularly the case when a place is sold as an authentic commodity to target tourist flows and generating a reorientation of the supply of commercial activities toward touristic needs at the expenses of proximity commerce. Furthermore, it is nowadays particularly relevant to mention the issues stemming from the platforms for short-term housing rentals such as Airbnb that contribute to generate overtourism and further exacerbate the adverse implications of touristification. More in detail, as mentioned in Franco and Santos (2021), these booking platforms intensify housing affordability issues for residents by reducing the supply of long-term housing rentals—especially in central areas—forcing local inhabitants to move to the outskirt of the cities or even to other places and contributing to gentrification issues (Cocola-Gant & Gago, 2019, Garcia-Lopez et al., 2020; Lee, 2016; Wachsmuth et al., 2017; Wachsmuth & Weisler, 2018). As Salerno and Russo (2020, p. 6) put it, short-term rents platforms might generate e phenomenon that they call *touristification of housing*. Not just small historic centers may change their identity but also medium size towns do it, when residents explicitly choose to relocate in the outskirts, leaving their facilities exclusively to tourist use.

If the issues related to overtourism apply to any type of destinations, cultural and art destinations are subject to specific challenges when they welcome large flows of tourists. Europe is particularly interested by this phenomenon as it hosts almost half of the UNESCO World Heritage Sites and it is endowed with many art cities. As De Luca et al. (2020) highlight, on the one hand, cultural tourism brings potential funds for supporting conservation efforts as well as the regeneration and preservation of peripheral areas. On the other hand, overtouristification of cultural venues, sites, facilities or cities poses the risks of loss of integrity and authenticity of the sites themselves as well as adverse implications in terms of loss of cultural identity and sense of belonging felt by the local community (see for instance Adie et al., 2020; Neuts & Nijkamp, 2012; Popp, 2012; Rasoolimanesh et al., 2019).

Overall, overtourism is a large-scale phenomenon that concerns many different places worldwide ranging from urban destinations to historical centers, from island, beaches and mountains to cultural sites and museums. It is a multi-dimensional concept as it is related to different issues from sociology to economy, from environment to gentrification. However, at the time of writing this book, the travel and tourism industry is going through an unprecedented crisis due to the outbreak of the COVID-19 pandemic that severely hit the world starting from 2020. Suddenly, in response to the spread of the virus, international movements in 2020 were cut to zero. Tourism and therefore overtourism were abruptly blocked: a counterposed situation with respect to the continuous and fast-growing increase in tourism flows registered before 2019. The following section is specifically dedicated at describing the situation of the tourism industry under these specific pandemic circumstances.

2.3.2 *Tourism and COVID-19 Pandemic: Present Challenges and Future Opportunities*

As highlighted in the Skift Research and McKinsey 2020 report titled *The travel industry turned upside down*, the COVID-19 pandemic is the greatest challenge that the modern tourism and travel industry has ever experienced. COVID-19 first emerged in China in December 2019 and rapidly spread to the whole world resulting in the declaration by the World Health Organization of, first, the outbreak of a Public Health Emergency of International Concern and, eventually, in March 2020, of a pandemic. The severe restrictions imposed by almost all the countries around the world in the attempt to face the health emergency caused—and are still causing—economic, social and political shocks. In fact, drastic measures have been taken by governments across the globe that locked down entire countries, preventing people from leaving their houses, prohibiting entry to their borders and introducing quarantines periods. As argued by Gössling et al. (2020), the context of global tourism moved essentially overnight from overtourism to no tourism at all.

Even though almost all the economic sectors have been hardly hit by the pandemic, tourism experienced an unprecedented crisis that is still ongoing at the time of writing. As reported by the UNWTO, following the World Health Organization declaration of the outbreak of the pandemic, 100% of the worldwide destinations have introduced travel restrictions and, by now, 27% of all destinations worldwide keep their borders completely closed for international tourism. If the international tourist arrivals were 1.5 billion in 2019, they dropped to 381 million in 2020 registering a 74% downturn with respect to the previous year and bringing international tourism back to 30 years ago levels. As a consequence, a loss of US$ 1.3 trillion in international tourism receipts has been registered and around 100 million jobs directly related to tourism are at risk (UNWTO website). As argued by the Skift Research and McKinsey report, COVID-19 challenges the tourism sector on two fronts: on the one hand, there is a direct impact as the very measures imposed to face the health emergency include travel limitations, transportation capacity reductions and physical distancing; on the other hand, the economic downturn linked with the COVID-19 combined with the uncertainty of the future evolution of the crisis led to a slowdown in travelers' activity. The same report highlights that the airline sector and the hotel sector, together with tours and activities organizations registered the most severe decline in revenues and they are not expected to reach pre-COVID-19 levels until 2023 or 2024.

The academic literature promptly started to analyze and explore the impact of COVID-19 on both tourism and economies worldwide as well as proposing some recovery forecasts analysis. Several studies reported the adverse impact of the pandemic on tourism sector (see for instance Dolnicar & Zare, 2020; Gössling et al., 2020; Qiu et al., 2020) and some others also pointed out that international tourism may have even contributed to spread the virus (Farzanegan et al., 2021). Based on this evidence and given the economic relevance of the sector, several studies are making the effort of proposing methods to forecast tourism recovery (see for instance Aronica et al., 2021; Assaf & Scuderi, 2020; Fotiadis et al., 2021; Karabulut et al., 2020; Sharma et al., 2021; Tsionas, 2020). Overall, a substantial uncertainty related to the evolution of the pandemic situation prevents from providing clear and straightforward forecasts. As discussed in Marques Santos et al. (2020) tourists' behaviors and choices are influenced by both economic (e.g., income reduction, unemployment or working hours reduction) and psychological factors (e.g., fear of contamination, scarce safety perceptions) that have been greatly impacted by the COVID-19 outbreak. It is not clear whether changes in travel behaviors will be limited to the short-term horizon or, instead, will continue in the long run.

Cultural tourism has also been subject to the travel limitations and anti-COVID-19 restrictions. As reported by the UNWTO Inclusive Recovery Guide dedicated at the socio-cultural impact of COVID-19 on cultural tourism, 90% of the countries closed or partially closed World Heritage Sites during 2020 and 70% of the world's museums were forced to temporarily shut down and more than 10% may never reopen. Furthermore, lockdowns and physical distances measures forced the cancelation of several events, rituals, food and music festivals around the world with adverse implications not only related to economies but also to socio-cultural aspects that damaged local communities. As highlighted by UNESCO (2020) artists and cultural professionals experienced a state of extreme economic and social fragility. UNWTO emphasizes the major role that cities have traditionally played in cultural tourism and the consequent enormous difficulties that the same cities must face due to restrictions and shutdowns of urban tourism. A considerable attempt has been made by cultural institutions and organizations to share their heritage and services online so that people could enjoy cultural experiences from home. During this challenging period culture has been proven of fundamental importance as millions of people participated in these different ways of experiencing culture in the search for a sense of comfort and source of inspiration for future travels (UNWTO).

Citing from the UNWTO Secretary-General "*This crisis is an opportunity to rethink the tourism sector and its contribution to the people and planet; an opportunity to build back better towards a more sustainable, inclusive and resilient tourism sector that ensure the benefits of tourism are enjoyed widely and fairly*" (Zurab Pololikashvili, UNWTO Secretary-General, UNWTO website). By the same token, the health emergency has been considered from many parts as an opportunity to reconsider tourism and to abandon unsustainable practices to move toward more sustainable, resilient and inclusive models to meet and contribute to the Sustainable Development Goals (SDGs). In fact, tourism has the potential to contribute to all the 17 SDGs and it is specifically mentioned in 3 of them (8, 12, 14). As evident from many forecasts and as proven right from the experience of previous crisis, tourism will rebound. However, several opportunities have been opened by this crisis for tourism to restart in a more sustainable way also considering and trying to solve the previous issues liked with overtourism as described in Sect. 2.3.1. Tourism success has been commonly defined in terms of growth in tourism numbers; however, this perspective has already been questioned before the COVID-19 crisis (see for instance Hall, 2019) because of overcrowding, climate, ecological and social issues directly associated with this approach. As argued by Gössling et al. (2020) the COVID-19 pandemic represents and opportunity and calls for a critical reconsideration of this volume growth model for tourism. The tourism sector needs to renovate in two main ways: on the one hand, new and innovative strategies are required that safeguard the health and safety of travelers and employees to restore consumer confidence (Sharma et al., 2021). On the other hand, more sustainable practices with respect to the pre-COVID period are desirable and expected. In this sense, several precautions and actions have been proposed by both institutions and scholars such as fostering the integration between urban and rural tourism proposing alternative, complementary and sustainable offers; implementing multi-level and participatory governance strategies; better communication directed both to tourists and residents and promoting inclusive approaches. The Joint Research Center proposed the following policy recommendations: make optimal use of policy initiatives already in place (e.g., measures to save jobs and improve skills; promotion of local tourism); carefully consider the implications of changing consumer preferences (shifting consumer preferences toward safety and healthy environment); increasing resilience through diversification (Marques Santos et al., 2020).

The same discussion in rethinking tourism in a more sustainable way is also ongoing in the cultural tourism field. UNWTO (2021) proposes some recommendations in the direction of promoting synergies, diversification and integration between urban and rural destinations and fostering community-based tourism through living heritage. Furthermore, the idea of the so-called *creative tourism* has been retrieved from many parts (see for instance Cruz et al., 2019) The concept of creative tourism has been proposed by Richards and Raymond (2000), and it is considered as a form of tourism in which travelers are offered the opportunity to develop their creative potential through the active participation in and experience of local skills, expertise and traditions. As argued by Russo and Richards (2016), a reposition of tourism is needed in which economic objectives take the second place while collaborative and relational forms of knowledge are put in the foreground together with the understanding of local values and identities (Cruz et al., 2019). The promotion of creative tourism is nowadays important as it also implies the possibility to valorize non-standard networks and routes, differentiating the touristic offer. Furthermore, in the context of cultural tourism the digital tools and the new technologies are a powerful occasion to be exploited to promote new and innovative ways to enjoy cultural facilities. Building a more resilient tourism and culture workforce thanks to the digital transition and harnessing technology to make cultural tourism more competitive are included as well in the UNWTO (2021) recommendations.

Based on the early subjective impressions coming from the half tourist season 2021 and reasoning from a tourist country like Italy, an evident desire of people for traveling, vacationing, visiting different places has filled destinations with tourists.

An also psychological urgency for going back to normal and coming back to previous times generated a reinforce of tourism demand even accompanied by higher spending availabilities for some. In terms of consumers' choices related to the ways of traveling, more individualistic types of decisions will be probably made. Private houses might be for instance preferred with respect to hotels; traveling by car could be chosen instead of using other means of transportation (an issue which should be promptly faced by public administrations). Another common trait in tourists' behaviors, by now strictly linked to COVID-19-related concerns, led some people to try to avoid over-popular, large destinations in favor of smaller, less well-known but precious sites and places. The impression is that this trend will continue in the future both as a result of changed consumers' preferences and administrations' strategies. Domestic tourism seemed to be largely chosen by travelers, whenever travel was possible, in 2020 and 2021 even when travel restrictions to other countries were not in place. This tendency is highly dependent on the evolution of the pandemic, but it could be true that if tourism is well dilute toward many different places, domestic tourism might remain highly predominant. In case of sufficient control of the pandemic and in the absence of drastic shifting in the tourism-related strategies, a "new normality" for tourism could very closely resemble the "old normality".

References

Adie, B. A., & Falk, M. (2020). Residents' perception of cultural heritage in terms of jobs creation and overtourism in Europe. *Tourism Economics, 27*(6), 1185–1201.

Adie, B. A., Falk, M., & Savioli, M. (2020). Overtourism as a perceived threat to cultural heritage in Europe. *Current Issues in Tourism, 23*(14), 1737–2174.

Albaladejo, I. P., & Gonzalez-Martinez, M. (2019). Congestion affecting the dynamic of tourism demand: Evidence from the most popular destinations in Spain. *Current Issues in Tourism, 22*(13), 1638–1652.

Amore, A., Falk, M., & Adie, B. A. (2020). One visitor too many: Assessing the degree of overtourism in established European urban destinations. *International Journal of Tourism Cities, 6*(1), 117–137.

Aronica, M., Pizzuto, P., & Sciortino, C. (2021). COVID-19 and tourism: What can we learn from the past? *The World Economy, 00*, 1–15.

Arslanturk, Y., Balcilar, M., & Ozdemir, Z. A. (2011). Time-varying linkages between tourism receipts and economic growth in a small open economy. *Economic Modelling, 28*, 664–671.

Assaf, A., & Scuderi, R. (2020). COVID-19 and the recovery of the tourism industry. *Tourism Economics, 26*(5), 731–733.

Balaguer, J., & Cantavella-Jordá, M. (2002). Tourism as a long-run economic growth factor: The Spanish case. *Applied Economics, 34*(7), 877–884.

Bernini, C., Cerqua, A., & Pellegrini, G. (2020). Endogenous amenities, tourists' happiness and competitiveness. *Regional Studies, 54*(9), 1214–1225.

Bernini, C., Cracolici, M. F., & Nijkamp, P. (2017). Place-based attributes and spatial expenditure behavior in tourism. *Journal of Regional Science, 57*(2), 218–244.

Biagi, B., Brandano, M. G., & Lambiri, D. (2015). Does tourism affect house prices? Evidence from Italy. *Growth and Change, 46*(3), 501–528.

Bramwell, B. (Ed.). (2004). *Coastal mass tourism—Diversification and sustainable development in Southern Europe*. Aspects of Tourism, Channel View Publications.

Brida, J. G., & Pulina, M. (2010). *A literature review on the tourism-led growth hypothesis*. Working Paper 2010/17, Centro di Ricerche Economiche Nord Sud (CRENoS).

Brida, J. G., & Scuderi, R. (2013). Determinants of tourist expenditure: A review of microeconometric models. *Tourism Management Perspectives, 6*, 28–40.

Bronzini, R., Ciani, E., & Montaruli, F. (2019). *Tourism and local growth in Italy*. Occasional Papers – Questioni di Economia e Finanza No. 509, Banca d'Italia.

Capò, J., Riera, F. A., & Rossellò, N. J. (2007). Dutch disease in tourism economies: Evidence from the Balearics and the Canary Islands. *Journal of Sustainable Tourism, 15*(6), 615–627.

Cellini, R., & Cuccia, T. (2013). Museum and monument attendance and tourism flow: A time series analysis approach. *Applied Economics, 45*(24), 3473–3482.

CHCfE Consortium. (2015). *Cultural heritage counts for Europe*. http://blogs.encatc.org/culturalheritagecountsforeurope//wp-content/uploads/2015/06/CHCfE_FULL-REPORT_v2.pdf, [29/10/2020].

Cocola-Gant, A., & Gago, A. (2019). Airbnb, buy-to-let investment and tourism-driven displacement: A case study in Lisbon. *Environment and Planning A: Economy and Space, 0*(0), 1–18.

Copeland, B. R. (1991). Tourism, welfare and de-industrialization in a small open economy. *Economica, 58*(232), 515–529.

Cortés-Jiménez, I. (2008). Which type of tourism matters to the regional economic growth? The cases of Spain and Italy. *International Journal of Tourism Research, 10*, 127–139.

Cracolici, M. F., & Nijkamp, P. (2008). The attractiveness and competitiveness of tourist destinations: A study of Southern Italian regions. *Tourism Management, 30*, 336–344.

Crouch, G. I., & Ritchie, J. R. B. (1999). Tourism, competitiveness, and societal prosperity. *Journal of Business Research, 44*(3), 137–152.

Cruz, A. R., Perestrelo, M., & Gato, M. A. (2019). Connecting the dots: Contributions to the creative tourism dynmics in Portugal. *Tourism & Management Studies, 15*(SI), 23–32.

Cuccia, T., & Cellini, R. (2007). Is cultural heritage really important for tourists? A contingent rating study. *Applied Economics, 39*(2), 261–271.

D'Eramo, M. (Ed.). (2017). *Il selfie del mondo. Indagine sull'età del turismo*. Feltrinelli.

De Luca, G., Dastgerdi, A. S., Francini, C., & Liberatore, G. (2020). Sustainable cultural heritage planning and management of overtourism in art cities: Lessons from atlas world heritage. *Sustainability, 12*(9), 3929.

De Micco, F., Cetron, M., Davies, O., & Guzman, J. (2021). Covid-19 impact on the future of hospitality and travel. *Journal of Hospitality and Tourism Research, 45*(5), 911–914.

Di Lascio, F. M. L., Giannerini, S., Scorcu, A. E., & Candela, G. (2011). Cultural tourism and temporary art exhibitions in Italy: A panel data analysis. *Statistical Methods & Applications, 20*(4), 519–542.

Dogru, T., & Bulut, U. (2018). Is tourism an engine for economic recovery? Theory and empirical evidence. *Tourism Management, 67*, 425–434.

Dolnicar, S., & Zare, S. (2020). COVID19 and Airbnb—Disrupting the disruptor. *Annals of Tourism Research, 83*, 102961.

Dritsakis, N. (2004). Tourism as a long-run economic growth factor: An empirical investigation for Greece using causality analysis. *Tourism Economics, 10*(3), 305–316.

Du Cros, H., & Kong, W. H. (2020). Congestion, popular world heritage tourist attractions and tourism stakeholder responses in Macao. *International Journal of Tourism Cities, 6*(4), 929–951.

English, D. B. K., Marcouiller, D. W., & Cordell, H. K. (2000). Tourism dependence in rural America: Estimates and effects. *Society & Natural Resources, 13*, 185–202.

European Commission and Council. (2020). *Cultural tourism in the EU macro-regions: Cultural Routes to increase the attractiveness of remote destinations*. https://rm.coe.int/routes4u-manual-attractiveness-remote-destination-cultural-tourism/16809ef75a%0A%0A, [20/10/2021].

Faber, B., & Gaubert, C. (2019). Tourism and economic development: Evidence from Mexico's coastline. *American Economic Review, 109*(6), 2245–2293.

Fang, Y., Yin, J., & Wu, B. (2018). Climate change and tourism: A scientometric analysis using CiteSpace. *Journal of Sustainable Tourism, 26*(1), 108–126.

Farzanegan, M. R., Gholipour, H. F., Feizi, M., Nunkoo, R., & Andargoli, A. E. (2021). International tourism and outbreak of Coronovirus (COVID-19): A cross-country analysis. *Journal of Travel Research, 60*(3), 687–692.

Fotiadis, A., Polyzos, S., & Huan, T. T. C. (2021). The good, the bad and the ugly on COVID-19 tourism recovery. *Annals of Tourism Research, 87*, 1–14.

Franco, S. F., & Santos, C. D. (2021). The impact of Airbnb on residential property values and rents: Evidence from Portugal. *Regional Science and Urban Economics, 88*, 103667.

Fusco, G. L., & Nijkamp, P. (2009). *Cultural tourism and sustainable local development*. Ashgate.

García-López, M. À., Jofre-Monseny, J., Martínez-Mazza, R., & Segú, M. (2020). Do short-term rental platforms affect housing markets? Evidence from Airbnb in Barcelona. *Journal of Urban Economics, 119*, 103278.

Gomez-Vega, M., Herrero-Prieto, L. C., & Valdivia Lopez, M. (2021). *Clustering and country destination performance at a global scale: Determining factors of tourism competitiveness*. Tourism Economics, early access.

Gössling, S., Scott, D., & Hall, M. (2020). Pandemic, tourism and global change: A rapid assessment of COVID-19. *Journal of Sustainable Tourism, 29*, 1–20.

Groizard, J. L., & Santana-Gallego, M. (2018). The destruction of cultural heritage and international tourism: The case of the Arab countries. *Journal of Cultural Heritage, 33*, 285–292.

Guccio, C., Lisi, D., Martorana, M., & Mignosa, A. (2017). On the role of cultural participation in tourism destination performance: An assessment using robust conditional efficiency approach. *Journal of Cultural Economics, 41*, 129–154.

Hall, C. M. (2019). Constructing sustainable tourism development: The 2030 agenda and the managerial ecology of sustainable tourism. *Journal of Sustainable Tourism, 27*(7), 1044–1060.

Hohl, A. E., & Tisdell, C. A. (1995). Peripheral tourism—Development and management. *Annals of Tourism Research, 2*(3), 517–534.

Huang, C. H., Tsaur, J. R., & Yang, C. H. (2012). Does world heritage list really induce more tourists? Evidence from Macau. *Tourism Management, 33*(6), 1450–1457.

Kadiyali, V., & Kosovà, R. (2013). Inter-industry employment spillovers from tourism inflows. *Regional Science and Urban Economics, 43*, 272–281.

Karabulut, G., Bilgin, M. H., Demir, E., & Doker, A. C. (2020). How pandemics affect tourism: International evidence. *Annals of Tourism Research, 84*, 102991.

Lee, D. (2016). How Airbnb short-term rentals exacerbate Los Angeles's affordable housing crisis: Analysis and policy recommendations. *Harv. L. & Pol'y Rev, 10*, 229.

Liu, H., & Song, H. (2017). New evidence of dynamic links between tourism and economic growth based on mixed-frequency granger causality test. *Journal of Travel Research, 57*(7), 899–907.

Marques Santos, A., Madrid Gonzales, C., Haegeman, K., & Rainoldi, A. (2020). *Behavioural changes in tourism in times of COVID-19—Employment scenarios and policy options*. JRC Science for policy report. Publications Office of the European Union, Luxembourg.

Marrocu, E., & Paci, R. (2013). Different tourists to different destinations. Evidence from spatial interaction models. *Tourism Management, 39*, 71–83.

Marrocu, E., Paci, R., & Zara, A. (2015). Micro-economic determinants of tourist expenditure: A quantile regression approach. *Tourism Management, 50*, 13–30.

Massidda, C., & Etzo, I. (2012). The determinants of Italian domestic tourism: A panel data analysis. *Tourism Management, 33*(3), 603–610.

Milano, C., Novelli, M., & Cheer, J. M. (2019). Overtourism and degrowth: A social movements perspective. *Journal of Sustainable Tourism, 27*(12), 1857–1875.

Morley, C., Rosselló, J., & Santana-Gallego, M. (2014). Gravity models for tourism demand: Theory and use. *Annals of Tourism Research, 48*, 1–10.

Naranpanawa, N., Rambaldi, A. N., & Sipe, N. (2018). Natural amenities and regional tourism employment: A spatial analysis. *Papers in Regional Science, 98*, 1731–1757.

Narayan, P. K. (2004). Economic impact of tourism on Fiji's economy: Empirical evidence from the computable general equilibrium model. *Tourism Economics, 10*(4), 419–433.
Neuts, B., & Nijkamp, P. (2012). Tourist crowding perception and acceptability in cities: An applied modelling study on Bruges. *Annals of Tourism Research, 39*(4), 2133–2153.
Nunkoo, R., Seetanah, B., Jaffur, Z. R. K., Moraghen, P. G. W., & Sannassee, R. V. (2020). Tourism and economic growth: A meta-regression analysis. *Journal of Travel Research, 59*(3), 404–423.
Oh, C. O. (2005). The contribution of tourism development to economic growth in the Korean economy. *Tourism Management, 26*(1), 39–44.
Paci, R., & Marrocu, E. (2014). Tourism and regional growth in Europe. *Papers in Regional Science, 93*(Supplement 1), S25–S50.
Panzera, E., de Graaff, T., & de Groot, H. L. F. (2020). European cultural heritage and tourism flows: The magnetic role of superstar world heritage sites. *Papers in Regional Science, 100*(1), 101–122.
Paramati, S. R., Alam, M. S., & Chen, C. F. (2017). The effects of tourism on economic growth and CO_2 emissions: A comparison between developed and developing economies. *Journal of Travel Research, 56*(6), 712–724.
Park, J. Y., & Jang, S. S. (2014). An extended gravity model: Applying destination competitiveness. *Journal of Travel & Tourism Marketing, 31*(7), 799–816.
Park, S., Woo, M., & Nicolau, J. L. (2019). Determinant factors of tourist expenses. *Journal of Travel Research, 59*(2), 267–280.
Patuelli, R., Mussoni, M., & Candela, G. (2013). The effects of world heritage sites on domestic tourism: A spatial interaction model for Italy. *Journal of Geographical Systems, 15*(3), 369–402.
Petit, S., & Seetaram, N. (2018). Measuring the effect of revealed cultural preferences on tourism exports. *Journal of Travel Research, 58*(8), 1262–1273.
Pompili, T., Pisati, M., & Lorenzini, E. (2019). Determinants of international tourist choices in Italian provinces: A joint demand–supply approach with spatial effects. *Papers in Regional Science, 98*(6), 2251–2273.
Popp, M. (2012). Positive and negative urban tourist crowding: Florence, Italy. *Tourism Geographies, 14*(1), 50–72.
Porter, M. E. (1990). *The competitive advantage of nations*. Collier Macmillan.
Qiu, R. T. R., Park, J., Li, S., & Song, H. (2020). Social costs of tourism during the COVID-19 pandemic. *Annals of Tourism Research, 84*, 102994.
Rasoolimanesh, S. M., Taheri, B., Gannon, M., Vafaei-Zadeh, A., & Hanifah, H. (2019). Does living in the vicinity of heritage tourism sites influence residents' perceptions and attitudes? *Journal of Sustainable Tourism*. https://doi.org/10.1080/09669582.2019.1618863
Ribaudo, G., & Figini, P. (2016). The puzzle of tourism demand at destinations hosting UNESCO world heritage sites: An analysis of tourism flows for Italy. *Journal of Travel Research, 56*(4), 521–542.
Richards, G., & Raymond, C. (2000). *Creative tourism*. Project: CREATOUR – Creative Tourism Destination Development in Small Cities and Rural Areas.
Ridderstaat, J., Croes, R., & Nijkamp, P. (2014). Tourism and long-run economic growth in Aruba. *International Journal of Tourism Research, 16*, 472–487.
Riganti, P., & Nijkamp, P. (2008). Congestion in popular tourist areas: A multi-attribute experimental choice analysis of willingness-to-wait in Amsterdam. *Tourism Economics, 14*(1), 25–44.
Russo, A. P., & Richards, G. (Eds.) (2016). *Reinventing the local in tourism—Producing, consuming and negotiating place*. Channel View Publications, Bristol – Buffalo – Toronto.
Saeporsdottir, A. D., & Hall, C. M. (2020). Visitor satisfaction in wilderness in times of overtourism: A longitudinal study. *Journal of Sustainable Tourism, 29*(1), 123–141.
Salerno, G. M., & Russo, A. P. (2020). Venice as a short-term city. Between local trends and local lock-ins. *Journal of Sustainable Tourism*. https://doi.org/10.1080/09669582.2020.1860068
Salifou, C. K., & ul Haq, I. (2017). Tourism, globalization and economic growth: A panel cointegration analysis for selected West African States. *Current Issues in Tourism, 20*(6), 664–667.

Seetanah, B. (2011). Assessing the dynamic economic impact of tourism for island economies. *Annals of Tourism Research, 38*(1), 291–308.

Sharma, A., Shin, H., Santa-Maria, M. J., & Nicolau, J. L. (2021). Hotels' COVID-19 innovation and performance. *Annals of Tourism Research, 88*.

Singh, D. R., Wright, A. S., Hayle, C., & Craigwell, R. (2010). Is the tourism-led growth thesis valid? The case of the Bahamas, Barbados, and Jamaica. *Tourism Analysis, 15*(4), 435–445.

Soukiazis, E., & Proença, S. (2008). Tourism as an alternative source of regional growth in Portugal: A panel data analysis at NUTS II and III levels. *Portuguese Economic Journal, 7*(1), 43–61.

Szromek, A. R., Hysa, B., & Karasek, A. (2019). The perception of overtourism from the perspective of different generations. *Sustainability, 11*(24), 7151.

Throsby, D. (2009). Tourism, heritage and cultural sustainability: Three 'golden rules'. In L. Fusco Girard, & P. Nijkamp (Eds.), *Cultural tourism and sustainable local development*. Ashgate.

Tsionas, M. G. (2020). COVID-19 and gradual adjustment in the tourism, hospitality, and related industry. *Tourism Economics*, 1–5.

UNESCO. (2020). *Museums around the world—In the face of COVID-19*. UNESCO World Heritage Centre.

UNWTO. (2017). *2017 International year of sustainable tourism for development*. http://www.tourism4development2017.org/why-tourism/, [29/10/2020].

UNWTO. (2018). *Tourism highlights—2018 edition*. https://www.e-unwto.org/doi/pdf/10.18111/9789284419876, [22/10/2021].

UNWTO. (2019). *International tourism highlights 2019 edition*. https://www.e-unwto.org/doi/pdf/10.18111/9789284421152, [21/10/2021].

UNWTO. (2021). UNWTO inclusive recovery guide—Sociocultural impacts of COVID-19, Issue 2: Cultural tourism. https://www.e-unwto.org/doi/book/10.18111/9789284422579, [28/09/2021].

Van Blarcom, B. L., & Kayahan, C. (2011). Assessing the economic impact of a UNESCO world heritage designation. *Journal of Heritage Tourism, 6*(2), 143–164.

Wachsmuth, D., & Weisler, A. (2018). Airbnb and the rent gap: Gentrification through the sharing economy. *Environment and Planning A, 50*(6), 1147–1170.

Wachsmuth, D., Kerrigan, D., Chaney, D., & Shillolo, A. (2017). *Short-term cities: Airbnb's impact on Canadian housing markets. A report from the Urban Politics and Governance Research Group*. School of Urban Planning, McGill University.

World Tourism Organization. (2018a). *European Union tourism trends*. https://www.e-unwto.org/doi/book/10.18111/9789284419470, [20/11/2020].

World Tourism Organization. (2018b). *Tourism and culture synergies*. https://www.e-unwto.org/doi/book/10.18111/9789284418978, [20/11/2020].

World Tourism Organization (UNWTO); Centre of Expertise Leisure, Tourism & Hospitality; NHTV Breda University of Applied Sciences; and NHL Stenden University of Applied Science. (2018). *'Overtourism'?—Understanding and managing Urban tourism growth beyond perceptions, executive summary*. UNWTO, Madrid. https://www.e-unwto.org/doi/epdf/10.18111/9789284420070, [20/10/2021].

Yang, C. H., Lin, H. L., & Han, C. C. (2010). Analysis of international tourist arrivals in China: The role of world heritage sites. *Tourism Management, 31*(6), 827–837.

Zuo, B., & Huang, S. (2017). Revisiting the tourism-led economic growth hypothesis: The case of China. *Journal of Travel Research, 57*(2), 151–163.

Chapter 3
From Cultural Heritage to Economic Development Through Tourism

3.1 Cultural Heritage, Tourism and Economic Development in the Public Debate

The paramount importance of cultural heritage for individuals, societies and countries and its ability to affect countless aspects of human beings' lives is nowadays strongly recognized by many different academic disciplines as well as public and international institutions, cultural associations, networks, policymakers and civil societies (Sciacchitano, 2019). With its complex system of integrated values such as aesthetic, symbolic or historic values (for a comprehensive analysis on cultural heritage values see Throsby, 2001), cultural heritage influences cultural, social, environmental and economic structures of the territories in which it is located (CHCfE Consortium, 2015). The essential role of cultural heritage has been very recently stressed in Europe, 2018 being designated "*European Year of Cultural Heritage*".

Within this context, opportunities and advantages for local communities and societies stemming from cultural heritage have been highlighted and a significant number of institutional bodies have been involved in the initiatives (i.e., the European Commission, the European Parliament, the Council of the European Union, the Committee of the Regions and the European Economic and Social Committee). As highlighted by Sciacchitano (2019), succeeding the European Year of Cultural Heritage, the European Commission developed for the first time a *European Framework for Action on Cultural Heritage*, revealing the need to recognize and make explicit the key role of heritage within European policies and programs. More specifically, cultural heritage is referred to as a *common good* and a *shared resource* able to generate social and economic improvements (European Commission, 2019, p. 4). The potential socio-economic relevance of cultural heritage was already acknowledged by the European Commission. Citing from the report Getting Cultural Heritage to Work for Europe: "*cultural heritage must be seen as a special but integral component in the production of the European GDP and innovation, its growth process, competitiveness and in the welfare of European society*" (European Commission, 2015, p. 6). According to the European Commission, together with culture, society

E. Panzera, *Cultural Heritage and Territorial Identity*, Advances in Spatial Science,
https://doi.org/10.1007/978-3-030-94468-1_3

and environment, economy is one of the four areas in which cultural heritage could potentially exert its influence (CHCfE Consortium, 2015).

The most evident and noticeable link between cultural heritage and economic development is tourism. During the 70s and, more extensively, the 80s heritage tourism began its development (CHCfE Consortium, 2015). As highlighted by the OECD, local cultural assets, including cultural heritage, started to be considered as elements of territorial attractiveness, differentiation and competitiveness and cultural heritage and tourism began to be considered as inextricably linked (Noonan & Rizzo, 2017; OECD, 2008). Following the European Year of Cultural Heritage, a pan-European dialogue on tourism and cultural heritage was launched by the Network of European Regions for Sustainable and Competitive Tourism (NECS-TouR) demonstrating the substantial interest in the phenomenon of heritage tourism and the intrinsic synergy between cultural heritage and tourism activities. As the Declaration argues, the joint combination of cultural heritage and tourism as well as acting as a European social cohesion facilitator and as a promoter of diversity awareness and acceptance is also able to act as an engine for local economic development (Network of European Regions for Competitive and Sustainable Tourism (NECSTouR), 2018). In fact, tourism is an important and fast-growing sector for the European Union. 538 million international tourists, corresponding to 40% out of the total number of world's tourists, visited Europe in 2017. Tourism grew for the eighth consecutive year showing an 8% increase from 2016 to 2017; it generates 10% of European GDP and accounts for 9% of total employment (UNWTO, 2018). In 2018 the Travel and Tourism sector contributed to the European GDP with a greater impact than the banking, automotive manufacturing, agriculture and mining sectors (World Travel & Tourism Council, 2019).

Even though synergies between cultural heritage and economic development and between cultural heritage, tourism and local economic growth are strongly professed and widely recognized in the public debate, it is hard to quantitatively validate and prove these links, especially when an attempt at generalization is looked for. In fact, in many cases, the impact of cultural heritage on economic growth appears to be taken for granted revealing the need for developing the economic analysis of this relationship. When the effects of the presence of cultural heritage on economies have been measured, the scope of the analysis is limited to specific countries (see for instance Greffe, 2004) or single heritage sites (see for instance Plaza & Haarich, 2015) and many channels are taken into account simultaneously (e.g., renovation and conservation activities, cultural and creative industries and tourism, among others). Out of many different potential channels of impact, tourism is the most considered and studied by the economic literature. However, either the relationship between cultural heritage and tourism or the one between tourism and economic growth have been deepened, resulting in an incomplete and fragmented analysis of the story. In other words, when the focus is on the link between heritage and tourism, the economic impact seems to be taken for granted and, on the other hand, when the relationship analyzed is the one between tourism and economic growth, the role of cultural heritage in tourism attractiveness is unknown.

The aim of this chapter is to understand if the great interest showed by the economic literature toward the tourism channel is justified by the fact that tourism is indeed a functioning and relevant channel through which cultural heritage plays a role in local economies. The analysis will be focused on understanding whether local tourism attractiveness is an actual and important trigger that allows us to consider cultural heritage as a resource able to stimulate economic growth. The chapter contributes to the literature, overcoming the previous mentioned limitations in three main ways: (a) empirically demonstrating that cultural heritage does have a positive role as an attractor for tourist flows; (b) empirically demonstrating that cultural heritage does have an impact on economic growth *through* tourism (potentially leading to both positive and negative consequences on local communities or heritage conservation); (c) extending the scope of the analysis to European regions (NUTS2 level) allowing for generalization of the results (see Chapter 2 for the conceptual and theoretical reasonings behind these mechanisms).

The following figure (Fig. 3.1) shows the conceptual framework of the analysis. The direct link between material cultural heritage and economic growth encompasses all the potential channels previously described through which an impact might be exerted, tourism excluded. The role of tourism is of particular interest and it has been therefore separated from the other channels in order to explore the relevance of its mediating role between tangible forms of heritage and regional economic growth.

The chapter is structured as follows: Sect. 3.2 describes the empirical methodology adopted, the data used for the quantitative analysis and the results obtained and Sect. 3.3 concludes.

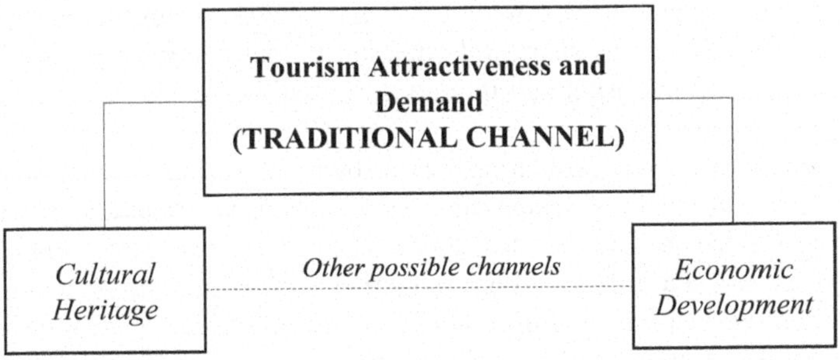

Fig. 3.1 Cultural heritage and economic development through tourism: the conceptual logical mechanism

3.2 The Role of Tourism Mediating Between Cultural Heritage and Local Development: The Empirical Strategy

3.2.1 Model Specifications

The present section presents the empirical strategy put in place in order to test the effectiveness of the tourism channel as a mediator between material cultural heritage and regional economic growth.

Following Cerisola (2019a, 2019b), a path model, i.e., a structural equation model for observed variables, is used to test the assumptions. This empirical strategy has been chosen because of its ability to detect both direct and indirect effects of a variable of interest (in our case a heritage-related variable) on an independent variable (as per our case economic growth). In other words, it is presumed that an intervening or mediator variable transmits some of the causal effects of a prior variable to subsequent variables (Kline, 2015). In Cerisola (2019a, 2019b) creativity is the mediator variable between tangible cultural heritage and development (in terms of employment growth rate), in this case, instead, tourism is the intervening variable between heritage and economic growth in terms of GDP per capita growth rate. A heritage-related variable is specified to influence economic growth both directly (and this link includes all the other potential channels such as, among others, maintenance and renovation activities, excluding tourism) and indirectly *through* tourism demand. In fact, it is presumed that tourism demand is influenced by regional endowment of cultural heritage and that in turn tourism affects economic growth. As highlighted in Nunkoo and Ramkissoon (2012), the structural equation model being a rigorous statistical tool allows complex and articulate models simultaneously encompassing multiple relationships to be tested.

Since we are interested in estimating the role that cultural heritage has on economic growth through tourism the starting point of the analysis is a standard growth regression model (see Barro & Sala i Martin, 2004). The use of a structural equation model, then, allows us to add a full set of regressors that explain tourism demand, which is one of the regressors of the structural growth equation. In other words, building on a typical regression growth model we jointly include regressors explaining growth (among which tourism and cultural heritage) and regressors explaining tourism (including cultural heritage). A structural equation model is therefore applied to 260 European NUTS2 regions[1] in three periods of time. The following specifications have been adopted to test, through a linear maximum likelihood estimation, the role of tourism as a mediating element between cultural heritage and regional economic growth:

[1] French overseas regions corresponding to codes FRA1, FRA2, FRA3, FRA4, FRA5, Spanish overseas regions corresponding to codes ES63, ES64 and PT20 and PT30 have been excluded from the analysis.

$$\Delta\text{GDPpc}_{rt} = \alpha + \beta_1\text{tourism demand}_{r,(t-1)} + \beta_2\text{cultural heritage}_r + \beta_3 X_{r,(t-1)} + \beta_4\text{time fixed effects} + \beta_5\text{regional fixed effects} + \varepsilon_{r,t} \quad (3.1a)$$

$$\text{Tourism demand}_{r,(t-1)} = \alpha + \beta_1\text{cultural heritage}_r + \beta_2 Z_{r,(t-2)} + \beta_3\text{time fixed effects} + \beta_4\text{regional fixed effects} + \varepsilon_{r,(t-1)} \quad (3.1b)$$

where ΔGDPpc_{rt} in Eq. (3.1a) is the GDP per capita growth rate in three distinct periods, i.e., 2014–2016, 2015–2017, 2016–2018. *Tourism demand* and *cultural heritage* represent the variables of interest. *Tourism demand* is measured as the number of tourist arrivals per capita in European regions and *cultural heritage* is measured both as the number of UNESCO cultural World Heritage Sites (WHS)[2] per square kilometer of land and as regional density of monuments. A set of explanatory variables ($X_{r,(t-1)}$) is added to the structural equation in order to include the standard regressors as in the empirical growth literature together with time and regional fixed effects (see for instance Temple, 1999; Barro, 1997). All the explanatory variables (whenever possible and when not time-fixed as in the case of tangible cultural heritage) have been one-year lagged with respect to the first year of each growth period.

As for the tourism demand equation or sub-equation—Eq. (3.1b)—the independent variable of interest is represented by the heritage-related variable (i.e., *cultural heritage*) and a set of control variables ($Z_{r,(t-2)}$) has been included to take into account the factors that are usually considered by the literature to have an impact on tourism attractiveness (for a comprehensive analysis of the standard included determinants of tourism demand see for instance Peng et al., 2014; Witt & Witt, 1995). The explanatory variables have been 1 year lagged with respect to the dependent variable in an attempt to support the causal direction and eliminate the possible correlation between the error term and the regressors (Paci & Marrocu, 2014).

The next section describes in detail the data used to perform the analysis.

3.2.2 *Data Description*

In order to carry out the econometric analysis, a database has been built on 269 European NUTS2 regions. The dependent variable of the structural equation (Eq. 3.1a) is the average annual GDP per capita growth rate. Even though the variables of interest are *tourism demand* and *cultural heritage* endowment, it goes without saying that economic growth does have other determinants as theorized and tested by models

---

[2] UNESCO categorize the sites according to their characteristics as cultural, natural or mixed sites. Following the aim of the present analysis only cultural UNESCO World Heritage Sites are considered.

dedicated to explaining economic growth (see for instance Barro, 1997). Therefore, a set of regressors has been included to control for the standard relevant factors considered by the economic growth literature:

- The *initial level of per capita GDP*. The variable is included to ascertain the initial level of wealth, and it is expected to be associated with a negative coefficient in the presence of a regional convergence process (see for instance Barro & Sala i Martin, 1992; Temple, 1999).
- *Human capital*—measured as the share of graduates over active population—and *innovation*—measured as the number of patent applications per resident. As well explained in Camagni and Capello (2009) because of the *hypermobility* that currently marks the traditional factors of production, i.e., capital and labor, regional development is nowadays highly reliant on other place-specific and more intangible factors such as skills, innovation, cultural elements and, in general terms, knowledge. We therefore included in the structural growth equation a variable proxying human capital accounting for regional accumulation of knowledge and a variable proxying innovation or technological capital (for human capital see, among others, Barro, 2001; Lucas, 1988; for innovation and technological capital see Fagerberg et al., 1997; Rodríguez-Pose & Crescenzi, 2008).
- *Population density* and *accessibility*. The demographic structure of a region together with physical accessibility surely influences regional growth (as for the relationship between population density and growth see for instance Ciccone & Hall, 1996; see Caragliu et al., 2011 for the role of accessibility). However, the casual direction is uncertain: on the one hand, urbanization economies and higher endowment of infrastructure allow innovation and knowledge to spread and transmission mechanisms can be fostered (Parr, 2002). On the other hand, congestion and crowding out effects might arise, leading to negative consequences.
- *Population* and *industrial structure*. Population is included to check for possible size-effects and the share of employed people in the manufacturing sector over active population takes into account the regional industrial structure.

As previously mentioned, the main variables of interest are *tourism demand* and *cultural heritage*. Tourism demand is proxied using the number of per capita tourist arrivals in European NUTS2 regions and is collected from the Eurostat database.[3]

As for the heritage-related variable, collecting and finding data on the endowment of cultural heritage, even when the type of heritage considered is restricted to the tangible one, is a rather complex task. As mentioned in Cicerchia (2019) the available European cultural statistics come from different data collections which means that a specific univocal collection dedicated to cultural data is still missing. Citing from Cicerchia (2019, p. 107) "*Other areas, instead remain uncovered: cultural diversity, cultural participation, and, paradoxically, cultural heritage. Some are indeed difficult to measure with statistics. Others are not difficult, but still suffer from a negative*

[3] An arrival is defined by Eurostat as a person (tourist) who arrives at a tourist accommodation establishment, i.e., hotels; holiday and other short-stay accommodation; camping grounds, recreational vehicle parks; and trailer parks.

political priority". As also highlighted by ESPON within the project on the Role and Spatial Effects of Cultural Heritage and Identity, with respect to other sectors, data collection is less advanced in the cultural field being the nature of cultural heritage multifaceted, subjective and submitted to different national or regional regulation criteria and definitions (ESPON project 1.3.3, 2004–2006).

As per the present analysis two distinct measures of tangible cultural heritage are tested: regional endowment of UNESCO cultural World Heritage Sites (WHS) and regional endowment of monuments (expressed as a standardized measure of monuments density elaborated from ESPON data).

The first measure of tangible cultural heritage sites is represented by the regional number of cultural UNESCO World Heritage Sites (WHS) divided by square kilometer of land. The model is firstly tested with this heritage-related measure since it is the most widely used indicator of cultural heritage throughout the literature. The main advantage of the measure is its coherent and consistent nature since the criteria defined by UNESCO to be nominated WHS need to be met by each site belonging to whichever region or country. More specifically, monuments, groups of buildings and sites are included in the category of cultural heritage sites and only those recognized as being of outstanding value for humanity and respecting at least one out of ten criteria specified by UNESCO can be labeled as UNESCO WHS. However, this measure does not come without controversies related to potential biases. As highlighted both by Frey and Steiner (2011) and Bertacchini and Saccone (2012), the selection of the sites depends on the ability to submit a valid application and it might be influenced by the political or economic power of the countries that apply for nominations and by the composition of the World Heritage Committee. Besides, it is not to be strictly considered as an indicator of the *endowment* of cultural heritage. In fact, the presence of UNESCO WHS is more related to exceptional quality and increased visibility of the site given by the UNESCO label. If a region does not include a cultural UNESCO WHS, it does not mean that the region lacks tangible cultural heritage sites. The following map (Fig. 3.2) shows the distribution of the UNESCO cultural WHS per square kilometer, across European regions in 2014.

The second measure of tangible cultural heritage comes from the ESPON project previously mentioned named *the Role and Spatial Effects of Cultural Heritage and Identity* and it is based on the number of regional monuments per square kilometer. More specifically, monuments are defined as *historical buildings (churches, palaces and castles, old mansions, bridges, fountains,* etc.*) and sites (caves, archaeological remains, battlefields,* etc.*)* (ESPON project 1.3.3, 2004, p. 8). Since these data are collected from national and regional listing systems, the main related issue regards an intrinsic inconsistency of the measure due to differences in national or regional definitions of monuments and data availability. In order to get a more coherent and comparable proxy for regional endowment of cultural heritage, we calculated a country-standardized regional measure according to the following formula:

$$\text{Tangible Cultural Heritage}_{r,c} = \frac{\frac{\text{Number of monuments}_r}{\text{Land Area}_r}}{\frac{\text{Number of monuments}_c}{\text{Land Area}_c}}$$

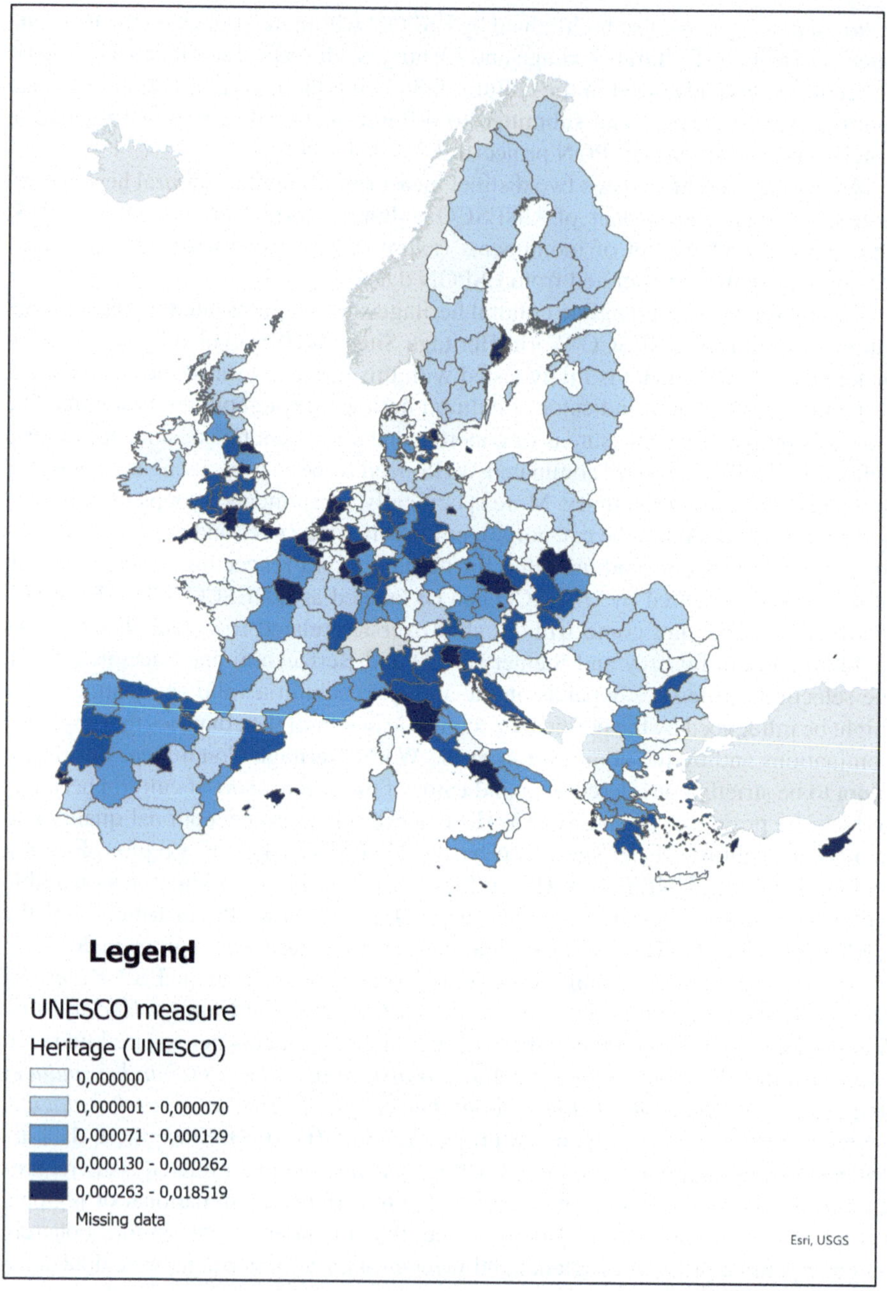

Fig. 3.2 Regional distribution of UNESCO cultural WHS per land square kilometer across European regions (*Source* UNESCO)

where r is the European NUTS2 region, c is the country to which the region belongs, and *Land Area* represents the usable land. The rationale behind the scaling of the ESPON measure of cultural heritage by area (expressed by square kilometer of land) refers to the decision of measuring the intensity with which the inhabitants are exposed to immovable heritage. The choice is therefore related to the attempt at capturing the type of environment that characterizes a local area in terms of intensity of cultural heritage. In other words, the indicator is built to try to assess the probability that an individual will encounter a piece of tangible cultural heritage on his/her way. The same measure is used by Cerisola (2019a, 2019b) to measure regional intensity of cultural heritage and by Cicerchia (2002) to capture the idea of the so-called *museo diffuso* (widespread museum) in Italy.

The year in which the endowment of monuments is registered is 2003 and, because of the essentially time-invariant nature of material heritage, we can reasonably assume that the number does not change through the years. The following map (Fig. 3.3) shows the distribution of this heritage measure across Europe, ranging from a minimum of 0.016 corresponding to the Flevoland region in The Netherlands to a maximum of 38.56 corresponding to Prague region in the Czech Republic.[4]

Besides being included as regressors in the structural equation model, *tourism demand* and *cultural heritage* variables are included in the sub-equation as well. Tourism demand is the dependent variable and cultural heritage is one of the regressors. Following well-established literature aiming at capturing the determinants of tourism demand, the main standard explanatory variables have been added to the equation, including:

- *Accessibility.* Availability of infrastructures and a good level of physical accessibility are essential conditions to guarantee that tourists can travel from their origin to the region of destinations (Khadaroo & Seetanah, 2008). The measure used in the analysis is a composite indicator of regional accessibility integrating different modes of transport (air, road and rail).
- *GDP per capita.* The variable is included to measure destinations wealth and absorptive capacity. It is usually associated with a positive pull effect on tourists because a high-income region is assumed to be able to provide higher quality public and tourist services (see for instance Eilat & Einav, 2004; Llorca-Vivero, 2008; Marrocu & Paci, 2013).
- *Capital City.* It checks for the presence in the region of the national capital city and its strength of attractiveness (Fourie & Santana-Gallego, 2011).
- *Mediterranean coast.* A dummy variable checking for the presence in the region of a portion of Mediterranean coast takes into consideration the attractiveness of

[4] Note that these numbers refer to the relative regional density of monuments with respect to the country to which they belong. Considering, for instance, Flevoland and Prague's corresponding heritage measure values we cannot say that Prague is endowed with a higher density of monuments than Flevoland. What we can affirm, instead, is that Prague, with respect to the Czech Republic, registers a 38.56 higher density of monuments and Flevoland a 0.016 greater density of monuments with respect to The Netherlands.

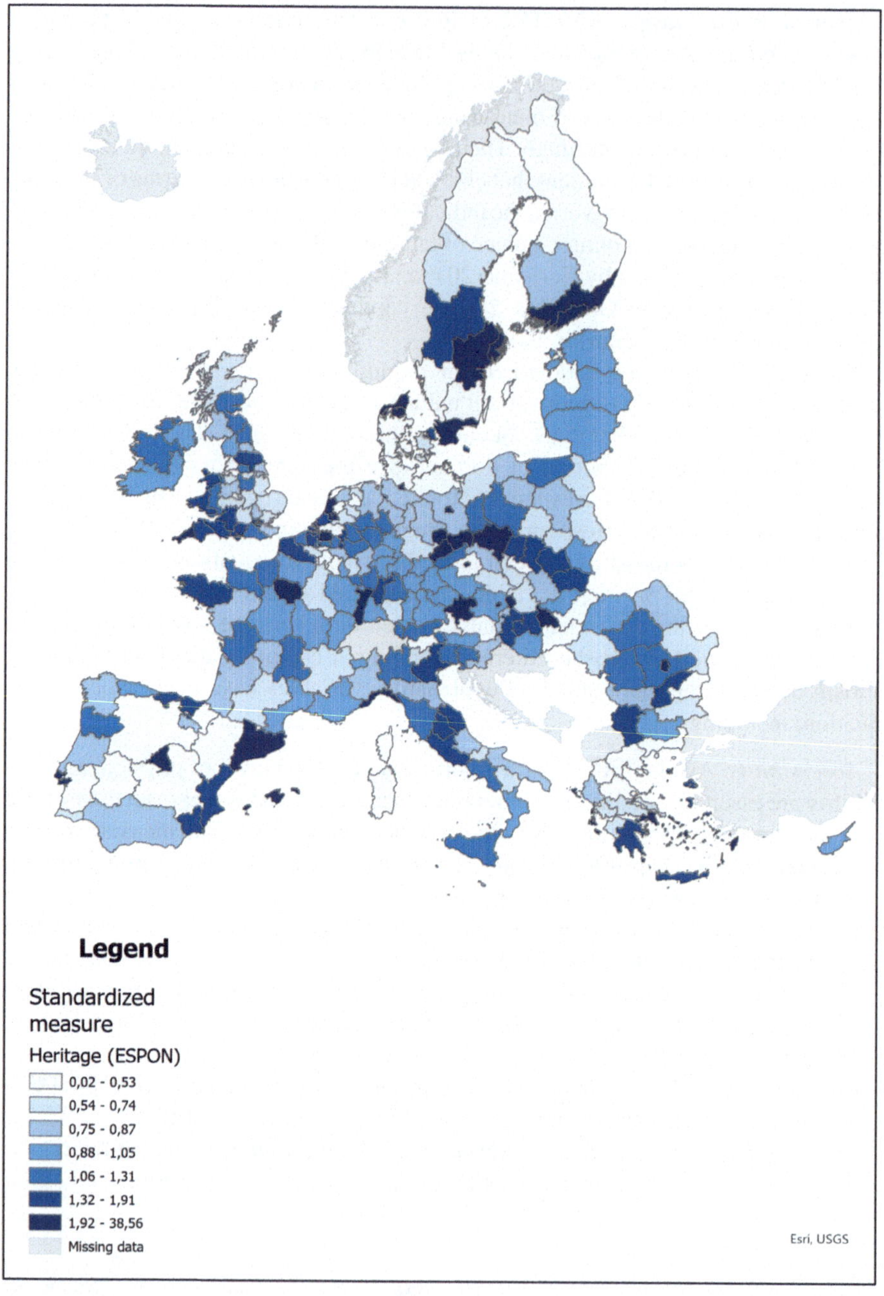

Fig. 3.3 The regional distribution of the standardized regional endowment of monuments across European regions (*Source* ESPON)

the region due to natural endowment (Patuelli et al., 2013) and the opportunity of sun and beach type of tourism (Marrocu & Paci, 2013).

- *Financial and Business Services.* The share of people employed in financial and business services over active population proxies and controls for business travel.
- *Crime rate.* This regressor captures the role of public safety and takes into consideration the potential discouraging effect that a high criminality rate exerts on tourist arrivals (Massidda & Etzo, 2012; Patuelli et al., 2013).
- *Tourism supply capacity.* The number of available beds[5] to accommodate tourists in each region of destination is included to monitor the availability of sufficient tourism infrastructures able to sustain and respond to tourism demand avoiding supply constraints (Khadaroo & Seetanah, 2008; Witt & Witt, 1995; Yang et al., 2010).
- *Population.* It takes the size of the region into account.

The following table (Table 3.1) summarizes and describes the variables included in the model.

3.2.3 Empirical Results

The empirical results are firstly presented in a synthetic graphical way focusing on the main variables of interest. The first tested heritage-related variable is the UNESCO cultural World Heritage Sites. Figure 3.4 shows the standardized coefficients of the specification corresponding to Eqs. 3.1a and 3.1b. The full set of coefficients associated to all the variables included in the model is presented in Table 3.3.

As evident from the results, a direct link between UNESCO cultural WHS and economic development does not seem to be significant. On the contrary, the coefficient associated with the heritage-related variable is positive and significant when included in the model to explain tourism demand, meaning that the regional presence of UNESCO cultural WHS does have an influence on tourist arrivals. The same positive and significant relationship is found between tourist arrivals and regional economic development. Having in mind that no direct effect is proved to be true by the model, the following table (Table 3.2) shows direct, indirect and total effects of the UNESCO cultural WHS on economic growth *mediated* by tourism demand showing that an indirect positive and statistically significant effect of tangible forms of cultural heritage on economic growth *through* tourism does exist. In other words, when mediated by tourism attractiveness, the endowment of UNESCO cultural WHS is able to influence local regional economic dynamics. Tourism is found to be, on average, a significant channel through which tangible heritage stimulates economic growth, all the other channels being encompassed in the direct effect that is not associated with a significant coefficient. The predominant role of tourism in this mechanism is therefore confirmed, meaning that material forms of cultural heritage

[5] The number of beds refers to the number of available beds provided by hotels, holiday and other short-stay accommodation; camping grounds, recreational vehicle parks and trailer parks.

Table 3.1 Structural equation model (cultural heritage, tourism and economic development): detailed variables description

Variable name	Description	Year(s)	Source
Structural equation			
GDP per capita growth rate	Measure of economic growth: average annual GDP per capita growth at constant 2005 prices	2014–2016 2015–2017 2016–2018	EUROSTAT
UNESCO (cultural World Heritage Sites)	Number of UNESCO cultural World Heritage Sites per square kilometer of land	2012 2013 2014	UNESCO
Monuments (per km^2)	Measure of tangible cultural heritage endowment: regional number of monuments per square kilometer standardized by country	2003	ESPON
Arrivals per capita	Measure of regional tourism demand: number of arrivals per inhabitant	2013 2014 2015	EUROSTAT
Human capital	Share of population with tertiary education per active population	2013 2014 2015	EUROSTAT
Population density	Measure of urbanization/agglomeration economies	2013 2014 2015	EUROSTAT
Innovation	Number of patent applications to the EPO per resident	2010 2011 2012	EUROSTAT
Industrial structure	Manufacturing share: manufacturing sector employment share per active population	2013 2014 2015	EUROSTAT
Population	Measure of regional economy size	2013 2014 2015	EUROSTAT
Accessibility	Measure of regional accessibility and infrastructure endowment: composite indicator of regional accessibility integrating different modes of transport (air, road and rail)	2006	ESPON

(continued)

Table 3.1 (continued)

Variable name	Description	Year(s)	Source
Quality of government	Composite indicator including core features of quality of government (impartiality, bureaucratic, quality and corruption) as well as broader measures (rule of law and transparency)	2010 2013 2017	University of Gothenburg
GDP per capita	Measure of regional wealth: GDP per capita at current prices	2013 2014 2015	EUROSTAT
Sub-equation			
UNESCO (cultural World Heritage Sites)	Number of UNESCO cultural World Heritage Sites per square kilometer of land	2012 2013 2014	UNESCO
Monuments (per km^2)	Measure of tangible cultural heritage endowment: regional number of monuments per square kilometer standardized by country	2003	ESPON
Mediterranean coast	Measure of regional attractiveness led by natural environment: dummy variable equal to 1 for regions with Mediterranean coast 0 otherwise		Own calculation
Financial and business services	Measure of the regional relevance of financial and business services: financial and business services sector employment share per active population	2012 2013 2014	Cambridge Econometrics
Crime rate	Measure of regional safety: crude death by assault rate expressed in deaths per 100.000 inhabitants	2012 2013 2014	EUROSTAT
Tourism supply capacity	Measure of regional ability to provide satisfactory essential facilities for tourists: number of beds per capita	2012 2013 2014	EUROSTAT

(continued)

Table 3.1 (continued)

Variable name	Description	Year(s)	Source
Accessibility	Measure of regional accessibility and infrastructure endowment: composite indicator of regional accessibility integrating different modes of transport (air, road and rail)	2006	ESPON
GDP per capita	Measure of regional wealth: GDP per capita at current prices	2012 2013 2014	EUROSTAT
Capital City	Measure of regional attractiveness led by the presence of a capital city: dummy variable equal to 1 for regions with a capital city and 0 otherwise		Own calculation

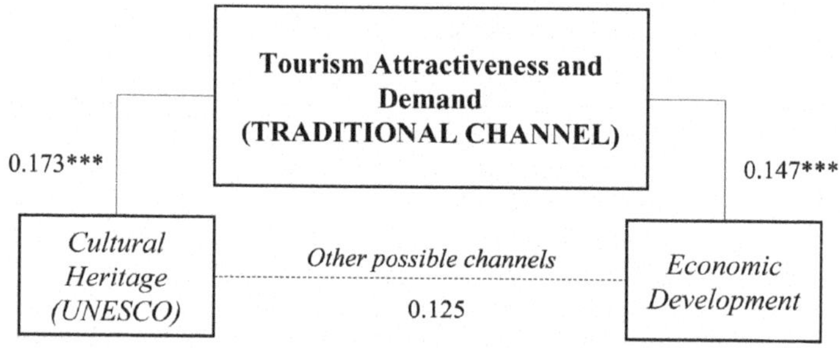

Fig. 3.4 UNESCO World Heritage Sites and economic development through tourism: the standardized coefficients. Significance levels: *** $p < 0.01$, ** $p < 0.05$, * $p < 0.1$

Table 3.2 Direct, indirect and total effects of UNESCO cultural World Heritage Sites per square kilometer of land on regional economic growth through tourism demand

	Direct effects (on GDP growth rate)	Indirect effects (on GDP growth rate)	Total effects (on GDP growth rate)
UNESCO cultural World Heritage Site	0.125	0.0255*	0.038
	(0.061)	(0.0105)	(0.062)
Observations	780	780	780

Standard errors in parentheses and standardized coefficients. *** $p < 0.01$, ** $p < 0.05$, * $p < 0.1$

are able to significantly influence local economies through their use or consumption. As for the magnitude of the coefficient, since the tables and the figures report the standardized coefficient, the magnitude can be directly interpreted. In other words, the coefficient associated with cultural heritage (UNESCO sites) as an explanatory variable of tourism attractiveness (0.173) can be interpreted as a corresponding increase in tourism demand when 1 more UNESCO site is present in the region. In turn, as tourism attractiveness increases by 1 unit, all the other factors being equal, the GDP growth rate increases by 0.147. The direct impact of cultural heritage on GDP growth is instead non-significant. It goes without saying that it is extremely difficult to build a new heritage site, however, two main aspects emerge from the empirical results. First, if a region is endowed with a higher number of already built heritage sites, a positive relationship exists between those sites and economic growth through tourism, and it is therefore advantageous for the region to preserve and valorize them. Secondly, since the UNESCO sites are analyzed here, it can be argued that tangible forms of cultural heritage have the potential of being labeled as UNESCO World Heritage Sites. Given the results obtained through the Structural Equation Model, it can be argued that the effort in embarking on the procedure of applying for getting the UNESCO label is worthwhile. Especially for regions with "hidden gems" which receive a low number of visitors.

The following table (Table 3.3) shows the full set of results with all the coefficients corresponding to the variables included in the model. Consistently with some previous literature on growth and tourism-led-growth (see for instance Paci & Marrocu, 2014; Soukiazis & Proença, 2008) the coefficient corresponding to the initial level of per capita GDP is negative and significant, demonstrating the presence of a convergence process among European regions. Education appears to be a significant determinant of regional economic growth together with the industrial structure, the initial size of the economies and multimodal accessibility of the regions. On the contrary, innovation and population density are associated with positive but non-significant coefficients probably because of high correlation with other variables (for instance between human capital and innovation) or because their effects are included in the more comprehensive GDP per capita coefficient. Looking at tourism demand determinants, multimodal accessibility and the exposure of the region on the Mediterranean coast are associated with a significant negative coefficient possibly due to congestion and overcrowding reasons. In agreement with some previous literature (see for instance Culiuc, 2014), GDP per capita of destination regions positively influences tourist arrivals and the same is true for the share of people employed in financial and services sector. These results suggest that, on average, movements of travelers across Europe are mainly toward richer regions, more agglomerated areas and significantly influenced by tourism for business purposes. Lastly, the variable accounting for tourist supply capacity presents a positive and significant coefficient indicating that regional ability to provide enough accommodation facilities is a crucial input for the expansion of tourism demand (see for instance Yang et al., 2010).

In order to check for potential omitted paths in the fitted model, the command *estat mindices* has been run in STATA after the structural equation model, and no modification indices have been indicated by the program.

Table 3.3 Structural equation model results (heritage-related variable: UNESCO cultural World Heritage Sites per square kilometer of land)

	(1)	(2)
	Structural equation GDP per capita growth	Tourism demand tourist arrivals per capita
Arrivals per capita	0.147***	
	(0.034)	
GDP per capita	−0.607***	
	(0.117)	
Human capital	0.155**	
	(0.070)	
Population density	0.058	
	(0.101)	
Innovation	0.048	
	(0.047)	
Industrial structure	0.078*	
	(0.045)	
Population	0.072**	
	(0.034)	
UNESCO	0.013	0.173***
	(0.061)	(0.059)
Accessibility	0.112*	−0.152***
	(0.067)	(0.041)
Capital city	0.088	−0.098
	(0.146)	(0.759)
GDP per capita (lagged)		0.346***
		(0.060)
Population		−1.534**
		(1.210)
Mediterranean coast		−0.415***
		(0.089)
Financial and business services (lagged)		0.139***
		(0.040)
Crime rate (lagged)		0.031
		(0.023)

(continued)

Table 3.3 (continued)

	(1)	(2)
Tourism supply capacity (lagged)		0.872***
		(0.017)
Time fixed effects	YES	YES
Regional fixed effects (NUTS1 level)	YES	YES
Constant	−0.349***	−1.764
	(0.207)	(1.492)
Observations	780	780

Standard errors in parentheses *** $p < 0.01$, ** $p < 0.05$, * $p < 0.1$
Overall R-squared: 0.95.
R-squared structural equation: 0.49.
R-squared tourism equation: 0.91.

3.2.4 *Robustness Check*

In order to check for the robustness of the results, the same structural equation model (Eqs. 3.1a and 3.1b) has been run using the alternative measure of tangible forms of cultural heritage that has been described in Sect. 3.2.2, i.e., regional standardized density of monuments. As well as being a robustness check of the model to different measures, it is also a test for the functioning of the mechanism using a conceptually different heritage-related variable that is able to take into account a higher number of heritage sites and a wider variety of typologies.

In Fig. 3.5, the standardized coefficients related to the effect of the standardized measure of monuments are displayed.

As in the case of the UNESCO cultural World Heritage Sites using a different measure of material cultural heritage does not change the results. A significant positive coefficient is still associated to the heritage-related measure meaning that regions

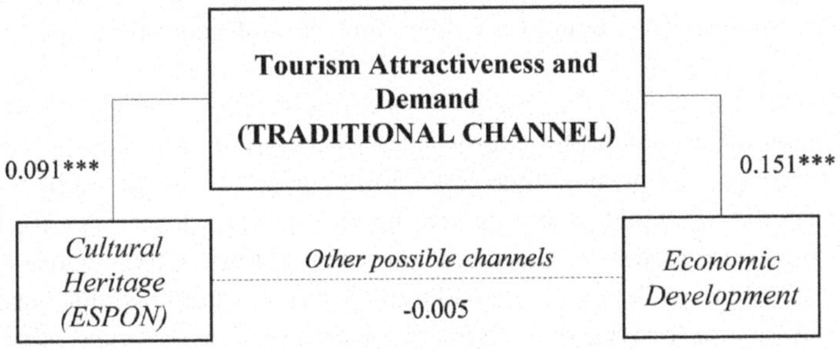

Fig. 3.5 Monuments and economic development through tourism: the standardized coefficients. Significance levels: *** $p < 0.01$, ** $p < 0.05$, * $p < 0.1$

Table 3.4 Direct, indirect and total effects of the standardized ESPON measure of monuments

	Direct effects (on GDP growth rate)	Indirect effects (on GDP growth rate)	Total effects (on GDP growth rate)
Standardized measure of monuments	−0.0051	0.0135***	0.0085
	(0.0333)	(0.0039)	(0.0326)
Observations	780	780	780

Standard errors in parentheses *** $p < 0.01$, ** $p < 0.05$, * $p < 0.1$

endowed with cultural heritage are more attractive for tourists and tourism demand plays a positive influence on regional economic development. Table 3.4 shows direct, indirect and total effects proving once more that a positive link between cultural heritage and economic development does exist where *mediated* by the tourism sector.

3.3 Conclusions

Cultural heritage is widely recognized as a common resource able to influence and stimulate local economies and the most analyzed and mentioned channel through which this mechanism works is tourism. This chapter empirically demonstrates that the predominant interest toward tourism showed by the economic literature is indeed justified, tourism attractiveness being a crucial channel through which tangible forms of cultural heritage actualize their impacts on economic growth in European regions. Applying a structural equation model using two different heritage-related measures results in confirming the role of tourism as mediator in this mechanism. Other channels represented by diverse heritage-related activities (e.g., conservation or renovation activities) seem to be weaker and less significant in transferring the economic potential of cultural heritage to effective local economic growth (further dedicated research is needed in this direction). The logic of use and consumption of heritage prevails on other heritage-related activities when an actual effect on local economies is expected. In fact, tourism is a strong economic sector able to activate upstream and downstream activities, benefit local production and generate employment and income.

Nevertheless, controversial consequences for economies, societies and environments and several fallouts might emerge from overtourism. Even though tourism is beneficial for employment, unskilled labor forces might be attracted by this sector and by the ancillary related activities leading to potential downsides for the local economies in the long run. Furthermore, the overexploitation of material cultural heritage could lead to its deterioration and tourists overcrowding could cause congestion or discomfort for local people. Tourist pressures might force local inhabitants or firms to move from central locations and the risk of the so-called *Disneyfication* of heritage might be encountered. The need for adequate policies targeted at regulating the tourism sector is therefore of primary importance. Both heritage sites and local communities' well-being and quality of life must be preserved and guaranteed by local government.

What seems to be of crucial importance is the implementation of planning strategies able to control and limit the potentially negative aspects of tourism assuring the right balance between conservation and usage of heritage sites and between economic benefits and socio-cultural dynamics. Furthermore, because of the relevance in terms of human capital, innovation and skilled labor force of other heritage-related sectors, e.g., conservation and renovation activities, more attention needs to be granted by local government to support these kinds of activities and make them able to influence local economies. Finally, more research is needed to investigate whether it is possible to detect and measure positive economic spillovers stemming from socio-cultural values related to cultural heritage such as sense of belonging or social capital reinforcement. The following part of the book will be dedicated to exploring the role of one of these intangible channels: territorial identity.

References

Barro, R. J. (2001). Human capital and growth. *American Economic Review, 91*(2), 12–17.

Barro, R. J., & Sala i Martin, X. (1992). Convergence. *Journal of Political Economy, 100*(2), 223–251.

Barro, R. J., & Sala i Martin, X. (Eds.). (2004). *Economic growth.* The MIT Press.

Barro, R. J. (Ed.). (1997). *Determinants of economic growth: A cross-country empirical study.* The MIT Press.

Bertacchini, E., & Saccone, D. (2012). Toward a political economy of World Heritage. *Journal of Cultural Economics, 36*(4), 327–352.

Camagni, R., & Capello, R. (2009). Knowledge-based economy and knowledge creation: The role of space. In U. Fratesi & L. Senn (Eds.), *Growth and innovation of competitive regions* (pp. 145–165). Springer.

Caragliu, A., Del Bo, C., & Nijkamp, P. (2011). Smart cities in europe. *Journal of Urban Technology, 18*(2), 65–82.

Cerisola, S. (2019). A new perspective on the cultural heritage-development nexus: The role of creativity. *Journal of Cultural Economics, 43*(1), 21–56.

Cerisola, S. (2019). *Cultural heritage.* Edward Elgar Publishing Limited.

CHCfE Consortium. (2015). *Cultural heritage counts for Europe.* http://blogs.encatc.org/culturalheritagecountsforeurope//wp-content/uploads/2015/06/CHCfE_FULL-REPORT_v2.pdf, [29/10/2020].

Ciccone, A., & Hall, R. (1996). Productivity and the density of economic activity. *American Economic Review, 86*(1), 54–70.

Cicerchia, A. (2002). *Il bellissimo vecchio. Argomenti per una geografia del patrimonio culturale.* Franco Angeli.

Cicerchia, A. (2019). Evidence-based policy making for cultural heritage. *SCIentific RESearch and Information Technology, 9*(1), 99–108.

Culiuc A. (2014), *Determinants of international tourism.* Working Paper No. 14/82, International Monetary Fund (IMF).

Eilat, Y., & Einav, L. (2004). Determinants of international tourism: A three-dimensional panel data analysis. *Applied Economics, 36*(12), 1315–1327.

ESPON. (2004–2006). *The role and spatial effects of cultural hritage and identity*. https://www.espon.eu/sites/default/files/attachments/fr-1.3.3_revised-full_August2006.pdf, [23/11/2020].
European Commission. (2015). *Getting cultural heritage to work for Europe*. https://op.europa.eu/en/publication-detail/-/publication/b01a0d0a-2a4f-4de0-88f7-85bf2dc6e004, [29/10/2020].
European Commission. (2019). *European framework for action on cultural heritage*. https://op.europa.eu/en/publication-detail/-/publication/5a9c3144-80f1-11e9-9f05-01aa75ed71a1, [29/10/2020].
Fagerberg, J., Verspagen, B., & Caniëls, M. (1997). Technology, growth and unemployment across European regions. *Regional Studies, 31*(5), 457–466.
Fourie, J., & Santana-Gallego, M. (2011). The impact of mega-sport events on tourist arrivals. *Tourism Management, 32*(6), 1364–1370.
Frey, B. S., & Steiner, L. (2011). World heritage list: Does it make sense? *International Journal of Cultural Policy, 17*(5), 555–573.
Greffe, X. (2004). Is heritage an asset or a liability? *Journal of Cultural Heritage, 5*(3), 301–309.
Khadaroo, J., & Seetanah, B. (2008). The role of transport infrastructure in international tourism development: A gravity model approach. *Tourism Management, 29*(5), 831–840.
Kline, R. B. (Ed.). (2015). *Principles and practice of structural equation modeling* (4th ed.). The Guilford Press.
Llorca-Vivero, R. (2008). Terrorism and international tourism: New evidence. *Defence and Peace Economics, 19*(2), 169–188.
Lucas, R., Jr. (1988). On the mechanics of economic development. *Journal of Monetary Economics, 22*(1), 3–42.
Marrocu, E., & Paci, R. (2013). Different tourists to different destinations. Evidence from spatial interaction models. *Tourism Management, 39*, 71–83.
Massidda, C., & Etzo, I. (2012). The determinants of Italian domestic tourism: A panel data analysis. *Tourism Management, 33*(3), 603–610.
Network of European Regions for Competitive and Sustainable Tourism (NECSTouR). (2018). *Barcelona declaration of tourism and cultural heritage: "Better places to live, better places to visit"*. https://necstour.eu/better-places-to-live-better-places-to-visit, [23/11/2020].
Noonan, D., & Rizzo, I. (2017). Economics of cultural tourism: Issues and perspectives. *Journal of Cultural Economics, 41*(2), 95–107.
Nunkoo, R., & Ramkissoon, H. (2012). Structural equation modelling and regression analysis in tourism research. *Current Issues in Tourism, 15*(8), 777–802.
OECD. (2008). *The impact of culture on tourism*. https://www.oecd.org/industry/the-impact-of-culture-on-tourism-9789264040731-en.htm, [29/10/2020].
Paci, R., & Marrocu, E. (2014). Tourism and regional growth in Europe. *Papers in Regional Science, 93*(Supplement 1), S25–S50.
Parr, J. B. (2002). Agglomeration economies: Ambiguities and confusions. *Environment and Planning A: Economy and Space, 34*(4), 717–731.
Patuelli, R., Mussoni, M., & Candela, G. (2013). The effects of World Heritage Sites on domestic tourism: A spatial interaction model for Italy. *Journal of Geographical Systems, 15*(3), 369–402.
Peng, B., Song, H., Crouch, G. I., & Witt, S. F. (2014). A meta-analysis of international tourism demand elasticities. *Journal of Travel Research, 54*(5), 611–633.
Plaza, B., & Haarich, S. N. (2015). The Guggenheim Museum Bilbao: Between regional embeddedness and global networking. *European Planning Studies, 23*(8), 1456–1475.
Rodríguez-Pose, A., & Crescenzi, R. (2008). Research and development, spillovers, innovation systems, and the genesis of regional growth in Europe. *Regional Studies, 42*(1), 51–67.
Sciacchitano, E. (2019). European year of cultural-heritage. A laboratory for heritage-based innovation. *SCIentific RESearch and Information Technology, 9*(1), 1–14.
Soukiazis, E., & Proença, S. (2008). Tourism as an alternative source of regional growth in Portugal: A panel data analysis at NUTS II and III levels. *Portuguese Economic Journal, 7*(1), 43–61.
Temple, J. (1999). The new growth evidence. *Journal of Economic Literature, 37*(1), 112–156.
Throsby, D. (Ed.). (2001). *Economics and culture*. Cambridge University Press.

UNWTO. (2018). *Tourism highlights—2018 edition.* https://www.e-unwto.org/doi/pdf/10.18111/9789284419876, [22/10/2021].

Witt, S. F., & Witt, C. A. (1995). Forecasting tourism demand: A review of empirical research. *International Journal of Forecasting, 11*(3), 447–475.

World Travel & Tourism Council. (2019). Benchmarking research trends 2019. https://wttc.org/Research/Economic-Impact/Benchmarking, [23/11/2020].

Yang, C. H., Lin, H. L., & Han, C. C. (2010). Analysis of international tourist arrivals in China: The role of World Heritage Sites. *Tourism Management, 31*(6), 827–837.

Part II
From Cultural Heritage to Local Development: The Role of Territorial Identity

Chapter 4
A New Framework for Definitions and Measures of Territorial Identity

4.1 Territorial Identity and Cultural Heritage: Introduction and Relevance of the Topic

The paramount relevance of European cultural heritage is nowadays widely acknowledged. Policymakers, scholars, professionals and citizens find themselves in agreement regarding the valuable influence that cultural heritage is able to exert on societies.

Even though each European Member State holds responsibility for heritage-related policies, the European Union—acting as a supporting, guarantor and coordinating agent—keeps stressing and highlighting the fundamental role of cultural heritage for Europe. Article 3.3 of the Treaty of European Union states that "*the Union shall respect its rich cultural and linguistic diversity and shall ensure that Europe's cultural heritage is safeguarded and enhanced*". Without neglecting each single European country's specificities and uniqueness in terms of the forms and types of cultural heritage they are endowed with, treating heritage as a collective and shared European resource enables the full appreciation of its potential and the development of synergies and connections to enhance cultural heritage conservation and valorization all around Europe. As stated in Article 167 of the Treaty, the EU "*shall contribute to the flowering of the cultures of the Member States, while respecting their national and regional diversity and at the same time bringing the common cultural heritage to the fore*".

The EU's compelling interest toward heritage has been demonstrated throughout the years with several initiatives, conventions, funds, projects and events the last of which being the European Year of Cultural Heritage in 2018, aimed at promoting a sense of belonging to a common European space. As highlighted by Sciacchitano (2019), following the European Year of Cultural Heritage, the European Commission developed for the first time a European Framework for Action on Cultural Heritage, revealing the need to recognize and make explicit the key role of heritage within European policies and programs.

E. Panzera, *Cultural Heritage and Territorial Identity*, Advances in Spatial Science,
https://doi.org/10.1007/978-3-030-94468-1_4

The reasons why European cultural heritage is believed to be of essential value and relevance stem from several positive spillovers associated with the presence of different forms and expressions of cultural heritage. In fact, both public institutions and academic literature ascribe to cultural heritage synergies with, for instance, knowledge and education (CHCfE Consortium, 2015), a function of driver toward social cohesion and inclusion (Council of Europe, 2005), individuals' well-being (European Commission, 2019), creativity and innovation (European Commission, 2018). Furthermore, the role of cultural heritage as an engine for territorial development and economic growth has been acknowledged (see for instance *Getting Cultural Heritage to Work for Europe*, European Commission, 2015), and the perception of heritage as an economic driver is in continuous expansion. The paramount importance of cultural heritage and its tight relationship with the territory in which it is located has been highlighted by the European Union for many years. In fact, the European Spatial Development Perspective report, which can be considered as one of the main European documents adopting a territorial perspective, was drafted in 1999 and it is worth noting that it begins and concludes mentioning European culture and identities and European cultural heritage[1] (European Commission, 1999).

One of the strongest and most recurrent associations is the one between cultural heritage and identity. Since cultural heritage is at once inherited from the past and a legacy for future generations, it is considered as a source of sense of belonging and cultural identity (CHCfE Consortium, 2015). Citing from the report "Cultural Heritage Counts for Europe", "*cultural heritage can lead to a greater national awareness, social cohesion, sense of a place and identity*" (CHCfE Consortium, 2015, p. 148). As argued in Dalmas et al. (2015) cultural heritage carries strong interrelations between contemporaneity and cultural tradition inherited from the past. The peculiar and essential characteristics of heritage can be identified in the memory which is embedded in it and the identity which is carried and infused by it (Vecco, 2010). Heritage is therefore perceived as storage of collective memory and as a vehicle of identity. As Tosco (2014) pointed out, the past dimension is not enough to define a cultural outcome as being cultural heritage. It is the present society that elects, safeguards and promotes certain kinds of cultural expressions crowning them as legitimate parts of its cultural heritage. This aspect shows the intertwined relationship between cultural heritage as a storage of history and past identities that shape the present ones and the role that current identities, values and beliefs play in deciding which heritage should be considered as such.

By means of official documentation, reports and strategic guidelines the European Union has oftentimes emphasized the role of cultural heritage as a vehicle of European identity, cohesion and sense of belonging. Furthermore, cultural heritage is acknowledged as a core element of the European way of life, being embedded in our territories and being a determinant of who Europeans are and therefore representing a force able to strengthen a sense of attachment to a European family (eTwinning, 2018). Why does identity hold such a relevant role in the public arena? Why is the

[1] See Art. (1) and Art. (326).

relationship between cultural heritage and identity mechanisms so often stressed and emphasized?

It is nowadays a fact that the European Union's citizens and regions face enormous challenges mainly due to two distinct phenomena, the first being globalization and the second being the new technological paradigm. Even though both globalization and technological progress have been sources of growth and development, it is also true that the new established order has not equally benefitted everyone. Globalization has contributed to founding a highly competitive context resulting also in reduced power of unions and wage setters (Saraceno & Fitoussi, 2019) and to facilitating the relocation of value chains changing their territorial patterns (Camagni, 2020). At the same time, technological progress has ended up favoring high-skilled and well-educated workers and penalizing low-skilled ones or those performing routine intellectual jobs threatened by automation and smart machines (Iammarino et al., 2017).

Consequently, inequality and insecurity about economic and personal stability has increased dramatically, together with severe discrepancy between expectations and actual opportunities. The financial crisis that hit the European Union from 2008 onwards, the vast migration flows involving the European countries, the blossoming of new forms of employment contracts all contribute to exacerbate feelings of uncertainty and discontent. Within this context of uncertain future, the question of identity becomes crucial. As highlighted by Francis Fukuyama in his recently published book entitled "*Identity*", it is possible to attribute what is going on in world politics today to a request for recognition of one's identity. Using his words "*According to Hegel, human history was driven by a struggle for recognition. He argued that the only rational solution to the desire for recognition was universal recognition, in which the dignity of every human being was recognized. Universal recognition has been challenged ever since by other partial forms of recognition based on nation, religion, sect, race, ethnicity, or gender, or by individuals wanting to be recognized as superior. The rise of identity politics in modern liberal democracies is one of the chief threats that they face, unless we can work our way back to more universal understanding of human dignity, we will doom ourselves to continuing conflict*" (Fukuyama, 2018, p. 10).

A claim for identity recognition is at the heart of the rise of consensus and stands for populist and nationalist parties mainly opposed to European integration that, over the last decade, has almost doubled (Dijkstra et al., 2018). This evidence has brought to light profound and severe feelings of discontent and disappointment overflowing in the European Union's citizens and territories. The phenomenon is of such a broad range and relevance that an ad hoc expression has been coined, namely *geography of discontent* (McCann, 2020; Rodríguez-Pose, 2017) and concerns for the future of the European Union have been disclosed. As Dijkstra et al. (2018) argue, long-term economic and industrial decline, low education levels and lack of local employment opportunities are the main causes explaining the growing consensus toward populist or nationalist parties. As a reaction to these unfavorable and uncertain conditions, identity is felt to be as a psychological anchor holding a nostalgic attachment for a past imagined strong and cohesive national community without the risks and downsides of modern society.

On the other hand, identity formation and reinforcement are considered of fundamental importance for the European Union. The promotion of European identity—as added not as in contrast with other territorial identities such as national or regional—is essential to foster and ensure the process of European integration. As argued in the European Identity Study, to reach the legitimation of any political system it is necessary that a sentiment of sameness and some form of identification are perceived by the members of that system (Prutsch, 2017). According to this study the process of European identity building should be grounded both on cultural ("*Europe as a cultural community of shared values*", p. 5) and political bases ("*Europe as a political community of shared democratic practices*", p. 5).

Following these reflections, identity means at the same time closure and openness, exclusion and inclusion, cultural legacy and future development. It can be related to the single individual, to a collectivity, a society, a territory and a political system. Identity is plural and multiple identities can coexist at the same time.

Since the debate and the literature related to identity are very rich and multi-faceted, the continuation of this chapter will be dedicated to deepening the concept of identity. Furthermore, because of the economic and quantitative approach of this book, the main objective of this chapter is related to the proposal of a new framework for measuring territorial identity and therefore being able to include it in an empirical analysis aimed at exploring its role in the relationships between cultural heritage and economic development. Accordingly, this chapter will be specifically dedicated to investigating the concept of identity and trying to find ways of measuring it. After having defined the concept and proposed an innovative way of measuring it, the logic and hypotheses behind the functioning of the relationships between cultural heritage, identity and economic development will be presented. The following chapters (Chapters 5 and 6) will explore in detail synergies and connections between identity and, respectively, cultural heritage and economic development following the logic presented at the end of this chapter.

The following sections will be structured as follows: Sect. 4.2 presents an overview of the concept of identity, clarifying how it has been treated by the literature so far; Sect. 4.3 discusses the concept of territorial identity and illustrates its peculiarities and characteristics as suggested by the existing literature; Sect. 4.4 proposes an original taxonomy of different ways in which territorial identity can occur within the borders of the European Union and discusses in detail each identified category; Sect. 4.5 presents the proposed way to measure territorial identity and a map of European regions according to their specific typology of territorial identity; and Sect. 4.6 concludes presenting the logic and the conceptual framework stemming from the proposed taxonomy and grounding the continuation of the book.

4.2 The Concept of Identity in the Existing Literature

Defining *identity* is a challenging and ambitious endeavor taken over by a multiplicity of disciplines. As argued by Fligstein et al. (2012), psychologists, sociologists, anthropologists and political scientists have shown their interest in investigating formation and attributes of the concept. Even though identity enters the ordinary language, its meaning is not sufficiently developed or fully captured by the definitions proposed by the dictionary (Fearon, 1999). In fact, the concept is elusive (Schilde, 2014), chaotic and vague (Paasi, 2002) and the essence of the meaning itself depends on the context in which it is discussed and the disciplines that analyze it. Furthermore, as highlighted in Paasi (2002) the notion of identity is close to that of, among others, social capital, trust, solidarity, social relations and sense of belonging. It is not something given, fixed or unchangeable, it is rather a social construct (Fearon, 1999) and an abstraction (Paasi, 2002) through which different elements are combined and unified and others are ruled out.

Starting from the second half of the twentieth century, the discourse on identity begins to emerge and to be established in the academic field. The psychologist Erik H. Erikson (1902–1994) is considered to be among the first scholars to investigate the notion of identity both in relation to the personal dimension and, more importantly, the social sphere. The idea that identity exists on two separate but integrated levels, namely individual and group, started to emerge. As Fearon (1999, p. 23) argues, personal identity can be defined as a "*set of aspects or attributes of a person. Physical attributes, membership in social categories, person specific beliefs, goals, desires, moral principles, or matters of personal style; aspects or attributes of the person that the person is conscious of and which distinguish the person from at least some others*". As claimed by Parekh (2009), the overall identity of a person is the result and combination of both personal and social identity.

The concept of social identity can be described as a complex unstable social process of categorization (Paasi, 2002; Revilla et al., 2013). Groups or communities define and recognize themselves as "us" distinguished by or opposed to others. The process of identity formation, reinforcement or transformation might assume the form both of a spontaneous process led by common history, language, ethnicity and cultural heritage or an intention or will of social institutions (Capello, 2018). As well explained in Capello (2018), two main elements are highlighted by the literature as the foundations of collective identity, namely similarity and solidarity. Citing from Fligstein et al. (2012, p. 108) "*collective identities refer to the idea that a group of people accept a fundamental and consequential similarity that causes them to feel solidarity among themselves*". Similarity refers to a condition of sameness, common to the members of a group or collectivity. The awareness of sharing the same values, attitudes, ways of living and being part of a common history, territory but also gender or sexual orientation feed a sense of similarity within the group. Solidarity refers to behavioral or process-oriented practices (Caporaso & Kim, 2009). In fact, solidarity embodies feelings of togetherness and sense of loyalty to a group that culminate in concrete demonstrative social actions. As Li and Brewer (2004) pointed out, the perception of experiencing common problems and the adoption of a cooperative and collective way of problem-solving favor the formation of a coherent social group (Caporaso & Kim, 2009).

As Risse (2002) explains, besides the dual nature of identity—being at the same time both at an individual (or related to the inner self) and a group level (or related to the outer self)—individuals simultaneously hold multiple identities occasionally even in conflict with one another. Social identities can be built based on personal lifestyles, gender, sexual orientation, work environment, political affiliation, religion, ethnicity, nation, region or town of belonging. The identification process tends to be associated with positive emotions given by the identification itself (Lawler, 2008). Whenever a disappointment perception comes out, the individual tries to leave the group (Tajfel & Turner, 1979). The identification with several and different groups or units follows diverse needs such that of stable inclusion in a larger community or that of distinctiveness and uniqueness with respect to other social categories (Brewer, 2001).

It has to be noted that if, on the one hand, identity brings people together building solid bonds and strengthening loyalty and sense of membership and belonging, on the other hand, it represents a powerful means of exclusion and othering. As Fearon (1999) argues, no matter the specific given definition, identity is always associated with a demand for recognition that, developing into an inclination to prevail and an affirmation of superiority, becomes a dangerous tool for segregation, resentment and hostility. The powerful role of identity can be better understood when a third dimension (added to the personal and social ones), of a political nature, is introduced. This political dimension involves "*an evolving concept of dignity, in which recognition is due not just to a narrow class of people, but to everyone. The broadening and universalization of dignity turns the private quest for self into a political project*" (Fukuyama, 2018, p. 38). The political dimension becomes particularly relevant when the identity discourse is associated with the territorial and institutional elements, whether they are the European Union, the nation, the region, the province or the city, especially when inhabitants or institutions establish emotional links with their territories that become symbols and instruments for recognition. The following section is dedicated to examining the concept of territorial identity—the main focus of the present research—understanding its meanings, sources and implications.

4.3 The Concept of Territorial Identity in the Existing Literature

When the territorial dimension is associated with the concept of identity the notion of territory assumes a relevant importance. There can be territorial identification toward a neighborhood, a village, a region, a nation or a supranational area. As explained in Raagma (2002) territorial identity concerns the social territorial system including people, traditions, culture and landscape, and it embraces emotional links between the inhabitants and the territory. As highlighted in Paasi (2002) each territory has an objective identity—using his words "*identity of a region*"—given by a specific territorial shape and characteristics, very different from "*regional identity*" which involves territorial consciousness and which generates an emotional tie between the inhabitants and their spatial context. Further traits of territorial identity include, as argued in Capello (2018), a certain degree of convergence between private and collective interests which consequently fuel sentiments of loyalty and sense of belonging. Furthermore, identification, attachment and bonding with a territory are fed by the same two fundamental elements that we previously discussed: similarity and solidarity (see for instance Revilla et al., 2013 and Capello, 2018).

Before delving into the sources and the formation process of territorial identity a clarification on the concept of territory is due. In the last two decades, the term *territory* has entered the public and academic fields considered as being more appropriate and exhaustive than *space* or *region*. As well explained in Camagni (2008, p. 32), several elements are embraced by the term *territory* namely:

- *a system of localized externalities, both pecuniary (where their advantages are appropriated through market transactions) and technological (when advantages are exploited by simple proximity to the source);*
- *a system of localized production activities, traditions, skills and know-how;*
- *a system of localized, proximity relationships, which constitute a "capital"—of a social psychological and political nature—in that it enhances static and dynamic productivity of local factors;*
- *a system of cultural elements and values which attribute sense and meaning to local practices and structures and defines local identities; they acquire an economic value whenever they either can be transformed into marketable products—goods, services and assets—or boost internal capability to exploit local potentials;*
- *a system of rules and practices defining a local governance model.*

All these elements are included in the concept of territorial capital[2] defined as the set of all assets—material and immaterial; private, public and collective; cognitive, social and relational—which constitute the development potential of each territory (Camagni, 2008).

[2] The OECD defines and discusses the concept of Territorial Capital within the OECD Territorial Outlook. Citing from the document: "*these factors may include the area's geographical location, size, factor of production endowment, climate, traditions, natural resources, quality of life or the agglomeration economies provided by its cities but may also include its business incubators and industrial districts, or other business networks that reduce transaction costs. Other factors may be "untraded interdependencies" such as understanding, customs and informal rules that enable economic actors to work together under conditions of uncertainty, or the solidarity, mutual assistance and co-opting ideas that often develop in clusters of small and medium-sized enterprises working in the same sector. Lastly, according to Marshall, there is an intangible factor, "something in the air", called the "environment" and which it is the outcome of a combination of institutions, rules, practices, producers, researchers and policymakers, that make a certain creativity and innovation possible*" (OECD, 2001, p. 15).

Territorial identity originates from the shared consciousness of the presence of these localized specificities and values, determining at the same time the character of local communities, their sense of belonging, their pride and demand for recognition. When territorial identity is included in this conceptual framework, two important consequences are achieved. First, territorial identity is conceived as a potential asset of economic development, leading, like almost all immaterial elements of territorial capital, to an increase in the efficiency of traditional, material production factors. Second, no less importantly, territorial identity can be measured (as are almost all other elements of territorial capital) and treated quantitatively as a development factor, among others.

Variations in the intensity of territorial identity might be due to its formation process. As explained in Paasi (1986) four elements contribute to the formation of territorial identity:

- existence or constitution of a territorial shape;
- presence of a symbolic shape (constituted by shared practices such as economy, culture, media or governance) that contributes to develop narratives of identity. This element includes symbols such as the name of the territorial unit or the flag;
- a certain number of institutions to preserve territorial and symbolic shape;
- established social practices and consciousness.

The four elements do not occur in a predetermined sequence and they can also take place simultaneously (Raagma, 2002). Furthermore, territories and territorial identities are social constructs which interact and combine with each other, change over time and influence and are influenced by political actions. As highlighted in Marks (1999), formation, shifts and transformations of territorial identities derive from macro-societal factors such as wars, culture, economic and political interests and institutions. However, objective evidence that associates these factors with territorial identity is missing. In fact, the process is influenced and framed by institutions that formalize pre-existing networks and territories. At the same time, the process is also guided by actors having prior or other territorial identities that influence their perceptions and are biased by political discourses.

It has to be noted that an important distinction is made between territorial identity and appreciation or recognition of political institutions. A positive relation with institutions can be associated to a partial connotation of territorial identity, the one concerning civic identification. As Bruter (2003) points out, civic identity refers to a feeling of citizenship within a certain political system characterized by rules, laws and rights which are shared and respected. Institutions are interpreted as guarantors of civil rights and political participation embedded in a democratic political culture (Prutsch, 2017). To achieve a full sense of territorial identity its cultural connotation needs to be embraced together with the civic one. Fundamental elements are the recognition of common cultural legacies and historical experiences (Prutsch, 2017), identification with a human group, abstracted from the political system (Bruter, 2003) and perception of shared cultural and social similarities (Capello & Perucca, 2019).

A further element of complexity stemming from the discourse on territorial identity is given by the fact that identification mechanisms, perceptions of common cultural or historical grounds and recognition of political institutions acquire different meanings when associated with different territorial levels (Paasi, 2002). Citing from Fligstein et al. (2012, p. 112) "*one can think of European identity as nested in national identities, regional identities and even more local identities such as cities or neighborhood, not in conflict but complementary and activated under certain social conditions. [...] Territorial identities are different from country to country and change over time*". Multiple territorial identities exist, coexist and are nested within each other (Díez Medrano & Gutiérrez, 2001). They can be thought of as imagined communities of loyalty (Schilde, 2014) and the meaning of territorial identity changes according to the person who feels it (Caporaso & Kim, 2009). As highlighted in Bettini (2016), cultures and communities are variable and complex mechanisms and do not represent a herald of selected survivals, there are no specific roots for people or communities.

Taking into consideration different elements and peculiarities of territorial identity, the following section proposes and describes in detail an original taxonomy of different ways or modes in which territorial identity can occur within the borders of the European Union.

4.4 Modes of Expression of Territorial Identities: An Original Classification

As highlighted in previous sections, territorial identity is a complex and multifaceted concept. It encompasses distinct elements and it can be plural and multilevel.

In the context of this work, territorial identity is interpreted as the perception of sameness felt and experienced by the inhabitants of a specific territory. In other words, all the people living in a same territory share a similarity condition that constitutes the basic requirement for territorial identity. This sameness characteristic can be expressed in different ways according to two main aspects. The first aspect is related to a behavioral dimension. In fact, similarity is the basic condition for the identification of individuals with a group; however, different behavioral attitudes within the same group might stem from this condition. More specifically, the perception of being similar to a certain group of people can be associated with a feeling of solidarity which takes place whenever a certain correspondence between private and common interests is recognized by the participating individuals. Depending on the presence of this solidarity feeling, different behaviors can be put in place by the individuals. If solidarity is absent, individualistic attitudes happen within a certain group. In this case, individuals base their territorial identity on a merely objective similarity given by the condition of living in the same territory, with the same rights and duties and the same economic, institutional and cultural frameworks. On the contrary, when solidarity is present, people put in place cooperative and reciprocal behaviors; they tend to trust each other and to act in accordance with the recognition of a common interest between the private and the common sphere.

The second aspect according to which different typologies of territorial identity can be expressed is the geographical scale of its reach. In fact, the fundamental feeling of sameness can be felt and experienced toward different geographical levels (e.g., the neighborhood, the city, the region, the nation or the European Union) either exclusively or simultaneously. This aspect determines whether certain groups of people living in a territory are open toward other spatial levels or instead are closed and not disposed to include and integrate the others.

To conceive a classification of different typologies or modes of expression of territorial identities, the two previously mentioned main aspects are formalized as follows:

- the founding elements of identity (behavioral aspect): following the literature (see for instance Capello, 2018 and Fligstein et al., 2012) identity is composed of two essential ingredients, namely *similarity* and *solidarity*.

  Similarity means that, as a result of a more or less spontaneous process of territorial institutionalization or formalization, the inhabitants of a territory share specific actual and contingent characteristics and peculiarities. Similarity can be referred to shared values, norms and beliefs but also merely to shared geographical borders, historical memories, common institutional and economic frameworks and common rights and duties.

  Solidarity means that the inhabitants of a region recognize a common and collective interest that encourages them to put in action supportive and mutually beneficial behaviors. Solidarity constitutes the foundation for a cohesive territorial collectivity and feeds loyalty and sense of belonging to a place and a community. The awareness of a certain kind of convergence between private and collective interests originates favorable practices for both the individual and the community and it adds complexity to a plain similarity feeling.
- the spatial reach of founding networks (geographical scale aspect): as highlighted in the literature, different territorial identities can be nested within each other (see for instance Díez Medrano & Gutíerrez, 2001). The founding networks are intended as relationships, interactions and shared feelings entertained by inhabitants inside and/or outside their specific region or territory. These relationships and interactions happen thanks to purposeful networks among individuals and institutions with multiple contents—economic, social, cognitive, political and cultural (Nooteboom, 2019). The strength and complexity of these relationships depend on the contextual multiplicity of contents, on frequency and continuity of contacts and on dedicated investments—economic or emotional. All this may end in a strong symbolic value enhancing the generation of identity.

The *founding elements of identity* and the *spatial reach of founding networks* have been considered as, respectively, horizontal and vertical axes of a matrix (reported in Fig. 4.1). More specifically, the *founding elements of identity* are differentiated in *similarity only* and *similarity and solidarity* and refer to the behavioral dimension of identity. The *spatial reach of founding networks* is instead expressed as *exclusively local*, reflecting a closed and self-centered type of territorial identity, or *simultaneously local and European*, reflecting a more open and absorptive type of

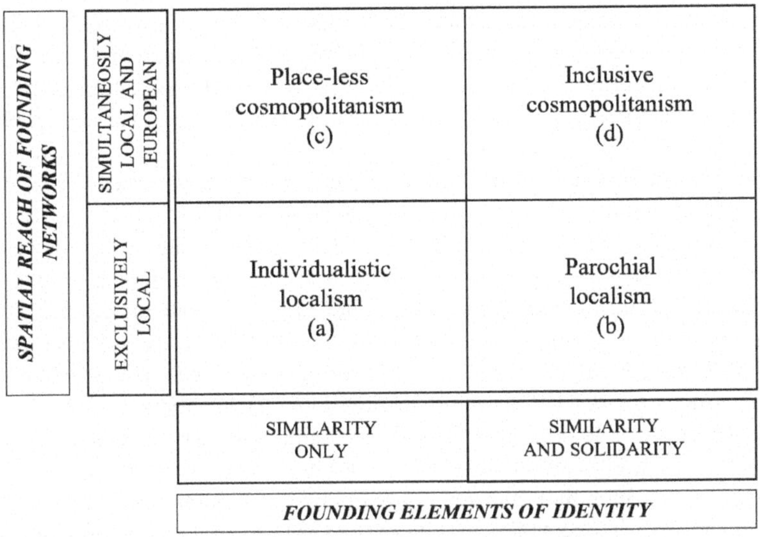

Fig. 4.1 Modes of expression of territorial identity: an original taxonomy

spatial reach of the founding networks. The following figure (Fig. 4.1) represents an attempt of classification of different ways in which territorial identity(ies) occur(s) (a preliminary version of the classification has been proposed in Camagni et al., 2020).

With reference to the specificity of the European Union, the following four typologies of territorial identity can be identified and characterized.

a. Individualistic localism: the first category is characterized by similarity only (as per the founding elements of identity) and exclusively local spatial reach of the founding networks. It is defined as individualistic because the inhabitants of the territory only perceive some forms of objective similarities with others mainly given by the fact of living in the same place, sharing the same geographic borders, being embedded in the same territorial characteristics and sharing the same institutional and economic contexts. Since the element of solidarity is missing, the identity portrayed in this category is fragile, weak and inactive. Similarity without solidarity characterizes a collectivity in which individuals or groups coexist in parallel yet without integrating or blending. The individualist dimension is confirmed by the fact that the spatial reach of the founding networks is exclusively local. The already weak perception of sameness and sharing does not cross the local frontiers.
b. Parochial localism: the second category is characterized by both similarity and solidarity and again by an exclusively local spatial reach of the founding networks. The community living in this territory is endowed with a strong and active local identity. People trust each other, perceive that they have a common interest and feel a sense of loyalty to the place in which they live. Similarity and solidarity found a cohesive, unified and strengthened collectivity ready to

act to consolidate and protect its shared interests. The exclusively local reach of the founding networks generates a condition of exclusive parochialism meaning that the territorial community is self-centered, closed and restricted giving no space to inclusion, admission or perceived proximity with external people and places.

c. Place-less cosmopolitanism: the third category is characterized by similarity only and simultaneously local and European spatial reach of the founding networks. As in case (a), inhabitants of territories ending up in this category share just a basic sense of similarity resulting in the identification with their pure living space, having uncertain bonds with the other inhabitants; togetherness or loyalty feelings are absent. On the other hand, the key characteristic of this category is the simultaneous local and European spatial reach of the founding networks that opens up the possibility to talk about cosmopolitanism. However, the sole presence of similarity without solidarity does not allow for the full complexity of an identitarian sentiment. Inhabitants are attached to the territory in which they live and contemplate the supranational territorial level in an abstract intellectual way rather than a sentimental and emotional one.
d. Inclusive cosmopolitanism: the fourth category is characterized by similarity and solidarity and simultaneously local and European spatial reach of the founding networks. In this case the community shares the same territorial conditions, values and beliefs and, at the same time, is moved by solidarity links among its members. Elements of internal and external integration, trust, loyalty and cohesion are present resulting in a strongly compact community. However, as opposed to case (b), the simultaneously local and European spatial reach of the founding networks allows for inclusion and openness toward others and other territorial levels. In this case cosmopolitanism fully reveals its potential as the supranational territorial level is considered as a source of cohesion and solidarity, possibly leading to higher political stability.

Overall, the main aim of the development of this taxonomy is related to detecting the identitarian characteristics of a specific territorial community (the regional community in this work). The adjective "territorial" is referred to a reference community and the meaning of the term is not just physical or geographical but also socio-economic and cultural. Groups of people are locally concentrated in certain territories (regions) and experience proximity in terms of institutional, economic, social, cultural and normative conditions. These local communities present peculiarities in terms of their felt and collectively expressed identity. Starting from the idea that these local, regional communities are glued by specific idiosyncratic characteristics (*similarity*), each of them might present different territorial/regional identities. More in detail, some of them, even though possibly very attached to their region, might feel inclusive and open attitudes toward the outside and they might consider themselves as European citizens, as well as national, or regional residents. Some others, instead, may consider themselves as being (collectively) very far from the status of European citizens and identify only with the local level. On the other hand, different sentiments and behaviors might be associated with the similarity condition: local communities can either show solidarity toward the others (when they perceive a certain correspondence between private and public interest) or demonstrate more individualistic and self-interested attitudes.

The following section describes the method proposed to measure these different identified typologies of territorial identity.

4.5 Measuring Territorial Identities: An Application to European Regions

As previously mentioned, the approach of this work is economic and quantitative. Furthermore, the objective of this part (Part B) of the book is the exploration of the role of territorial identity as a bridge between the endowment of cultural heritage and local economic development.

From this objective derives the need to try to measure territorial identity and, more specifically, investigate how the four different identified typologies of territorial identity are spread across the European Union and its regions. In fact, as in Part A, the geographical level considered for the empirical analysis is the regional one. The reasons justifying this choice mainly relate to two aspects. On the one hand, the regional level allows us to take into consideration a sufficiently disaggregated level to detect and consider the specificities, peculiarities and differentiated characteristics of territories (including territorial identities) within the national boundaries. On the other hand, a limit of data availability prevents from considering a more disaggregated territorial level. In fact, since the scope of the analysis is the whole European Union, to guarantee a reliable degree of comparability, the regional level (NUTS2) represents the most suitable one.

Therefore, following the taxonomy of different modes of expressions of territorial identities presented in Fig. 4.1, data gathered through the Eurobarometer surveys[3] have been considered to classify European regions according to their specific type of territorial identity.

More specifically, two Eurobarometer questions have been selected to represent and measure the dimensions expressed on the horizontal and vertical axes in the matrix for the classification of different typologies of territorial identity.

The *founding elements of identity* are measured according to the answers to the following Eurobarometer question:

> *On the following list, which are the three most important values for you personally?*

[3] Eurobarometer is a series of surveys conducted on behalf of the European Commission since the 1970s. These surveys aim at monitoring the public opinion in the European Union member and candidate countries on different topics such as, among others, attitudes toward European integration, social conditions, health, culture, the economy, or the environment. The survey results are regularly published in official reports by the European Commission or by the European Parliament (Gesis.org; European University Institute).

Among the possible answers "*Solidarity, support for others*" has been selected.

The *spatial reach of founding networks* is measured according to the following Eurobarometer question:

For each of the following statement, please tell me to what extent it corresponds or not to your opinion: You feel you are a citizen of the EU.
1—No, definitely not;
2—No, not really;
3—Yes, to some extent;
4—Yes, definitely.

A decision has been made to choose to consider European citizenship over a more general feeling of being European to take into account the identification and association with the European Union as an institution. By doing so, a stronger political meaning is grasped. The recognition and appreciation of the institution can be interpreted as the conversion of a cultural sentiment into a political one, closest to the social/political human being. Nationalist parties are indeed against the institutions rather than the more general, geographical conception of Europe.

It has to be noted that for each Eurobarometer survey the sample size is 1000 meaning that each survey has 1000 respondents per country. In order to have a more representative sample for the present analysis, four Eurobarometer surveys have been considered jointly resulting in a sample size of 4000 respondents per country. It also has to be noted that the number of individuals interviewed is proportional to the number of inhabitants of each NUTS2 region belonging to the various countries.

The following table (Table 4.1) indicates the codes and the years of the Eurobarometer rounds that have been taken into consideration:

Two main time spans have been taken into consideration: the Eurobarometer surveys corresponding to the years 2012, 2014, 2015 and 2016 have been grouped under the label *Partial recovery from 2008 financial crisis*; the Eurobarometer surveys corresponding instead to the years 2017 and 2018 have been grouped under the label *Full recovery from 2008 financial crisis.*

The following steps have been undertaken to assign a typology of territorial identity to each European NUTS2 region:

Table 4.1 Eurobarometer rounds considered in the analysis

Eurobarometer No.	Year	Time Span
77.3	2012	Partial recovery from 2008 financial crisis
82.3	2014	
84.3	2015	
86.2	2016	
87.3	2017	Full recovery from 2008 financial crisis
88.3	2017	
89.1	2018	
90.3	2018	

1. For each of the selected Eurobarometer questions, the individual answers of four Eurobarometer rounds have been grouped;
2. Each individual answer has been assigned to the corresponding European NUTS2 region according to the information provided by the Eurobarometer surveys;
3. For each NUTS2 region and for each considered question, the average of individual answers of four Eurobarometer rounds has been computed;
4. For each question considered, the European average of individual answers of the same four Eurobarometer rounds has been computed;
5. For each country and for each considered question, the average of individual answers of the same four Eurobarometer rounds has been computed;
6. For each question considered, a class (corresponding to one of the four identified typologies of territorial identity as explained in Fig. 4.1) has been assigned to each NUTS2 region resulting from a comparison between the regional average value and the European average value;
7. For each question considered, a class (corresponding to one of the four identified typologies of territorial identity as explained in Fig. 4.1) has been assigned to each NUTS2 region resulting from a comparison between the regional average value and the national average value.

The following figure (Fig. 4.2) graphically shows the method of the territorial identity categories assignment both comparing the regional average values with the European average value (a) and with the national average value (b).

Following this procedure, each European region has been associated with the corresponding typology of territorial identity that emerges from the Eurobarometer surveys considered. Figure 4.3 shows a map of European NUTS2 regions with their corresponding typology of identity assigned according to the European average value (which is the method presented in Fig. 4.2 (a)).

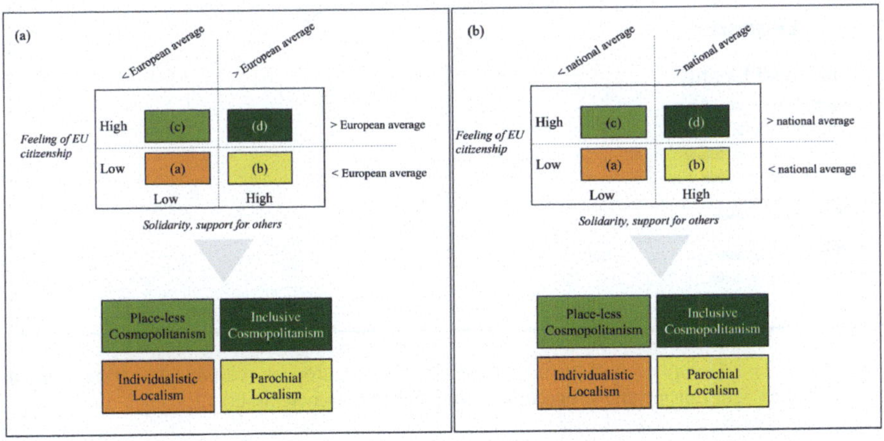

Fig. 4.2 Method for territorial identity categories assignment to European NUTS2 regions

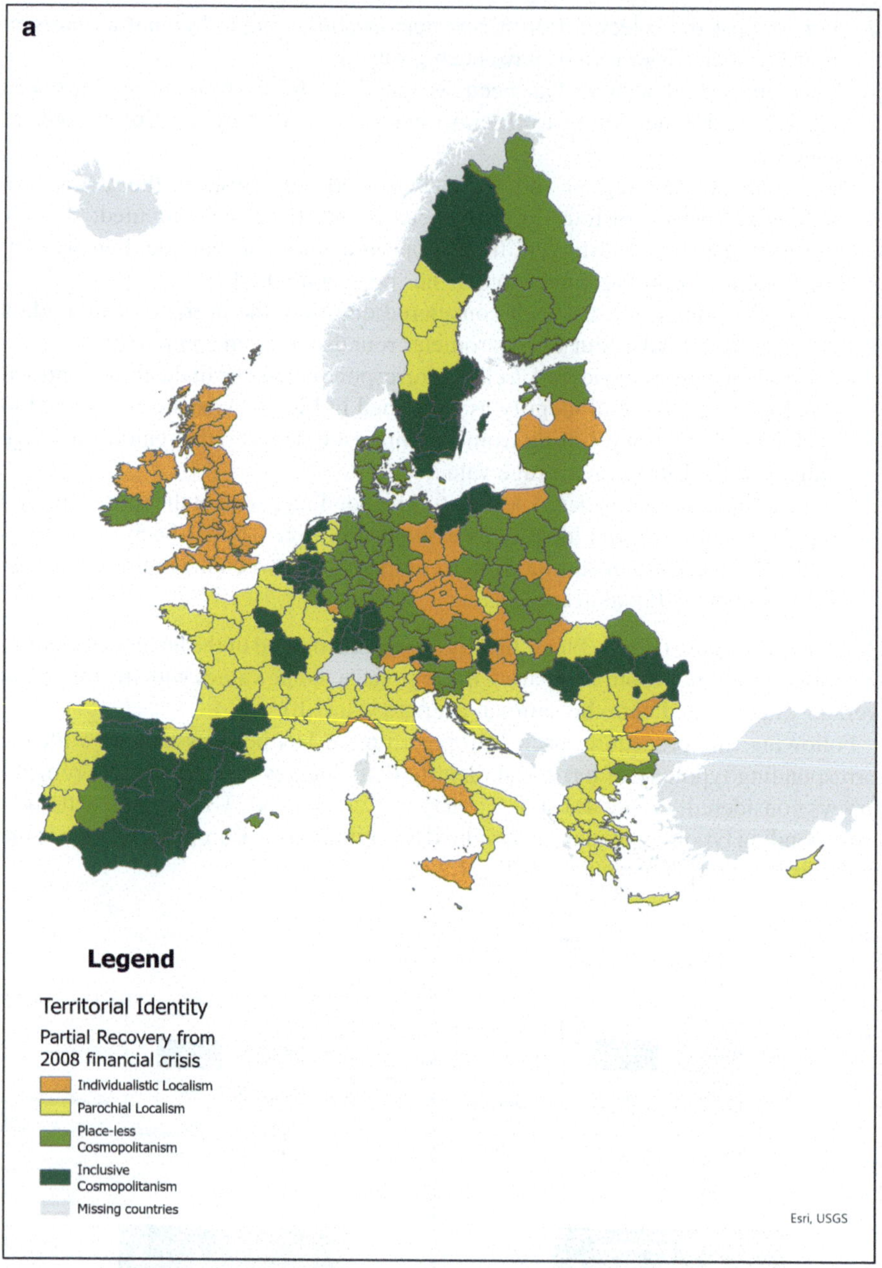

Fig. 4.3 Modes of expression of territorial identity across European regions comparing regional average values with European average value (*Source* Eurobarometer data)

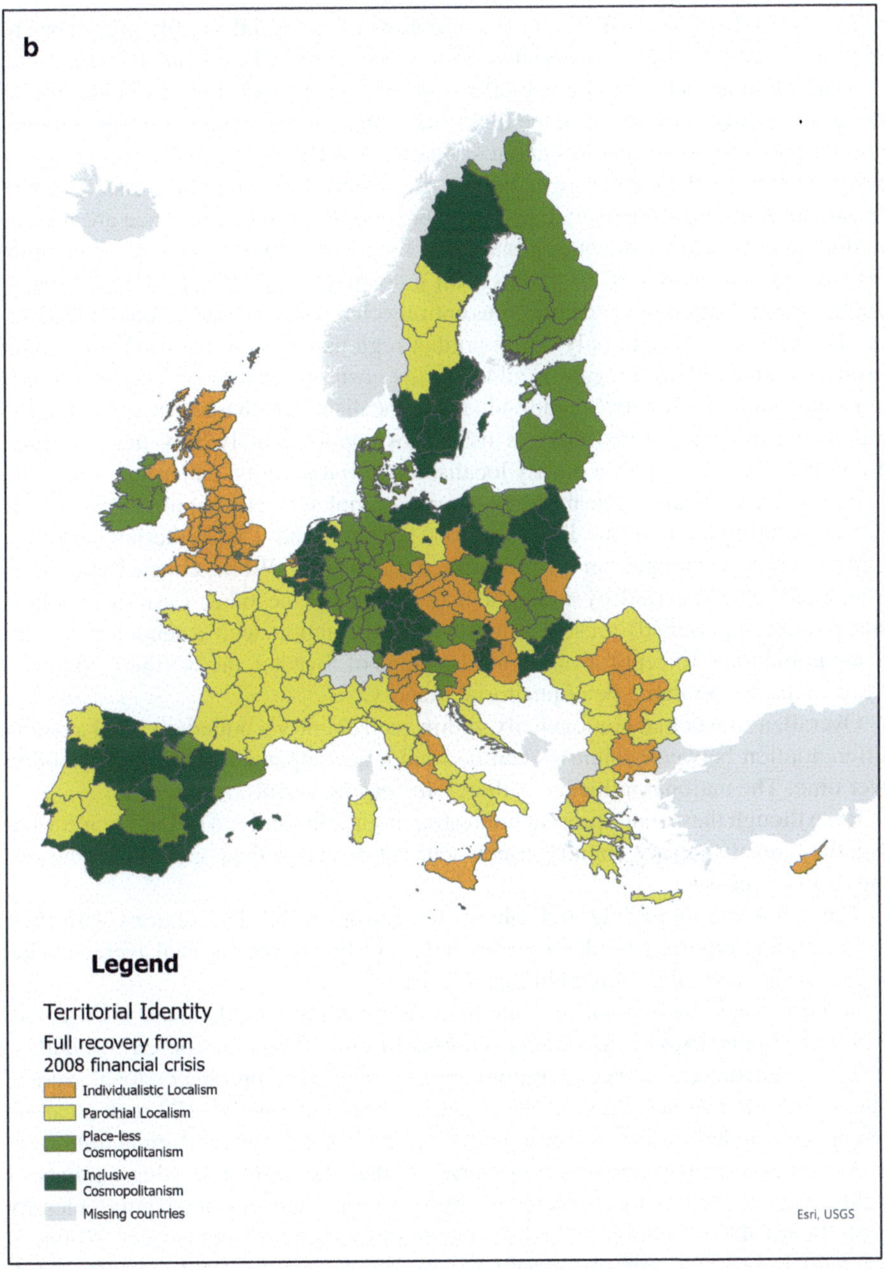

Fig. 4.3 (continued)

As evident from Fig. 4.3, if a specific typology of territorial identity is assigned to each region comparing the regional average value with the European average value, a strong predominance of country effects is evident. In fact, regions belonging to the same country show, most of the times, the same color, showing a strong national component in regional feelings about solidarity and belonging to the Union. Spain is almost entirely dark green, revealing its predominant cosmopolitan character and the situation remains relatively constant over time. Portugal and France are instead predominantly yellow, showing a parochial localist identity condition. Over time, France seems to lose its few regions with a cosmopolitan attitude (Ile de France, Bourgogne and Aquitaine) and becomes entirely characterized by parochial localism. On the contrary, Portugal only cosmopolitan regions (Algarve and Lisbon) remain cosmopolitan and Norte region is added to the cosmopolitan ones. The situation is constantly split in UK between individualistic localism that characterizes most of the country and the London area which is instead cosmopolitan. Italy, Slovenia, Romania, Bulgaria and Greece show a mostly localist territorial identity, either individualistic or parochial. Germany appears to be almost completely cosmopolitan except for the surrounding areas of the Berlin region. Belgium and The Netherlands show a predominantly cosmopolitan territorial identity as well. While Czech Republic is completely characterized by individualistic localism, the other Eastern countries (not already mentioned) present a more varied situation with a tendency toward cosmopolitanism. Except for two central regions of Sweden, the Northern countries present a cosmopolitan type of territorial identity.

Overall, a substantial homogeneity within each country's boundaries and a strong differentiation between countries can be found, accompanied by a robust stability over time. The national influence is therefore very powerful.

Even though these maps present interesting highlights and can be largely informative, they mostly capture country effects without detecting the regional peculiarities and distinctiveness.

The following maps (Fig. 4.4) shows the European NUTS2 regions with their corresponding typology of identity assigned according to the national average value (which is the method presented in Fig. 4.2 (b)).

In these maps the regional specificities are much more evident and highlighted. Within the boundaries of each single country, different typologies of territorial identity coexist. In this case, since the typologies are assigned comparing regional average values with the national ones, all the countries with only one NUTS2 region can no longer be included (Malta, Luxembourg, Cyprus, Estonia, Latvia, Lithuania).

A common trait to almost all countries is that the regions hosting capitals or highly influential cities are characterized by a cosmopolitan type of territorial identity (with the notable exception of Budapest and—only in the second period—Sofia). It is interesting to note that fast-growing industrial regions fall into the same class: the regions of Katowice, Krakow and Danzig in Poland; the border areas of Hungary with EU15, south-western France and south-eastern England; Comunidad Valenciana in Spain; Tuscany and most of the Adriatic regions of the "Third Italy" down to Puglia.

An additional aspect worth analyzing is the stability of the typology over time, passing from the first to the second period, from the partial to the full recovery from

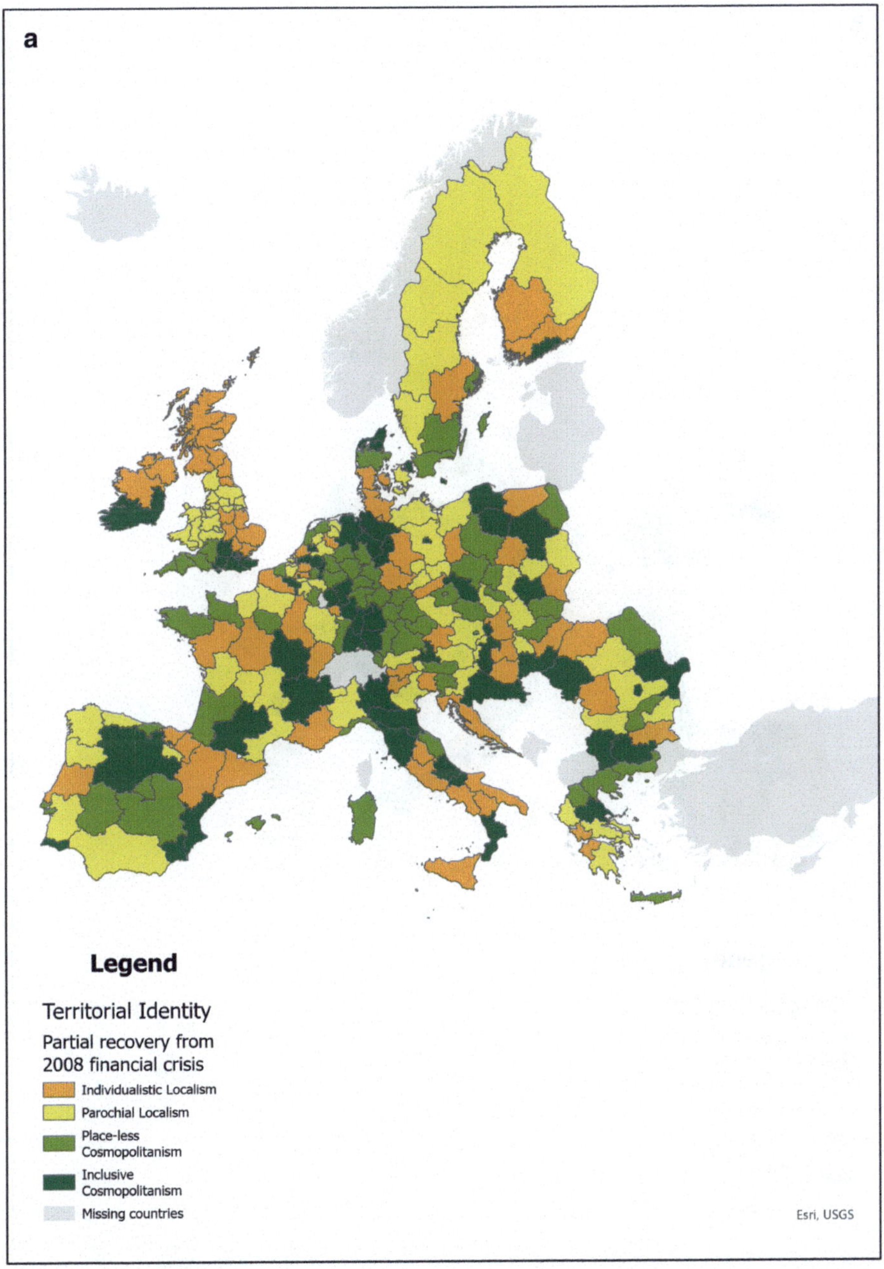

Fig. 4.4 Modes of expression of territorial identity across European regions comparing regional average values with national average values (*Source* Eurobarometer data)

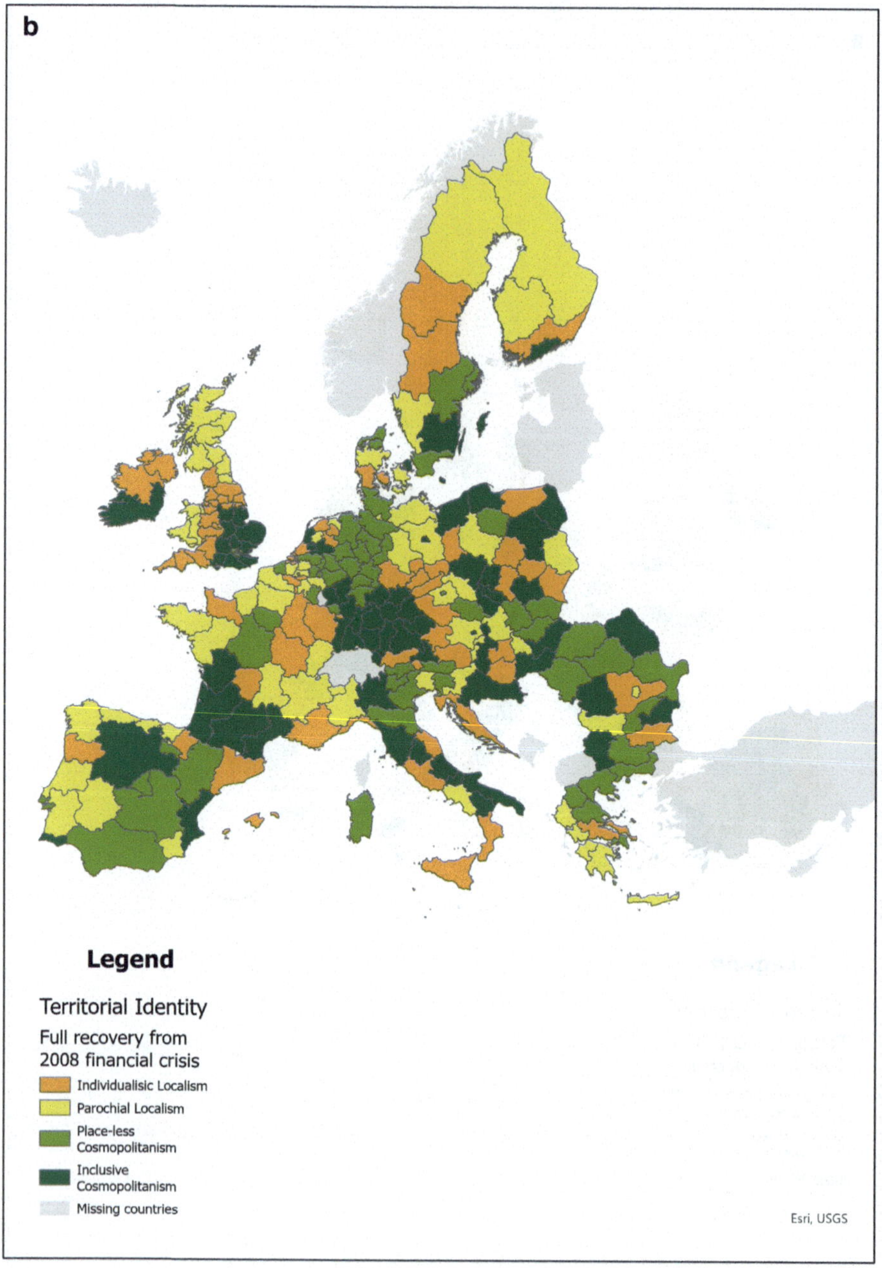

Fig. 4.4 (continued)

Full recovery from financial crisis (II period) / Partial recovery from financial crisis (I period)	**Individualistic Localism**	**Parochial Localism**	**Place-less Cosmopolitanism**	**Inclusive Cosmopolitanism**	Total N. of regions in each typology (I period)
Individualistic Localism	**24**	20	8	11	63
Parochial Localism	29	**30**	6	6	71
Place-less Cosmopolitanism	9	7	**28**	18	62
Inclusive Cosmopolitanism	3	4	20	**33**	60
Total N. of regions in each typology (II period)	66	60	62	68	**256**

Fig. 4.5 Transition Matrix among territorial identity classes—Number of regional changes between assignments in the first period (2012–2016, in rows) and assignments in the second period (2017–2018, in columns). The diagonal presents the number of regions that kept their territorial identity stable over time

the 2008 financial crisis. The following (Fig. 4.5) reports an analysis of the changes that happened over time with a Transition Matrix. The rows show the number of regions falling into the different typologies of territorial identity in the first period ending up in the different typologies in the second period. On the diagonal of the table, we find the number of regions that kept their classification stable over time and in the other cells the number of those which changed psychological condition.

Three main messages can be grasped from this table:

1. The highest values in both rows and columns can be found on the principal diagonal of the matrix, indicating regions that do not change their characterization in our typology. Looking at the total number of regions in each class in the first period (the total at the end of each row), "stable" regions represent between (more than) 1/3 to (more than) 1/2 of the total—this last share being present among initially "inclusive cosmopolitanism" regions, 33 out of a total of 60. On average, "stable" regions represent 45% of total regions analyzed (115/256). Therefore, it can be argued that, overall, there is a relevant stability over time across European regions in terms of their identitarian characterization in our typology.
2. Among the changes, the most frequent ones happen in a horizontal sense inside Fig. 4.1, namely either between individualistic localism and parochial localism or between place-less cosmopolitanism and inclusive cosmopolitanism. Horizontal movements from the first to the second period represent 34% of total regions, while vertical movements represent only 21% of cases. This means that the vertical axis, pointing out the alternative between a local and a local/European sense of belonging, represents a strong discriminatory criterion

among regions, relatively difficult to break, adding a further element of stability to the classification. Horizontal movements (changes) inside the upper or the lower boxes in Fig. 4.1, implying the opening or closure with respect to solidarity, happen more easily and more frequently than vertical ones. In conclusion, a clear identitarian separation exists between localism and cosmopolitanism, and the juxtaposition between the two typologies of territorial identity represents a quasi-structural element in the identitarian realm of European regions. The element regarding solidarity is instead more linked to a political dimension and appears to be more precarious and more easily influenced.

3. Concerning the direction of horizontal changes over time, a prevalence of movements in the direction of selfish and individualistic conditions can be detected with time, both in absolute terms (29 against 20 cases) and in percentage terms. A similar trend can be identified considering the shifts between place-less cosmopolitanism and inclusive cosmopolitanism: while 20 (or 1/3 over a total of 60 regions) change from inclusive to place-less cosmopolitanism, only 18 (or 29% over a total of 62 regions) move in the opposite direction.

To dig deeper into the peculiarities of each of the four identified typologies of territorial identity the following figure (Fig. 4.6) describes their characteristics (only the period related to a full recovery from the financial crisis is taken into account here).[4]

As evident from the graphs presented in Fig. 4.6, areas which present higher population density, greater presence of artificial land and a higher share of population with foreign citizenship perceive a *place-less cosmopolitan* typology of territorial identity. Greater accessibility and innovation are instead the characteristics of areas experiencing *inclusive cosmopolitanism*. The areas characterized by both the cosmopolitan categories are among the richest European regions in terms of GDP per capita. It is interesting to note that the higher tourist presence both in terms of arrivals per capita and overnight stays is to be found in areas characterized by *individualistic localism* possibly suggesting that tourist congestion might be associated with psychological reactions of closure and a shift toward more individualistic behaviors. This assumption will be further explored in the following chapter.

Overall, the maps reported in Fig. 4.4 allow us to identify and detect the regional specificities and, therefore, the categories of territorial identity assigned to each region comparing the regional condition with the national one. These will be taken into account in the rest of the book.

Having identified four different typologies of territorial identity and having proposed a way to measure them, the following section takes cultural heritage and economic development into consideration again and describes the main logic and assumptions that will guide the continuation of the book.

---

[4] Figure 4.6 is the result of an ANOVA analysis conducted on some specific socio-economic characteristics of the four typologies of territorial identity. The following graphs report the mean values of these characteristics in each category of territorial identity only if the considered variables present a statistically significance variance among the four categories. Tourist arrivals and tourist overnight stays do not present statistically significant differences among the mean values but they are reported anyway because of the interesting distribution of their mean values across the categories of territorial identity.

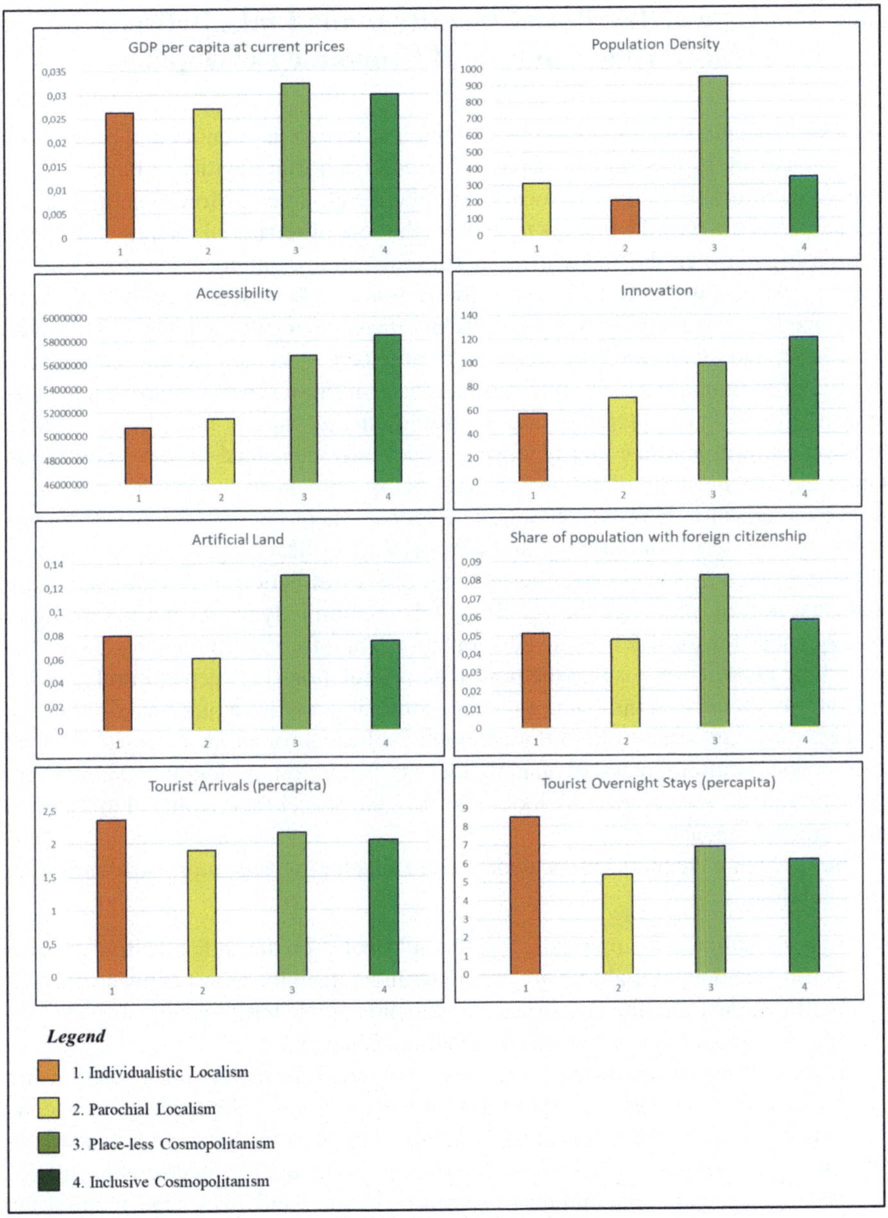

Fig. 4.6 Descriptive characteristics of the four typologies of territorial identity

4.6 The Role of Territorial Identity in the Links Between Cultural Heritage and Local Economic Development

Once we have clarified the meaning attributed to territorial identity and proposed a way to measure it, it is now possible to include territorial identity in the discourse related to cultural heritage and local economic development. More specifically, the main aim of Part B of the book is to explore the role of territorial identity within the relationship between the endowment of cultural heritage and local development.

As explained in Sect. 4.1 several connections, links and synergies have been recognized and identified between cultural heritage and territorial identity. However, these links and synergies have never been precisely systematized and empirically tested. Furthermore, the economic consequences of these synergies have been so far neglected by both the literature and the public institutions. In fact, the association between cultural heritage and identity is commonly presented as socio-cultural in nature expressing its implications on (and being influenced by) society or culture in its broader sense. However, economic implications might result as well from this nexus. In fact, territorial identity and territorial identification give rise to a variety of feelings such as trust or togetherness but also disaffection or resentment. These elements, in turn, influence the way in which economic dynamics work, leading to consequences for local economic development. Therefore, the main innovative idea behind the present work is that the powerful interrelations between cultural heritage and identity do have an influence on local economic growth. In other words, cultural heritage plays an active role in the economic sphere through its synergies with an indirect socio-cultural element, namely identity formation or identity enhancement. Even though the main conjecture looks justified, the proper functioning of this logical mechanism is unclear.

The following chapters will be dedicated to developing and empirically exploring two main issues:

1. to systematize and empirically test the links between the endowment of cultural heritage and territorial identity, trying to understand the nexus between cultural heritage, the founding and structural elements of territorial identity and the four identified typologies of territorial identity (Chapter 5);
2. to understand and empirically test the role of territorial identity in its relationship with cultural heritage as a catalyst for local economic development. More specifically, two alternative logical mechanisms will be explored: a *mediation mechanism* and a *synergy mechanism*. According to a mediation mechanism, cultural heritage generates and influences territorial identity and, in turn this identitarian feeling is supposed to determine some form of economic development. A mediation mechanism will be tested with territorial identity expressed according to the four typologies identified, exploring the potential differences deriving from their specificities. On the other hand, a synergy mechanism implies a simultaneous and interacting effect of different elements which, together with cultural heritage, determine the economic growth of places. The role of territorial identity—in its different typologies—in this case is interpreted as a context element

that, whenever present, is able to foster or strengthen the relationship between cultural heritage and local development. These alternative mechanisms will be tested in Chapter 6. Both can be justified ex-ante in theoretical terms, which one works in reality is a matter of empirical investigation.

References

Bettini, M. (Ed.). (2016). *Radici—Tradizione, identità, memoria.* Il Mulino.

Brewer, M. B. (2001). The many faces of social identity: Implications for political psychology. *Political Psychology, 22*(1), 115–125.

Bruter, M. (2003). Winning hearts and minds for Europe—The impact of news and symbols on civic and cultural European identity. *Comparative Political Studies, 36*(10), 1148–1179.

Camagni, R. (2008). Towards a concept of territorial capital. In R. Capello, R. Camagni, U. Fratesi, & B. Chizzolini (Eds.), *Modelling regional scenarios for an enlarged Europe* (pp. 33–47). Springer Verlag.

Camagni, R. (2020). Space, land rent and income distribution. *Scienze Regionali, Italian Journal of Regional Science, 3,* 343–372.

Camagni, R., Capello, R., Cerisola, S., & Panzera, E. (2020). The cultural heritage—Territorial capital nexus: Theory and empirics, *Il Capital Culturale,* Supplementi (11), Doi: 10.13138/2039-2362/2547.

Capello, R. (2018). Interpreting and understanding territorial identity. *Regional Science Policy and Practice, 11,* 141–158.

Capello, R., & Perucca, G. (2019). From cohesion policy implementation to European identity. *Regional Science Policy & Practice, 11*(4), 631–636.

Caporaso, J. A., & Kim, M. H. (2009). The dual nature of European identity: Subjective awareness and coherence. *Journal of European Public Policy, 16*(1), 19–42.

CHCfE Consortium. (2015). *Cultural heritage counts for Europe.* http://blogs.encatc.org/culturalheritagecountsforeurope//wp-content/uploads/2015/06/CHCfE_FULL-REPORT_v2.pdf, [29/10/2020].

Council of Europe. (2005). *Council of Europe framework convention on the value of cultural heritage for society (Faro Convention).* https://rm.coe.int/CoERMPublicCommonSearchServices/DisplayDCTMContent?documentId=0900001680083746, [26/11/2020].

Dalmas, L., Geromini, V., Noel, J. F., & Tsang, K. S. J. (2015). Economic evaluation of urban heritage: An inclusive approach under a sustainability perspective. *Journal of Cultural Heritage, 16*(5), 681–687.

Díez Medrano, J., & Gutiérrez, P. (2001). Nested identities: National and European identity in Spain. *Ethnic and Racial Studies, 24,* 753–778.

Dijkstra, L., Poelman, H., & Rodríguez-Pose, A. (2018). *The geography of EU discontent* (Working Paper 12/2018). Publications Office of the European Union, Luxembourg.

eTwinning. (2018). *Learning from the past, designing our future: Europe's cultural heritage through eTwinning.* Co-funded by the Erasmus + Programme of the European Union. https://www.etwinning.net/eun-files/Online%20%E2%80%93%20eTwinning%20publication%2024.09.2018.pdf, [26/11/2020].

European Commission. (1999). *ESPD—European Spatial Development Perspective: Towards balanced and sustainable development of the territory of the European Union.* Office for Official Publications of the European Communities.

European Commission. (2015). *Getting cultural heritage to work for Europe.* https://op.europa.eu/en/publication-detail/-/publication/b01a0d0a-2a4f-4de0-88f7-85bf2dc6e004, [29/10/2020].

European Commission. (2018). *A new European agenda for culture*. https://eur-lex.europa.eu/legal-content/EN/TXT/PDF/?uri=CELEX:52018DC0267&from=EN, [22/10/2021].

European Commission. (2019). *European framework for action on cultural heritage*. https://op.europa.eu/en/publication-detail/-/publication/5a9c3144-80f1-11e9-9f05-01aa75ed71a1, [29/10/2020].

Fearon, J. D. (1999). *What is identity (As we now use the word)?*. Stanford University, Department of Political Science.

Fligstein, N., Polyakova, A., & Sandholtz, W. (2012). European integration, nationalism and European identity. *Journal of Common Market Studies, 50*(S1), 106–122.

Fukuyama, F. (Ed.). (2018). *Identity: The demand for dignity and the politics of resentment*. Farrar, Straus and Giroux.

Iammarino, S., Rodríguez-Pose, A., & Storper, M. (2017). *Why regional develoment matters for Europe's economic future*. Publications Office of the European Union.

Lawler, S. (Ed.). (2008). *Identity—Sociological perspectives*. Polity Press.

Li, Q., & Brewer, M. B. (2004). What does it mean to be an American? Patriotism, nationalism, and American identity after 9/11. *Political Psychology, 25*(5), 727–739.

Marks, G. (1999). *Territorial identities in the European Union*. In J. J. Anderson (Ed.), *Regional integration and democracy: Expanding on the European experience* (pp. 69–91). Rowman and Littlefield.

McCann, P. (2020). Perceptions of regional inequality and the geography of discontent: Insights from the UK. *Regional Studies, 54*(2), 256–267.

Nooteboom, B. (2019, December 4). *Identity in the EU*. Presented at the Forum A new European industrial strategy oriented to the citizens and the territory for a reform towards post-neoliberal economic policies. Forum in partnership with European Economic and Social Committee, Brussels.

OECD. (2001). *OECD territorial outlook*.

Paasi, A. (1986). The institutionalization of regions: A theoretical framework for understanding the emergence of regions and the constitution of regional identity. *Fennia International Journal of Geography,* 105–146.

Paasi, A. (2002). Bounded spaces in the mobile world: Deconstructing "regional identity." *Tijdschrift Voor Economische En Sociale Geografie, 93*(2), 137–148.

Parekh, B. (2009). Logic of identity. *Politics, Philosophy & Economics, 8*(3), 267–284.

Prutsch. (2017). *Research for CULT committee—European identity, European parliament, policy department for structural and cohesion policies*. Brussels. https://www.europarl.europa.eu/RegData/etudes/STUD/2017/585921/IPOL_STU(2017)585921_EN.pdf, [26/11/2020].

Raagma, G. (2002). Regional identity in regional development and planning. *European Planning Studies, 1,* 55–76.

Revilla, J. C., Jeffreys, S., & Martínez, F. J. T. (2013). Collective identities in the age of restructuring: Old and new class, space and community-based identities in six European regions. *International Sociology, 28*(4), 391–408.

Risse, T. (2002, December 6–8). *The Euro and identity politics in Europe, paper presented at the conference "The Year of Euro"*. Nanovic Institute for European Studies, University of Notre Dame.

Rodríguez-Pose, A. (2017). The revenge of the places that don't matter (and what to do about it). *Cambridge Journal of Regions, Economy and Society," 11*(1), 189–209.

Saraceno, F., & Fitoussi, J. P. (2019). Inequality, growth and regional disparities. Rethinking European priorities. In C. Altomonte, & A. Villafranca (Eds.), *Europe in identity crisis—The future of the EU in the age of nationalism* (pp. 70–93). ISPI—Ledizioni LediPublishing.

Schilde, K. E. (2014). Who are the Europeans? European identity outside of European integration. *Journal of Common Market Studies, 52*(3), 650–667.

Sciacchitano, E. (2019). European year of cultural-heritage. A laboratory for heritage-based innovation. *SCIentific RESearch and Information Technology, 9*(1), 1–14.

Tajfel, H., & Turner, J. C. (1979). An integrative theory of intergroup conflict. In W. Austin & S. Worchel (Eds.), *The social psychology of intergroup relations* (pp. 33–47). Brooks/Cole.

Tosco, C. (Ed.). (2014). *I beni culturali. Storia, tutela e valorizzazione*. Il Mulino.

Vecco M. (2010). A definition of cultural heritage: From the tangible to the intangible. *Journal of Cultural Heritage, 11*, 321–324.

Chapter 5
The Role of Cultural Heritage in Shaping Territorial Identities

5.1 The Cultural Heritage-Territorial Identity Nexus: Introductory Notes

Cultural heritage and territorial identity can be easily associated, their connections and synergies being tight, strong and solid. Thanks to its symbolic power cultural heritage is a herald and a source of values that shapes and influences specific typologies of territorial identities. With its historic nature, cultural heritage represents and embodies a common past of a community and with its authenticity and social values it witnesses and transfers common interpretations of reality, shared wisdom, experiences and meanings. In other words, cultural heritage with its multiple and multifaceted values and peculiarities can inspire a sense of belonging, attachment, affection and connection to a territory.

As highlighted in Paasi (1986), territories and territorial consciousness do not emerge from nothingness, meaning that they are products of history and social action rather than the outcomes of autonomous forces. Following his perspective, a territory is "*comprehended as one expression of time–space specific relations and structures of society, being formed through the development of society, the latter with its structures also being a part of the global organization of socio-spatial reality*" (Paasi, 1986, p. 120). One out of the many elements that constitute this socio-spatial reality is cultural heritage with its primary constitutive value in identity formation. As proposed by Carta (2007), culture and cultural heritage embody the human being tending toward knowledge as the cognitive reason rooting behaviors of societies and representing historical identities. Citing from the report Cultural Heritage Counts for Europe "*culture has the power to connect people and become a strategic tool for the safeguarding of the identity and the authenticity of places and local community*" (CHCfE Consortium, 2015, p. 47).

The relationship between cultural heritage and territorial identity has been widely mentioned and recognized, but how exactly does this relationship function? And, more specifically, in what ways can cultural heritage influence the previously identified dimensions that, according to the present perspective, define territorial identity

E. Panzera, *Cultural Heritage and Territorial Identity*, Advances in Spatial Science,
https://doi.org/10.1007/978-3-030-94468-1_5

(i.e., the ones reported in Sect. 4.4: founding elements of territorial identity and spatial reach of founding networks)?

The aim of this chapter is to answer these questions and explore the role that cultural heritage has in shaping and influencing territorial identity and the four corresponding typologies identified in Sect. 4.4.

More in detail, Sect. 5.2 will be dedicated to conceptually develop the mechanisms through which cultural heritage might affect territorial identity with the aid of the literature that has already discussed these relationships; Sect. 5.3 specifically focuses on the role that cultural heritage plays in the fundamental dimensions of territorial identities as classified in Sect. 4.4 (i.e., *founding elements of territorial identity* and *spatial reach of founding networks*); Sect. 5.4 empirically tests the hypothesized relationship between cultural heritage and territorial identity by quantitatively analyzing the role that cultural heritage plays in the four modes of expression of territorial identity (*individualistic localism, parochial localism, place-less cosmopolitanism* and *inclusive cosmopolitanism*) resulting in confirming the assumption that heritage does have a role in this relationship even though differentiated according to the typology of territorial identity considered; Sect. 5.5 concludes.

5.2 The Cultural Heritage-Territorial Identity Nexus in the Existing Literature

Given the multiplicity of values recognized as founding elements of cultural heritage, territorial identity might be influenced by it in several manners and diverse aspects of territorial identities can be activated under different circumstances through the presence of cultural heritage. By considering the same perspective adopted in Sect. 4.1, identity can cover three diverse interdependent layers: individual, social and political. Accordingly, the role of cultural heritage in its connections with territorial identity can be also discussed following these three layers.

Firstly, cultural heritage has the power to influence the *individual* layer of territorial identity. It can be argued that cultural heritage in its creation, fruition and enjoyment leads to the satisfaction of human needs (Tweed & Sutherland, 2007). In fact, culture and cultural heritage are fundamental determinants of what makes life full and meaningful (https://www.iccrom.org/projects/heritage-and-wellbeing-what-constitutes-good-life). Cultural heritage enters the individual identity sphere representing and evoking personal memories or genealogical links that tie the person to the place in which he or she lives (Janssen et al., 2017). Place connection and place attachment are subjective feelings influenced by experiences, memories, emotions and engagement. In this sense, cultural heritage with its idiosyncratic nature is a powerful symbol eliciting these types of feelings. As highlighted in Huovinen et al. (2017), place awareness closely relates to experiences of participation and belonging to a place's-built-environment, strengthened by repeated activities such as walking familiar streets or crossing familiar squares. In this way, cultural heritage enters the intimate field of habits, emotional, often unconscious, ties and innate loyalty to a place. Besides, as highlighted by many scholars (see for instance Blake, 2000; Ferilli et al., 2016; Matarasso, 1997) cultural heritage positively contributes to improving individual well-being. In fact, cultural heritage contributes to creating a pleasant environment, giving an emotional touch to a place, establishing sustainable lifestyles and forming cosmopolitan attitudes (Adam, 2003).

The influence exerted by cultural heritage on territorial identities is not limited to the individual layer: the *social* layer of territorial identity is in fact very much related with the presence of heritage sites. In this sense, two main typologies of associations can be mentioned: one related to the sheer presence of cultural heritage representing a common and shared resource and the other one related to its fruition. The same emotional links mentioned before are fundamental as well when the discourse is shifted toward the social layer of territorial identity. As argued by Liu and Hilton (2005), the collective experience of a group is exhibited through cultural heritage which also represents the wisdom of the group and carries emotional implications. The territorial endowment of cultural heritage becomes a symbol of community values, shared meanings and joint interpretations of reality (Sable & Kling, 2001). Cultural heritage can be interpreted as a shared focal point creating ties, supporting networking and expressing and influencing a group's perspective (Bellandi & Santini, 2017). Furthermore, as highlighted in Ferilli et al. (2016), a special capability of bonding communities can be attributed to cultural heritage which is able to foster shared pride and sense of belonging to a specific type of local cultural identity. In fact, cultural heritage can bring unknown people together through the powerful role of common images and symbols. In turn, these feelings of pride and belonging empower the cohesive nature of the local community, instilling a sentiment of self-consciousness. On the other hand, following the reasoning of Ferilli et al. (2016), cultural heritage might also play a role in community bridging meaning that, through the knowledge of different typologies of heritage (i.e., different expressions of different cultures of different groups) made possible by the presence of heritage sites, a sort of tacit intercultural dialog is put in place through which mutual awareness and reciprocal understanding result in bringing different groups together. The same results of bonding and bridging communities and groups are obtained through participation in cultural events and fruition of cultural heritage. As mentioned in Macdonald (2013), specific kinds of experiences are offered through the fruition of cultural heritage that allows individuals to engage with the past and share their experience with other unknown people. In this sense, cultural heritage allows people to visit a site individually but, rather than feeling lonely, feeling part of a community. Furthermore, cultural heritage sites frequently become the venues of events organized for the community usually aiming at involvement, inclusion and sharing. As Furia et al. (2018) explain, these forms of noninstrumental social interactions lead to genuine forms of interpersonal relations allowing people to shape or reshape their social identities. Oftentimes cultural-heritage-related activities involve voluntary work which originates from intrinsic motivations to participate, to feel part of a community.

Cultural heritage can possibly also be associated with the *political* layer of territorial identity. Since heritage is characterized by an essential narrative dimension and by the possibility to associate stories and meanings to sites, districts or buildings (see Janssen et al., 2017), heritage and collective memory have always been mobilized by politics with the aim of establishing territorial authority and territorial identity (Borges, 2017). In fact, history embedded in cultural heritage provides both concreteness and temporality and represents an essential element in creating and cultivating the imagined community of, for instance, a nationhood (Liu & Hilton, 2005). As argued by Harvey (2001), government or ruling elites might decide to mobilize certain selected lessons from the past which in turn are able to influence people's attachment and loyalty to their place and community as well as condition the community's response to future challenges. Through associations with images, stories, meanings and narratives, cultural heritage might be used as an instrument for inventing or discovering a common past able to foster a strong collective territorial identity (Borges, 2017). For a region to be stable and growing, a cohesive identity is necessary, and its promotion can be influenced by the presence of emblematic heritage sites. As Adam (2003) pointed out, territorial symbols and special features such as heritage sites create images of differentiation from others. Besides, cultural heritage can be described as a set of signs that guide behaviors, elicit feelings and influence thoughts (Ünlü, 2019). As highlighted in Blake (2000), material forms of culture are considered as synonyms and symbols of cultural identity at a profound level. During armed conflicts or wars, the intentional destruction of heritage sites, especially when ethnic conflicts are involved, demonstrates the tight and permanent relationship between cultural heritage and identity perceived in political terms. Citing from Blake (2000, p. 84) "*The role of cultural heritage as a vehicle for the expression and even construction of a nation or group's cultural identity is a double-edged sword which can act both for the good and for the bad. It can lead to an aggressive assertion of identity, whether national or ethnic, which may cause and certainly foster armed conflict in which the destruction of cultural monuments – the symbols of the cultural identity of one of the parties to the conflict – often becomes a weapon of war. It also has great potential for creating cohesion within a group, be it a self-identified ethnic minority within a State, a nation State or even a supranational body*". The political dimension of the link between cultural heritage and territorial identity is particularly relevant for the European Union that tries to propose cultural heritage as a shared and common resource. However, at the same time, the EU recognizes the specificities and uniqueness of local heritage. Some controversy may arise from the political narratives associated with heritage: its characterization as part of a common, shared, universal heritage might be in contrast with the fact that a specific community produced that heritage and recognizes its identity in it. In a sense, it can be argued that much is asked of heritage which at the same time owns national, regional and global legacies and sometimes these aims are incompatible (Lowenthal, 1997). On the other hand, as pointed out in Gillman (2006), according to another point of view, it is incorrect that national or local cultures are valued over and above a universal community of citizens and to the whole of humankind.

More links can be identified between the endowment of heritage and territorial identities that impact on individual, social and political layers at the same time. Heritage sites are a fundamental tool for education and a living symbol of the past. Being aware of what happened in the past and acquiring knowledge about a place's history can guide and inspire territorial consciousness and can influence future development (Janssen et al., 2017). As Liu and Hilton (2005) affirm, knowledge of history and heritage offers us narratives about our origins, our nature and our destinations, it defines paths that support establishing the essence of a group's identity. The endowment of heritage contributes to our education and to evaluating authenticity, cultural experiences and historical anchoring (Bellandi & Santini, 2017). Furthermore, as argued and demonstrated by Cerisola (2019a, 2019b), cultural heritage functions as an inspirational element for creativity, providing territories with creative vocations and characterizations. Another potential link between heritage and territorial identity stems from the role that historical built environment sites have in combining the past with contemporary uses. As Janssen et al. (2017) argue, space, heritage sites and landscapes are a living ecosystem. Culture-led regeneration of territories grants cultural continuity, new dynamics of interpreting and experiencing heritage sites and intergenerational linkages (Gunay, 2010; Sable & Kling, 2001; Tweed & Sutherland, 2007). Regeneration activities related to heritage sites provide local communities with the possibility to rediscover their past with a contemporary interpretation of it that allows more people to be involved, more meanings to be put in place and more territorial self-awareness and attachment to be generated. Lastly, territorial identity can be influenced by the presence of heritage through the competitive advantage in the global arena that might be gained with heritage endowment (Gunay, 2010; Hribar et al., 2015). Cultural heritage being a location-specific element, it helps create place distinctiveness and territorial uniqueness, becoming a fundamental competitive resource. In fact, projects of culture-led regeneration or place identification function as attractors of people, businesses, institutions and resources fostering innovation and competitiveness. Cultural heritage sites are oftentimes included in place-marketing policies with the aim of renovating the image of the place increasing tourism and investments attractiveness and, therefore, fostering a sense of belonging and pride. (Adam, 2003; Ferilli et al., 2016).

Table 5.1 shows a summary of the typology of influences that the endowment of cultural heritage might exert on territorial identity.

Some limitations and negative consequences can also result from the presence of cultural heritage and from its relationship with territorial identity. The main ones are related to the validation of certain groups at the expense of some others that might feel excluded. In fact, a rhetoric of inclusion and exclusion emphasizing the distinctiveness of specific cultural identities and groups might result in closures and exclusion. Citing from Waterton and Smith (2010, p. 9) "*As it stands, the heritage sector is dominated by a particular notion of community, one that overlooks the fact that representations of reality can have powerful effects on any group under construction. It can lead to misrecognition, discrimination, lowered self-esteem and lack of parity in any engagement with heritage*".

Table 5.1 Influences of heritage on territorial identities

Individual layer
Heritage as a source of individual memories, emotions and well-being
Social layer
Heritage as a source of community cohesiveness and bonding
Heritage as a source of inclusiveness, bridging and openness
Heritage as a source of social interactions and participatory behaviors
Political layer
Heritage as a source of political communities, common narratives and shared roots
Individual, social and political layers
Heritage as a source of knowledge and education
Heritage as a source of creativity
Heritage as a source of culture-led regeneration activities that favor social capital
Heritage as a source of distinctiveness, uniqueness and competitiveness fostering pride and a sense of belonging

The following section focuses on the links and synergies between cultural heritage and territorial identity as defined and classified within the context of this book.

5.3 Founding Elements of Territorial Identity and Spatial Reach of Founding Networks: The Role of Cultural Heritage

Having discussed the main mechanisms through which the presence of cultural heritage influences territorial identities, an examination of the role that cultural heritage has on the dimensions used to define and categorize territorial identity will be carried out in this section. More specifically, the interest lies in discussing in greater detail the ways in which heritage interacts with the two identified dimensions that classify territorial identities according to the proposed taxonomy: *founding elements of territorial identity* and *spatial reach of founding networks*. The same matrix proposed in Sect. 4.4 to classify different typologies of territorial identity is proposed here again in Fig. 5.1.

The hypotheses proposed here and to be empirically tested relates to the positive role that the endowment of heritage can play in fostering solidarity and acceptance of nested territorial identities (namely both local and European).

Starting from solidarity, as previously discussed, heritage stimulates a sense of common interests and aspirations also with unknown people. As argued in Article 167

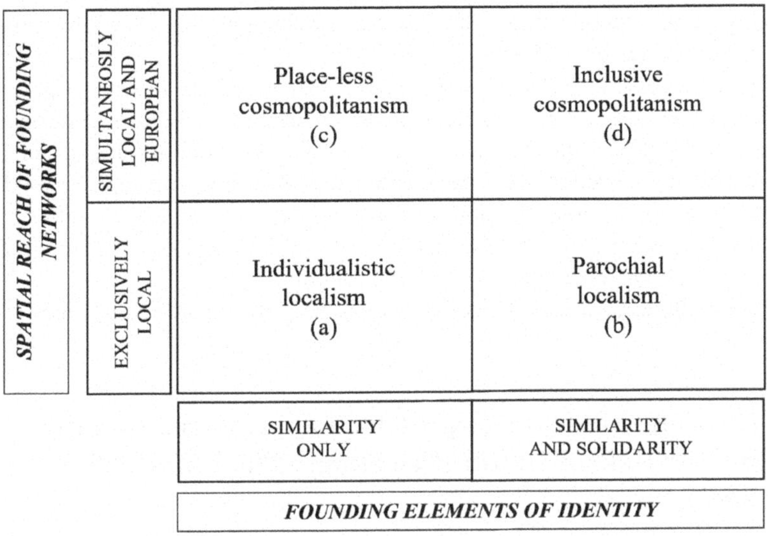

Fig. 5.1 Modes of expression of territorial identity(ies): an original taxonomy

of the EU Treaty, by adding to a territory a peculiar physiognomy and consequently promoting territorial development as a creative community, a touristic place or an entrepreneurial center, heritage generates social solidarity and civic pride among individuals. An enjoyable atmosphere and pleasant territorial images supported by the presence of heritage foster a sense of belonging, common territorial interests and ambitions. Because of its relationship with the territory in which it is located, heritage creates a strong sense of place generating or enhancing territorial awareness and a sort of spatial membership (European Commission, 1999; Gospodini, 2007). As proposed by the Faro Convention (2005), cultural heritage represents a driver for social cohesion and inclusion and serves as a framework for participation and engagement (Council of Europe, 2005). Turning the past into something visible, cultural heritage is able to materialize collective, social and popular memory and represents a physical support for local collective memory (Cerisola, 2019a, 2019b; Vecco, 2010).

As far as a multilevel local and European identity is concerned, as built heritage can be considered a product of manipulations representing a deliberate encoding of symbolic meanings, European institutions tend to consider heritage as a powerful tool for building a European community. Seeking to imprint identities on conserved forms of built heritage represents a quest for political legitimation. On the other hand, cultural heritage is a core element of the European way of life being embedded in our territories and being a determinant of who Europeans are and therefore representing a force able to strengthen a sense of attachment to a European family (eTwinning, 2018). The possibility to move more freely within Europe allows people to gain greater awareness and appreciation of diverse typologies of cultural heritage. Through the educational value of heritage and exploiting the chance to get new knowledge from it, people might feel a sense of belonging to a wider community or to more than one territorial level.

Refining the discourse by considering the four identified modes of expression of territorial identity, it can be noted that the presence of solidarity and the simultaneous sentiment of sameness felt toward both the local and the European spatial levels are the elements that distinguish and differentiate the four typologies. Therefore, by exploring the role that heritage has in enhancing solidarity and/or a more comprehensive feeling of territorial identity, it will be possible to grasp which are the most influenced typologies of territorial identity.

The following section is dedicated to empirically investigating these relationships.

5.4 The Four Modes of Expression of Territorial Identity and the Role of Cultural Heritage: The Empirical Analysis

5.4.1 The Role of Cultural Heritage in Shaping Territorial Identity: The Empirical Strategy

The present section presents the empirical strategy used in order to test the effectiveness of cultural heritage endowment as a source of territorial identity. More specifically, the aim is to empirically understand:

1. whether tangible forms of cultural heritage have a statistically significant effect in shaping territorial identities and
2. whether the four identified typologies of territorial identities (*individualistic localism, parochial localism, place-less cosmopolitanism and inclusive cosmopolitanism*) are equally or differently influenced by the endowment of cultural heritage.

As previously discussed (see Sect. 4.5), the data used to measure and classify different typologies of territorial identity are gathered from several rounds of Eurobarometer surveys. Two main questions have been considered in measuring the *founding elements of identity* and the *spatial reach of founding networks.* Respectively, the following questions have been used:

- *In the following list, which are the three most important values for you personally?*

Among the possible answers "*Solidarity, support for others*" has been selected.

- *For each of the following statement, please tell me to what extent it corresponds or not to your opinion: You feel you are a citizen of the EU.*

  1—No, definitely not
  2—No, not really
  3—Yes, to some extent

4—Yes, definitely

Eurobarometer surveys provide individual data related to these questions of interest together with information related to the spatial collocation of individuals. In other words, it is possible to associate each individual with the NUTS2 region in which they live. Using these two questions, a category of territorial identity (classified as in Fig. 4.1) has been assigned to each individual according to the following criteria:

- *Individualistic localism* has been assigned to individuals who did not mention solidarity as one of the three most important values for them personally and answered *No, not really* or *No, definitely not* when asked whether they feel they are citizens of the EU;
- *Parochial localism* has been assigned to individuals who mentioned solidarity as one of the three most important values for them personally and answered *No, not really* or *No, definitely not* when asked whether they feel they are citizens of the EU;
- *Place-less cosmopolitanism* has been assigned to individuals who did not mention solidarity as one of the three most important values for them personally and answered *Yes, to some extent* or *Yes, definitely* when asked whether they feel they are citizens of the EU;
- *Inclusive cosmopolitanism* has been assigned to individuals who mentioned solidarity as one of the three most important values for them personally and answered *Yes, to some extent* or *Yes, definitely* when asked whether they feel they are citizens of the EU.

Therefore, the empirical analysis aims at investigating whether the presence of cultural heritage in the region where individuals live influences the probability that the individuals will be allocated to a specific category of territorial identity. From an empirical perspective, the aim is to investigate the role played by cultural heritage in influencing the probability that individuals will choose one out of the four modes of expression of territorial identity.

The formal model underlying the present analysis can be written as follows:

$$\text{Modes of expression of territorial identity}_i = f(\text{cultural heritage}_r, \text{individual characteristics}_i, \text{regional characteristics}_r) \quad (5.1)$$

where the modes of expression of territorial identity (the dependent variable) can take four values (*individualistic localism, parochial localism, place-less cosmopolitanism* or *inclusive cosmopolitanism*). These alternative perceptions and modes of expression of territorial identity depend on a set of individual characteristics and on a set of regional characteristics which include territorial attributes such as the endowment of cultural heritage.

Focusing on the methodological technique used to estimate Eq. (5.1), a multinomial logit model is chosen as the empirical strategy to answer the two previously mentioned research questions. Multinomial logit models are in fact used when the dependent variable is discrete, as in this case. Each observation is the outcome of individual choices; there are more than two outcomes and there is no order of strength, meaning that the outcomes are unordered. Furthermore, three main characteristics define the dependent variable: (1) it can take only four specific, distinct and separable choice alternatives (*individualistic localism, parochial localism, place-less cosmopolitanism, inclusive cosmopolitanism*), (2) these alternatives are not nested and do not overlap, (3) there are no alternative-specific independent variables (see Thrane, 2015).

As explained in Greene (2002), unordered choice models can be motivated by a random utility model as follows:

$$U_{ij} = z_{ij}^{'}\theta + \varepsilon_{ij}$$

where i is the individual and j the choices. If the individual makes choice j, then U_{ij} is the maximum among the J utilities. Therefore, the statistical model is directed by the probability that the choice j is chosen, which is:

$$\text{Prob}\left(U_{ij} > U_{ik}\right) \quad \text{for all other } k \neq j$$

Citing from Greene (2002, p. 801), "*the model is made operational by a particular choice of distribution for the disturbances. As in the binary choice case, two models are usually considered, logit and probit. Because of the need to evaluate multiple integrals of the normal distribution, the probit model has found rather limited use in this setting. The logit model, in contrast, has been widely used in many fields, including economics, market research, politics, finance and transportation engineering*".

If Y_i is the random variable that indicates the choice made, the multinomial logit regression model is given by:

$$\text{Prob}(Y_i = j|x_{ir}) = \frac{e^{x_i\beta_j + z_r\alpha_j}}{\sum_{j=0}^{3} e^{x_i\beta_j + z_r\alpha_j}}, j = 0,1,2,3$$

where $\text{Prob}(Y_i = j|x_{ir})$ equals the probability that the individuals with characteristics x_i, living in regions with characteristics z_r choose the jth category of the dependent mode choice variable. x_i is a set of independent variables or regressors referring to individual characteristics; z_r is a set of explanatory variables referring to regional characteristics and β_j and α_j vectors of parameters to be estimated through a maximum likelihood technique.

The *individualistic localism* category is taken as a reference and since individuals in the sample are nested within regions, this hierarchical structure has been taken into account by clustering the error terms of the model for the individuals' region of residence. This procedure has been already undertaken by other studies that used similar datasets (see for instance Capello & Perucca, 2019; Lenzi & Perucca, 2016).

The following section describes the data used for the empirical analysis.

5.4.2 Data Description

The data included in the empirical model can be divided into two main categories: variables referred to individual characteristics and variables referred to regional characteristics. The list of all the variables included in the analysis together with a short description and the sources is reported in Table 5.2. The dependent variable is measured in 2012, 2014, 2015, 2016, 2017 and 2018 in line with the available Eurobarometer rounds (respectively 77.3, 82.3, 84.4, 86.2, 88.3, 90.3). The individual explanatory variables correspond to the same Eurobarometer years. The regional variables have instead been 1 year lagged (when not time invariant) with respect to the dependent variable to support a causality reasoning.

The explanatory variable of interest is represented by cultural heritage. More specifically, tangible forms of cultural heritage are considered for the empirical analysis. The data used are gathered from an ESPON project named "*The Role and Spatial Effects of Cultural Heritage and Identity*" in which data related to the number of monuments are available at the regional level. Within the context of the project, monuments include historic buildings (churches, palaces and castles, old mansions, bridges, fountains, etc.) and sites (caves, archeological remains, battlefields, etc.) (see ESPON project 1.3.3, 2004–2006). The year in which the number of monuments is registered is 2003, however, because of the essentially time-invariant nature of this type of tangible cultural heritage, it can be reasonably assumed that the number does not change over time. Since these data are collected from national and regional listing systems, the main issue regards an intrinsic inconsistency of the measure due to differences in national or regional definitions of monuments and data availability. In order to get a more coherent and comparable proxy for regional endowment of tangible forms of cultural heritage, a country-standardized regional measure has been computed according to the following formula:

$$\text{Tangible Cultural Heritage}_{r,c} = \frac{\frac{\text{Number of monuments}_r}{\text{Land Area}_r}}{\frac{\text{Number of monuments}_c}{\text{Land Area}_c}}$$

where r is the European NUTS2 region and c is the country to which the region belongs (the same measure has been used in the empirical analysis performed in Chapter 3. To have a more precise understanding of the issue related to the non-standardized data see Sect. 3.2.2).[1]

The choice of the other individual and regional variables to be included in the model has been undertaken by reading and analyzing the literature quantitatively

[1] UNESCO World Heritage Sites are not expressly considered in this part of the book because they are assumed to be much more correlated with tourism than with territorial identity. In fact, stemming from the results obtained in Part A, the hypothesis in Part B is that "common" heritage sites are the ones related to territorial identity. Nevertheless, all the empirical analyses have been performed also including a UNESCO WHS variable that always emerges as non-statistically significant and has not been reported in the results tables.

dealing with this topic. However, it has to be noted that the empirical literature is, so far, more devoted to the European identity discourse with the aim of understanding which are the determinants of positive attitudes toward integration rather than focusing on territorial identity in its broader sense. Besides, when solidarity is empirically discussed, the literature focuses on the determinants of support for redistributive policies or cohesion policies which are both diverse perspectives with respect to the meaning of solidarity that is considered in the present work. Stemming from this literature, the variables more coherent with the aim of this chapter have been considered.

Hooghe and Marks (2005) argue that three main families of explanations lie behind support to European integration. The first family of explanation concerns economic arguments and builds on citizens' evaluation of economic consequences in terms of costs and benefits of European integration. The second family is instead related to the social dimension and to the psychology behind membership of a group. Finally, a third family of explanation can be identified as political in nature and deals with understanding the role of political cues in mediating the effect of economic considerations and community sense of belonging. Furthermore, individuals can be influenced by collective economic, social or political circumstances, as well as by the same factors at the individual level and as argued by many scholars (e.g., Anderson, 1998; Christin, 2005; Eichenberg & Dalton, 1993; Hooghe & Marks, 2005; Rohrschneider, 2002), public opinion can be influenced by subjective evaluations as well as objective elements.

Expanding the same considerations and the same classification of explanations to analyze the determinants of the four modes of expression of territorial identity, the following list introduces the typologies of explanatory variables included in the model and the underlying reasoning.

- *Economic explanations*: economic circumstances play a role in determining each individual's feeling of territorial identity. In fact, both the founding elements of territorial identity (namely similarity and solidarity) and the openness to multilevel territorial identities are influenced by economic circumstances, expectations and statuses. As reported by Nelsen and Guth (2020), Jones et al. (2012), Lindberg and Scheingold (1970), economic interests together with strategic reasons and institutional factors contribute to the formation of permissive consensus toward European integration. Generally speaking, citing from Bremer et al., (2020, pp. 58–59) "*people may resist integration because they believe it implies more costs than benefits to their own state (and hence presumably to them individually)*". Objective and perceived material benefits, both at the individual and regional levels, contribute as well as strengthening or lowering solidarity-related attitudes. For instance, as Braun (2020) puts it, since small states or, more generally, small communities, rely on fewer votes, fewer financial means and fewer economic resources, they might feel stronger incentives for coalition-building and solidarity toward each other since they recognize a certain convergence between individualistic and common interests. Furthermore, as Nicoli et al. (2020) point out, support for specific forms of solidarity such as unemployment benefit schemes, may be driven by economic reasons in terms of the personal or common benefits that might be derived from the same policies. In other words, willingness to support redistributive policies across the European Union based on solidarity among countries and regions is influenced by the related individual advantages expected (Kuhn et al., 2018).

- *Social explanations*: as Karl Deutsch said in 1957, reaching successful integration implies a strong sense of community able to overcome borders and traditional divisions and animosities (see also Nelsen & Guth, 2020). A "*we-feeling*" is required to feel a sense of European citizenship fostered by social circumstances. As Smith (2009) argued, cultural raw materials such as ideas, traditions and symbols are needed to build new identities and to shape group consciousness. On the other hand, as Bremer et al. (2020) pointed out, processes of integration or recognition of multilevel territorial identities may be opposed when perceived as threats to national or local identities. By the same token, solidarity can also be influenced by social determinants depending on the meanings attributed to cooperation and solidarity (see for instance in Braun, 2020 the concept of *flexible solidarity*), the level of attachment to one's own local territory and the local capabilities and experiences of inclusion and exclusion.
- *Political explanations*: political determinants are also to be included in the analysis aimed at explaining the four identified modes of expression of territorial identity. Political factors such as trust in government and political parties and support for left, centrist or right-oriented parties, might influence both the feeling of EU citizenship and the inclination to express solidarity. As also mentioned in the previous sections, collective identities may be mobilized for political purposes (see for instance Börzel & Risse, 2020) and they can be shaped by practices of democratic participation (McNamara & Musgrave, 2020). As explained in Hooghe and Marks (2005), citizens' attitudes toward integration and solidarity are associated with their ideological placement and they are affected by the influence of elites and political parties.

Table 5.2 summarizes the explanatory variables included in the empirical analysis. More specifically, they have been divided according to the three families of explanations previously identified (economic, social and political) and for each family they have been further classified according to their regional or individual nature. The table reports the name, the description and the source of the variables together with the level (individual or regional).

The following section reports the results of the empirical analysis.

Table 5.2 Multinomial logit: list of explanatory variables for the empirical analysis

Name	Description	Source	Family	Level
Economic explanations				
GDP per capita	Measure of regional wealth: GDP per capita at constant 2005 prices	Eurostat	Economic	Regional
Human capital	Share of population with tertiary education per active population	Eurostat	Economic	Regional
Population density	Number of metropolitan areas	Eurostat	Economic	Regional
Tourist attraction	Measure of regional tourism demand: number of arrivals per inhabitant	Eurostat	Economic	Regional
Economic expectations at the country level	A scale from 1 to 3 has been created corresponding to the following Eurobarometer question: "*What are your expectations for the next twelve months: will the next twelve months be better, worse or the same, when it comes to the economic situation of your country?*" 1 corresponds to *worse* 2 corresponds to *same* 3 corresponds to *better*	Eurobarometer	Economic	Individual
Occupation	Dummy = 1 if the respondent is self-employed Dummy = 1 if the respondent is a manager/professional Dummy = 1 if the respondent is white collar Dummy = 1 if the respondent is a manual worker Dummy = 1 if the respondent is a house person Dummy = 1 if the respondent is unemployed Dummy = 1 if the respondent is retired Dummy = 1 if the respondent is a student	Eurobarometer	Economic	Individual

(continued)

Table 5.2 (continued)

Name	Description	Source	Family	Level
High level of education	Dummy variable equal to 1 if the respondent indicated *More than 20* to the question "*How old were you when you stopped full-time education*"	Eurobarometer	Economic	Individual
Job-related personal expectations	A scale from 1 to 3 has been created corresponding to the following Eurobarometer question: "*What are your expectations for the next twelve months: will the next twelve months be better, worse or the same, when it comes to your personal job situation?*" 1 corresponds to *worse* 2 corresponds to *same* 3 corresponds to *better*	Eurobarometer	Economic	Individual
Social explanations				
Ethnolinguistic Fractionalization	Measure of diversity within each region. The index has been calculated as follows: $ELF = 1 - \sum_i s_i^2$ where s_i is the share of the citizenship group i over the total population (see Alesina & La Ferrara, 2005) The available citizenship groups are: European Union foreign countries European foreign countries African countries North American countries Other American countries Asian countries Oceania countries Other countries	Eurostat Census data	Social	Regional
Perception of inclusiveness of the EU	Dummy equal to 1 if the respondent indicated *cultural identity* as an answer to the following question: "*What does EU mean to you personally?*"	Eurobarometer	Social	Individual

(continued)

Table 5.2 (continued)

Name	Description	Source	Family	Level
Perception of loss of cultural identity due to EU	Dummy equal to 1 if the respondent indicated *loss of cultural identity* as an answer to the following question: "*What does EU mean to you personally?*"	Eurobarometer	Social	Individual
Solidarity with poorer regions	Dummy equal to 1 if the respondent indicated *Solidarity with poorer region* as an answer to the following question: "*In your opinion among the following issues, which are those that most create a feeling of community among European citizens?*"	Eurobarometer	Social	Individual
Political explanations				
Quality of government	Composite indicator including core features of Quality of Government (impartiality, bureaucratic, quality and corruption) as well as measures that are broader (rule of law and transparency)	University of Gothenburg	Political	Regional
Trust in political parties	Dummy variable equal to 1 if the respondent answered *tend to trust* to the following question: "*I would like to ask you a question about how much trust you have in certain institutions. Please tell me if you tend to trust or tend not to trust political parties*"	Eurobarometer	Political	Individual
Trust in national government	Dummy variable equal to 1 if the respondent answered *tend to trust* to the following question: "*I would like to ask you a question about how much trust you have in certain institutions. Please tell me if you tend to trust or tend not to trust the national government*"	Eurobarometer	Political	Individual

(continued)

Table 5.2 (continued)

Name	Description	Source	Family	Level
Satisfaction with the national democracy	A scale from 1 to 4 has been created corresponding to the following Eurobarometer question: "*On the whole, are you very satisfied, fairly satisfied, not very satisfied or not at all satisfied with the way democracy works in your country?*" 1 corresponds to *not at all satisfied* 2 corresponds to *not very satisfied* 3 corresponds to *fairly satisfied* 4 corresponds to *very satisfied*	Eurobarometer	Political	Individual
Satisfaction with the EU democracy	A scale from 1 to 4 has been created corresponding to the following Eurobarometer question: "*On the whole, are you very satisfied, fairly satisfied, not very satisfied or not at all satisfied with the way democracy works in the EU?*" 1 corresponds to *not at all satisfied* 2 corresponds to *not very satisfied* 3 corresponds to *fairly satisfied* 4 corresponds to *very satisfied*	Eurobarometer	Political	Individual

(continued)

Table 5.2 (continued)

Name	Description	Source	Family	Level
Political self-placement	A scale from 1 to 10 has been created corresponding to the following question: "*In political matters people talk of "the left" and "the right". How would you place your views on this scale?*" where 1 indicates extreme left and 10 indicates extreme right	Eurobarometer	Political	Individual
Perception of personal political relevance in EU matters	A scale from 1 to 4 has been created corresponding to the following question: "*Please tell me to what extent you agree or disagree with the following statement: my voice counts in the EU: totally agree, tend to agree, tend to disagree, totally disagree*" 1 corresponds to *totally disagree* 2 corresponds to *tend to disagree* 3 corresponds to *tend to agree* 4 corresponds to *totally agree*	Eurobarometer	Political	Individual
Other factors				
Age	Age of the respondent	Eurobarometer	Other	Individual
Gender: female	Dummy equal to 1 if the respondent is a woman	Eurobarometer	Other	Individual
Rural area	Dummy equal to 1 if the respondent declares that they live in a rural area or village	Eurobarometer	Other	Individual

5.4.3 Empirical Results

Table 5.3 reports the empirical results of the adopted model. *Individualistic localism* is the baseline category and the three columns represented in Table 5.3 correspond to the other three identified typologies of territorial identity: (2) *Parochial localism*, (3) *Place-less cosmopolitanism* and (4) *Inclusive cosmopolitanism.*

The first interesting outcome to be discussed refers to the role of tangible forms of cultural heritage in influencing territorial identity. As evidenced in the results table, the coefficient associated with the cultural-heritage-related variable is positive and significant only in the case of *place-less cosmopolitanism.* In other words, a higher amount of tangible forms of cultural heritage is associated with an increased probability of feeling a *place-less cosmopolitanism* type of territorial identity rather than an *individualistic localism* type (which is the baseline category). This result tells us that the dimension defining territorial identity which is influenced the most by this specific type of cultural heritage is the multilevel nature of territorial identity rather than solidarity. Built heritage, cultural sites and cultural districts are in fact able to inspire a sense of belonging to a wider community even if individuals were not born in the specific place in which heritage sites are located. Tangible forms of cultural heritage are in fact able to animate and impress travelers, foreigners and cosmopolitan people who, through the influence of heritage, feel they are part of a larger community and feel like European citizens. By the same token, people living in territories endowed with immovable tangible heritage are more exposed and prone to welcoming new movers attracted by the same presence of heritage and therefore more used to getting in touch and will know and possibly accept and include different ways of living, different habits and different cultures. In this way, a multicultural and flexible atmosphere can be generated. Another way in which tangible forms of heritage influence a *place-less cosmopolitan* type of territorial identity is through its educational value. Getting to know the history, the values and the potential intercultural connections happened in a place and witnessed by the heritage sites is useful in shaping and fostering a sense of belonging to multiple territorial layers. However, as also highlighted in Kuhn et al. (2018), cosmopolitan people may be global, open and flexible without necessarily showing solidarity. Cultural heritage may in fact stimulate openness in privileged groups of people, inspired by neoliberal ideas supporting open borders and common humanity but still very reluctant to share their resources with other people. From these results, neither *parochial localism* nor *inclusive cosmopolitanism* is more influenced by the endowment of tangible forms of cultural heritage in comparison with *individualistic localism.*

This means that the solidarity dimension of territorial identity does not appear to be strongly associated with the sheer presence of immovable cultural heritage. This result could be explained by the fact that cultural heritage needs to be activated to trigger solidarity within the society. In other words, for solidarity to be instilled, there is the need of some activities and some actions dedicated to it and related to heritage. For instance, rather than the type of heritage considered in the

Table 5.3 The modes of expression of territorial identity as a function of individual and regional characteristics: empirical results

	(2)	(3)	(4)
	Parochial localism	Place-less cosmopolitanism	Inclusive cosmopolitanism
Cultural heritage	0.047 (0.050)	0.046* (0.027)	−0.015 (0.039)
Cultural heritage * tourist arrivals	−0.029 (0.030)	−0.033** (0.014)	−0.036** (0.018)
Family of explanations: economic collective			
GDP per capita	0.157* (0.088)	0.043 (0.056)	0.063 (0.081)
Education	0.054 (0.054)	−0.032 (0.056)	0.026 (0.072)
Number of tourist arrivals per capita	−0.014 (0.039)	−0.048 (0.047)	0.011 (0.065)
Economic expectations (country)	−0.068** (0.027)	0.022 (0.019)	0.010 (0.024)
Family of explanations: economic individual			
Self employed	−0.199*** (0.074)	0.038 (0.040)	−0.036 (0.058)
White collar	−0.174** (0.068)	0.070** (0.036)	0.049 (0.049)
House person	−0.092 (0.085)	−0.207*** (0.058)	−0.149** (0.073)
Unemployed	0.040 (0.062)	−0.242*** (0.042)	−0.305*** (0.063)
Manager/professional	−0.219*** (0.075)	0.109*** (0.033)	0.224*** (0.046)
Manual worker	−0.144*** (0.053)	−0.149*** (0.034)	−0.174*** (0.044)
Personal job expectations	−0.021 (0.036)	0.109*** (0.022)	0.076** (0.030)
High education level	0.053 (0.040)	0.389*** (0.027)	0.452*** (0.033)
Family of explanations: social collective			
Metropolitan areas	0.012 (0.043)	−0.033 (0.023)	−0.019 (0.038)
Ethnolinguistic fractionalization	−0.154* (0.064)	0.061 (0.048)	0.027 (0.069)
Family of explanations: social individual			
EU means cultural diversity	0.211*** (0.043)	0.547*** (0.029)	0.758*** (0.036)

(continued)

Table 5.3 (continued)

	(2) Parochial localism	(3) Place-less cosmopolitanism	(4) Inclusive cosmopolitanism
EU means loss of identity	−0.036 (0.043)	−0.574*** (0.027)	−0.686** (0.055)
Solidarity with poorer regions	0.654*** (0.056)	0.227*** (0.039)	0.887*** (0.059)
Family of explanations: political collective			
Quality of government	0.051 (0.069)	−0.005 (0.061)	0.042 (0.090)
Trust political parties	0.169*** (0.062)	0.083*** (0.031)	0.274*** (0.042)
Trust national government	0.056 (0.058)	0.252*** (0.030)	0.259*** (0.039)
Satisfaction with national democracy	−0.042 (0.033)	0.028 (0.024)	0.081*** (0.027)
Satisfaction with EU democracy	0.086** (0.037)	0.717*** (0.022)	0.628*** (0.031)
Family of explanations: political individual			
Political views	−0.095*** (0.012)	−0.019** (0.008)	−0.104*** (0.012)
My voice counts in the EU	0.088*** (0.022)	0.746*** (0.023)	0.784*** (0.029)
Other factors			
Age	−0.005*** (0.002)	−0.009*** (0.001)	−0.012*** (0.001)
Female	0.164*** (0.034)	−0.080*** (0.018)	0.045* (0.025)
Rural	0.049 (0.051)	−0.066* (0.026)	−0.033 (0.044)
Country Fixed Effects	Yes	Yes	Yes
Time Fixed Effects	Yes	Yes	Yes
Constant	−0.853*** (0.207)	−2.458*** (0.128)	−3.398*** (0.213)
Observations	119,628	119,628	119,628

Notes Robust standard errors in parentheses; ***$p < 0.01$, **$p < 0.05$, *$p < 0.1$
The coefficients are standardized
Reference categories: *individualistic localism* (dependent variable), *student* (occupation)

empirical analysis, museums could probably be a type of heritage which is seen to be much more related to solidarity formation, or actions of culture-led regeneration of neglected neighborhoods specifically intended to include people might prove to foster solidarity.[2]

Another interesting result deriving from the interpretation of the outcomes regards the coefficient associated with the interaction between tangible forms of cultural heritage and tourist attractiveness (in terms of the number of tourist arrivals per capita). Both the coefficients associated with the interaction term and related to cosmopolitan types of territorial identity (both *place-less* and *inclusive*) are negative and significant. This result can be interpreted as the negative effect of overtourism on local communities. In other words, when the number of tourists who visit local heritage sites becomes excessive, congestion problems might generate discomfort and stress for local people. The uncontrolled abuse of tangible forms of heritage sites linked to tourist activities disturbs both solidarity and the feeling of EU citizenship, leading people to shift toward individualistic and closed attitudes.

Other relevant outcomes of the analysis involve some of the additional control variables included. For instance, education, positive expectations referred to personal job situations, perception of the EU as supportive of cultural diversity together with trust in political parties, in national government and satisfaction with both national and EU democracies are positively related to a cosmopolitan type of territorial identity (both place-less and inclusive) with respect to the baseline category. A positive perception related to the individual relevance in EU matters and a more left-oriented political affiliation are associated with a less individualistic type of territorial identity. More specifically, considering the meanings attributed to the EU, individuals who believe that European Union means cultural diversity present a higher probability of being far from an individualistic type of identity. By looking at the magnitude of the coefficient, a relevant increase can be noted starting from *parochial localism* (0.211) passing through *place-less cosmopolitanism* (0.547) and arriving at *inclusive cosmopolitanism* (0.758). The same is valid for the perception of the EU as a loss of identity. The coefficient associated with *parochial localism* is not significant and is very small, and the magnitude of the coefficient increases (in absolute value) from the −0.574 associated with *place-less cosmopolitanism* to −0.686 associated with *inclusive cosmopolitanism*. The pattern of increased magnitude of the coefficients can also be found in the ones associated with satisfaction with EU democracy and perception of personal political relevance in EU matters (*my voice counts in the EU*). Individuals who perceive the EU as a source and a storage of cultural diversity, who are satisfied with the EU democracy, who perceive themselves as influential citizens of the EU and who do not consider the EU as a loss of identity present a low probability of feeling an individualistic type of territorial identity, a greater

[2] This discourse should be developed by considering, for instance, the existence of different typologies of museums, some of them more related and dedicated to local communities and some others able to attract visitors and tourists from elsewhere. The spatial location and networks of museums are also to be considered as extending the role of museums (see for instance de Graaf et al., 2009).

probability of feeling parochial localism, an even greater probability of being place-less cosmopolitan and the highest probability of feeling inclusive cosmopolitanism. While these variables are very much related to the identitarian dimension of the spatial reach of founding networks of territorial identity, other variables included are more linked with the behavioral dimension of solidarity. In fact, the coefficients associated to the variables indicating both trust in local political parties and solidarity with poorer regions present a greater magnitude when associated with *parochial localism* and *inclusive cosmopolitanism* compared with *place-less cosmopolitanism* and *individualistic localism.*

Even though some interesting findings can be highlighted from the results obtained and presented in Table 5.3, the interpretation of the coefficients estimated with multiple outcome models deserves some specific attention (Wulff, 2015). In fact, as also discussed in Cameron and Trivedi (2005) and Greene (2002), two main downsides related to mere interpretation of the coefficients can be mentioned. First, the interpretation is limited since it allows us to make statements related on the ability of a predictor to enhance the probability of one choice outcome with respect to the base category. In this way, the fact that outcomes are linked with each other is neglected and it is rather complex to detect the implications for each category. Second, and by the same token, the sign of each coefficient can be interpreted only in relation to and in contrast with the base category. In other words, only two categories can be compared. Citing from Wulff (2015, p. 305), "*the coefficient of a predictor with regard to a specific category tells us about how the predictor relates to the probability of observing a particular category relative to the base category*".

Therefore, even though some undeniably relevant information can be detected from the interpretation of the coefficients reported in Table 5.3, to face the interpretational issues just mentioned, the marginal effects related to the four identified categories of territorial identity have been calculated.

The marginal effects are defined as the slope of the prediction function at a given value of the explanatory variable and thus inform us about the change in predicted probabilities due to a change in a particular predictor. While the results reported in Table 5.3 represent a relative probability of the occurrence of a certain type of territorial identity with respect to the reference category, the marginal effects represent the overall probability of the occurrence of a certain outcome of the dependent variable (in this case either *individualistic localism, parochial localism, place-less cosmopolitanism* or *inclusive cosmopolitanism*) due to a change in the endowment of cultural heritage.

Table 5.4 reports the marginal effects corresponding to the cultural-heritage-related predictor variable.

As evident from Table 5.4, the endowment of tangible forms of cultural heritage has an influence on both *individualistic localism* and *place-less cosmopolitanism.* This influence goes in opposite directions. In fact, the presence of cultural heritage is associated with a lower probability for an individual to experience *individualistic localism* and a higher probability to feel *place-less cosmopolitanism.* Therefore, the interpretation deriving from the calculation of the marginal effects is in line with the ones provided for the coefficients reported in Table 5.3. Thanks to the multifaceted

Table 5.4 Multinomial logit marginal effects

	(1) Individualistic localism	(2) Parochial localism	(3) Place-less cosmopolitanism	(4) Inclusive cosmopolitanism
Cultural heritage	−0.0058* (0.0035)	0.0009 (0.0018)	0.012** (0.0047)	−0.0048 (0.0032)

Notes Robust standard errors in parentheses ***$p < 0.01$, **$p < 0.05$, *$p < 0.1$

values owned and transferred by cultural heritage, it is less likely that individuals living in territories endowed with more heritage sites experience an individualistic localism type of territorial identity. On the contrary, place-less cosmopolitanism is fed by the presence of tangible forms of cultural heritage. Accordingly, the presence of cultural heritage is able to influence the most identitarian aspect of territorial identity, which is the spatial reach of founding networks (see Sect. 4.5). A shift from individualistic toward cosmopolitan attitudes is made possible by the territorial endowment of cultural heritage. The lack or the presence of solidarity is instead less related to the endowment of tangible forms of cultural heritage. Since solidarity appears to be more political in nature, the sheer presence of heritage is not enough to stimulate solidarity. To do so, there is the need to activate, manage and handle heritage as a symbol or as a site specifically dedicated to fostering community-related behaviors.

5.5 Conclusions

Cultural heritage and territorial identities are strictly intertwined. In fact, heritage interacts with the formation, shaping and enhancement of territorial identities through diverse mechanisms such as encoding of symbolic meanings, creating a distinctive territorial image or landscape, fostering social cohesion and inclusion and contributing to generate new knowledge, among others. In this section, the relationships between the endowment of cultural heritage and the four identified modes of existence of territorial identities have been empirically explored, applying a multilevel multinomial logistic model.

The results confirm the expectations of strong relationships between the endowment of cultural heritage and the feeling of a sense of belonging to a wider community, while absence of cultural heritage is associated with a higher probability of belonging to the first typology of territorial identity (*individualistic localism*). In fact, tangible forms of cultural heritage are positively associated with a *place-less cosmopolitan* type of territorial identity characterized by a strong feeling of EU citizenship but with lower inclinations toward solidarity. This result shows that the sheer endowment of built heritage sites can infuse a "*we-feeling*" with a larger community which is able to cross national borders. However, the endowment of heritage must be "activated" to gain influence also on the solidarity dimension. Other interesting results of the analysis highlight that positive feelings related to the functioning of the EU democracy, to the perception of inclusive participation and to the protection of cultural diversity are associated to a lower probability for individuals to feel individualistic localism and to a higher probability of experiencing an inclusive cosmopolitan type of territorial identity. Other sensitivities related to trust in local political parties and to the perception of the EU as a powerful tool for showing solidarity to and supporting other regions are instead more related to parochial localism and inclusive cosmopolitanism categories. Furthermore, a higher degree of education, positive expectations on personal economic situations and a more left-oriented political affiliation result in a higher probability of feeling a cosmopolitan type of identity rather than individualistic ones.

The following chapter will be dedicated to explore the economic consequences stemming from the relationship between cultural heritage and diverse typologies of territorial identity.

References

Adam, B. (2003). Social policies for metropolitan regions—Identity, participation and integration. *European Planning Studies, 11*(6), 739–747.

Alesina, A., & La Ferrara, E. (2005). Ethnic diversity and economic performance. *Journal of Economic Literature, 43*(3), 762–800.

Anderson, C. J. (1998). When in doubt, use proxies: Attitudes toward domestic politics and support for European integration. *Comparative Political Studies, 31*(5), 569–601.

Bellandi, M., & Santini, E. (2017). Resilience and the role of arts and culture-based activities in mature industrial districts. *European Planning Studies, 25*(1), 88–106.

Blake, J. (2000). On defining the cultural heritage. *The International and Comparative Law Quarterly, 1*, 61–85.

Borges, L. A. (2017). Using the past to construct territorial identities in regional planning: The case of Mälardalen, Sweden. *International Journal of Urban and Regional Research, 41*, 659–675.

Börzel, T. A., & Risse, T. (2020). Identity politics, core state powers and regional integration: Europe and beyond. *Journal of Common Market Studies, 58*(1), 21–40.

Braun, M. (2020). Postfunctionalism, identity and the Visegrad group. *Journal of Common Market Studies, 58*(4), 925–940.

Bremer, B., Genschel, P., & Jachtenfuchs, M. (2020). Juncker's curse? Identity, interest, and public support for the integration of core state powers. *Journal of Common Market Studies, 58*(1), 56–75.

Cameron, A. C., & Trivedi, P. K. (Eds.). (2005). *Microeconometrics—Methods and applications*. Cambridge University Press.

Capello, R., & Perucca, G. (2019). From cohesion policy implementation to European identity. *Regional Science Policy & Practice, 11*(4), 631–636.

Carta, M. (Ed.). (2007). *L'armatura cultural del territorio*. Franco Angeli s.r.l.

Cerisola, S. (2019a). A new perspective on the cultural heritage-development nexus: The role of creativity. *Journal of Cultural Economics, 43*(1), 21–56.

Cerisola, S. (2019b). *Cultural heritage, creativity and economic development*. Edward Elgar Publishing Limited.

CHCfE Consortium. (2015). *Cultural heritage counts for Europe*. http://blogs.encatc.org/culturalheritagecountsforeurope//wp-content/uploads/2015/06/CHCfE_FULL-REPORT_v2.pdf, [29/10/2020].

Christin, T. (2005). Economic and political basis of attitudes towards the EU in central and east European countries in the 1990s. *European Union Politics, 6*(1), 29–57.

Council of Europe. (2005). *Council of Europe Framework Convention on the Value of Cultural Heritage for Society (Faro Convention).* https://rm.coe.int/CoERMPublicCommonSearchServices/DisplayDCTMContent?documentId=0900001680083746, [26/11/2020].

de Graaff, T., Boter, J., & Rouwendal, J. (2009). On spatial differences in the attractiveness of Dutch museums. *Environment and Planning A, 41*, 2778–2797.

Eichenberg, R. C., & Dalton, R. J. (1993). Europeans and the European Community: The dynamics of public support for European integration. *International Organization, 47*(4), 507–534.

ESPON. (2004–2006). *The role and spatial effects of cultural heritage and identity.* https://www.espon.eu/sites/default/files/attachments/fr-1.3.3_revised-full_August2006.pdf, [23/11/2020].

eTwinning. (2018). *Learning from the past, designing our future: Europe's cultural heritage through eTwinning.* Co-funded by the Erasmus+ Programme of the European Union. https://www.etwinning.net/eun-files/Online%20%E2%80%93%20eTwinning%20publication%2024.09.2018.pdf, [26/11/2020].

European Commission. (1999). *ESPD—European Spatial Development Perspective: Towards balanced and sustainable development of the territory of the European Union.* Office for Official Publications of the European Communities.

Ferilli, G., Sacco, P. L., Tavano, B. G., & Forbici, S. (2016). Power to the people: When culture works as a social catalyst in urban regeneration processes (and when it does not). *European Planning Studies, 25*(2), 241–258.

Furia, D., Crociata, A., & Agovino, M. (2018). Voluntary work and cultural capital: An explanatory analysis for Italian regional data. *Economics and Politics, 35*, 789–808.

Gillman, D. (Ed.). (2006). *The idea of cultural heritage.* Cambridge University Press.

Gospodini, A. (2007). Urban morphology and place identity in European cities: Built heritage and innovative design. *Journal of Urban Design, 9*(2), 225–248.

Greene, W. H. (Ed.). (2002). *Econometric analysis* (5th ed.). Prentice Hall.

Gunay, Z. (2010). Conservation versus regeneration?: Case of European capital of culture 2010 Istanbul. *European Planning Studies, 18*(8), 1173–1186.

Harvey, D. C. (2001). Heritage pasts and heritage presents: Temporality, meaning and the scope of heritage. *International Journal of Heritage Studies, 7*(4), 319–338.

Hooghe, L., & Marks, G. (2005). Calculation, community and cues—Public opinion on European integration. *European Union Politics, 6*(4), 419–443.

Hribar, M. Š., Bole, D., & Pipan, P. (2015). Sustainable heritage management: Social, economic and other potentials of culture in local development. *Procedia – Social and Behavioral Sciences, 188*, 103–110.

Huovinen, A., Timonen, E., Leino, T., & Seppälä, T. (2017). Changing urban identities on a discursive map. *City, Culture and Society, 11*, 20–28.

Janssen, J., Luiten, E., Renes, H., & Stegmeijer, E. (2017). Heritage as sector, factor and vector: Conceptualizing the shifting relationship between heritage management and spatial planning. *European Planning Studies, 25*(9), 1654–1672.

Jones, E., Menon, A., & Weatherhill, S. (Eds.). (2012). *The Oxford handbook of the European Union.* Oxford University Press.

Kuhn, T., Solaz, H., & van Elsas, E. J. (2018). Practising what you preach: How cosmopolitanism promotes willingness to redistribute across the European Union. *Journal of European Public Policy, 25*(12), 1759–1778.

Lenzi, C., & Perucca, G. (2016). Are urbanized areas source of life satisfaction? Evidence from EU regions. *Papers in Regional Science, 97*(S1), S106–S122.

Lindberg, L. N., & Scheingold, S. A. (Eds.). (1970). *Europe's would-be polity: Patterns of change in the European community.* Prentice-Hall.

Liu, H. J., & Hilton, D. J. (2005). How the past weighs on the present: Social representations of history and their role in identity politics. *British Journal of Social Psychology, 44*, 1–21.

Lowenthal, D. (1997). *The heritage crusade and the spoils of history.* Cambridge University Press.

Macdonald, S. (Ed.). (2013). *Memorylands—Heritage and identity in Europe today*. Routledge.
Matarasso, F. (1997). *Use or ornament? The social impact of participation in the arts*. Comedia.
McNamara, K. R., & Musgrave, P. (2020). Democracy and collective identity in the EU and the USA. *Journal of Common Market Studies, 58*(1), 172–188.
Nelsen, B. F., & Guth, J. L. (2020). Losing faith: Religion and attitudes toward the European Union in uncertain times. *Journal of Common Market Studies, 58*(4), 909–924.
Nicoli, F., Kuhn, T., & Burgoon, B. (2020). Collective identities, European solidarity: Identification patterns and preferences for European social insurance. *Journal of Common Market Studies, 58*(1), 76–95.
Paasi, A. (1986). The institutionalization of regions: A theoretical framework for understanding the emergence of regions and the constitution of regional identity. *Fennia International Journal of Geography, 164*, 105–146.
Rohrschneider, R. (2002). The democracy deficit and mass support for an EU-wide government. *American Journal of Political Science, 46*(2), 463–475.
Sable, A. S., & Kling R.W. (2001). The double public good: A conceptual framework for "shared experience" values associated with heritage conservation. *Journal of Cultural Economics, 25*, 77–89.
Smith, A. D. (2009). *Ethno-symbolism and nationalism: A cultural approach*. Routledge.
Thrane, C. (2015). Examining tourists' long-distance transportation mode choices using a multinomial logit regression model. *Tourism Management Perspectives, 15*, 115–121.
Tweed, C., & Sutherland, M. (2007). Built cultural heritage and sustainable urban development. *Landscape and Urban Planning, 83*(1), 62–69.
Ünlü, T. S. (2019). Urban memory and planning: Investigating the use of oral history. *European Planning Studies, 27*(4), 802–817.
Vecco, M. (2010). A definition of cultural heritage: From the tangible to the intangible. *Journal of Cultural Heritage, 11*, 321–324.
Waterton, E., & Smith, L. (2010). The recognition and misrecognition of community heritage. *International Journal of Heritage Studies, 16*(1–2), 4–15.
Wulff, J. N. (2015). Interpreting results from the multinomial logit: Demonstrated by foreign market entry. *Organizational Research Methods, 18*(2), 300–325.

Chapter 6
Cultural Heritage and Territorial Identity: The Economic Consequences of Their Synergies

6.1 Cultural Heritage, Territorial Identity and Economic Development: A New Conceptual Framework

If the previous chapter was dedicated to explaining and empirically proving how cultural heritage plays a role in shaping and influencing territorial identity, this section deepens the analysis of the economic spillovers potentially derived from synergies between heritage and territorial identity. In fact, when interpreted as an economic resource, cultural heritage plays a role as a catalyst for local development not only through tourist activities (as demonstrated in Part A of this book) but also through intangible, more sophisticated and socio-cultural channels which refer to territorial identity.

The main idea proposed here has been inspired by a table presented in the report *Cultural Heritage counts for Europe*. The report provides a comprehensive overview of the multiple relationships that cultural heritage entertains with the territories in which it is located. More specifically and according to their perspective, four domains on which cultural heritage exerts its impact can be identified, namely *economic*, *social*, *environmental* and *cultural*. By interacting with and influencing these four domains, cultural heritage is linked to and associated with sustainable development. Furthermore, sub-domains of impact have been identified by the report, each of which falls into one or more of the four main domains. The following table (Table 6.1) replicates the one proposed in the report. The intersections between the rows and the columns report an "x" whenever that specific combination has already been considered and analyzed so far by the literature.

Considering the column dedicated to the economic domain, various mechanisms are mentioned through which cultural heritage plays its role in economic dynamics. It can be noticed that the table is exhaustive in indicating and mentioning all the channels of synergies between the endowment of heritage and the economic sphere that have been discussed and empirically proved by the literature so far. For instance, the role of cultural heritage in generating new knowledge and skills and contributing to education and therefore influencing economic dynamics has been discussed, among

E. Panzera, *Cultural Heritage and Territorial Identity*, Advances in Spatial Science,
https://doi.org/10.1007/978-3-030-94468-1_6

Table 6.1 Upgraded Potential Areas of Cultural Heritage Impact (*Source* Cultural Heritage Counts for Europe and Author's own elaboration)

	Economic	*Social*	*Cultural*	*Environmental*
Image and symbol creation			X	
Visual attractiveness			X	
Architectural language			X	
Creativity and innovation	*Cerisola* (2019a, 2019b)		X	
Sense of place	Capello and Perucca (2017)	X	X	X
Cultural landscape			X	X
Reducing urban sprawl				X
Preserving embodied energy				X
Lifecycle prolongation				X
Education	X	X	X	
Skills	X	X	X	
Knowledge	X	X	X	
Creation of Identity	*Panzera*	X	X	
Regional attractiveness	X		X	X
Social cohesion	*Panzera*	X		
Community participation		X		
Continuity of social life		X		
Place branding	X	X		
Labor market	X	X		
Regional competitiveness	X	X		X
Real Estate market	X			
Gross Value Added	X			
Return on Investment	X			
Tax Income	X			
Housing Stock Management	X			X

others by Backman and Nilsson (2018). The economic dynamics influenced by regional attractiveness and place branding fostered by the presence of heritage and fed by tourism attractiveness are extensively discussed by the literature (see for instance Patuelli et al., 2013). A rich branch of the literature examines the role of heritage in the real estate market (see for instance Lazrak et al., 2014) as well as its role in generating gross value added or return on investment (see for instance Bowitz and Ibenholt, 2009).

Even though these channels are certainly accurate and relevant, one of the main ideas underlying this work is that other intangible and socio-cultural elements might generate positive economic consequences through their links with cultural heritage. Cerisola (2019a, 2019b) already started testing this reasoning both conceptually and empirically focusing on creativity, a channel indicated by the report but not referred to the economic area. According to Cerisola (2019a, 2019b), cultural heritage is instead able to have an impact also on economic dynamics through the mediating role of creativity, a hypothesis corroborated by her econometric analysis on Italian regions. Therefore, her name has been added to the table (Table 6.1).

Similarly, the aim of this book is to discuss the effects that cultural heritage has on the economic domain through other intangible mechanisms, which have been so far overlooked by the economic literature or analyzed only according to their social and cultural impacts. Identity, sense of place and social cohesion are embedded in the concept of territorial capital (as explained in Sect. 4.3), and consequently contribute, together with all other production factors, of a material and immaterial nature, to the development of places, cities and regions. The synergetic outcome that follows the presence of these unconventional factors has been labeled as the territorial relational surplus, given the strictly localized, interactive and collective form of the underlying processes leading to an economic surplus (Camagni, 2019).

A similar perspective has been adopted by Capello and Perucca (2017) in which the effects of local cultural characteristics have been analyzed as enhancers of the role of tangible cultural assets. The potential relationship between tangible forms of heritage and economic development is not place-neutral: the endowment of immaterial cultural assets such as social cultural values, individual cultural attitudes, sense of identification with cultural symbols or institutional behaviors related to culture, influence the role that material cultural heritage might have on local development. Accordingly, "*the role of tangible elements of cultural capital on economic growth is reinforced when they are embedded in specific cultural environments*" (ibidem, p. 110). Consequently, their names have been added to Table 6.1 corresponding to the interaction between sense of place and the economic sub-domain of impact.

The reasoning of both Cerisola (2019a, 2019b) and Capello and Perucca (2017) has been expanded here to include other intangible elements of territorial capital namely *territorial identity* declared in the four modes of expression as previously discussed (see Sect. 4.4). In other words, intangible, soft and socio-cultural territorial conditions are believed to influence the role that the endowment of tangible forms of cultural heritage can have in fostering socio-economic dynamics.

It has to be noted that, on the one hand, the relationship between cultural heritage, creativity and local economic development studied by Cerisola (2019a, 2019b) functions according to a logical mediation mechanism: cultural heritage inspires creativity which, in turn, is able to stimulate development. On the other hand, in the work carried out by Capello and Perucca (2017), cultural heritage and territorial cultural assets interact and create synergies that, in turn, influence economic dynamics. Since there are no a priori justifications or shared assumptions related to the functioning of these—similar but alternative—processes, both a mediation and a synergy mechanism will be tested empirically in a quantitative way.

The following figure (Fig. 6.1) graphically represents the two logical mechanisms tested.

According to the *mediation mechanism*, cultural heritage generates, shapes or enhances specific typologies of territorial identity. In turn, each influenced typology, in line with its diverse characteristics, generates economic development.

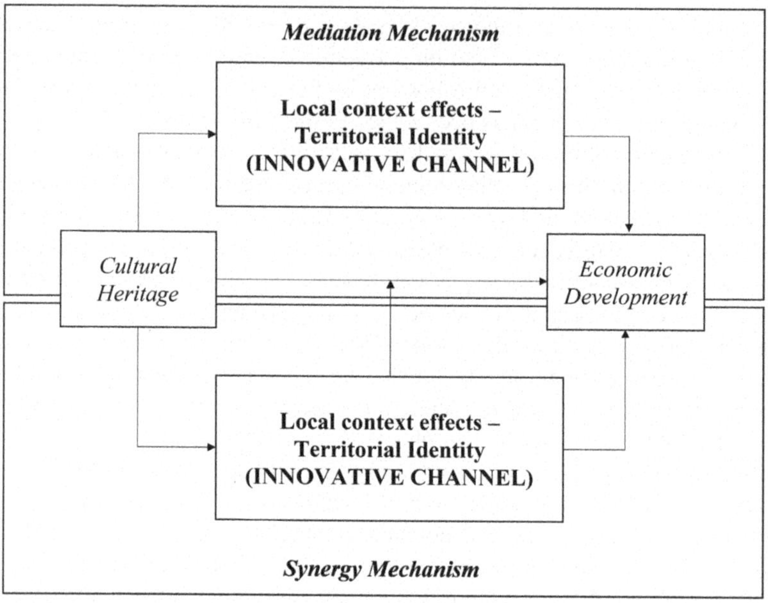

Fig. 6.1 Cultural heritage, territorial identity and economic development: The conceptual framework

On the other hand, according to a *synergy mechanism*, all the channels through which cultural heritage may affect economic development are encompassed in the analysis. The role of territorial identity is interpreted as a context element able to foster, enhance and strengthen the economic consequences stemming from the presence of cultural heritage. In other words, territorial identity, according to its specificities and peculiarities, represents a context externality able to influence the impact that cultural heritage has on local development.

Starting from the assumption that the endowment of cultural heritage and local economic development represents a nexus working not only through predominantly economic mechanisms, such as tourism, but also through intangible, socio-cultural-psychological local elements, after a brief overview aimed at conceptually explaining how the heritage/territorial identity interactions might function (Sect. 6.2), an econometric analysis will be performed in order to figure out whether a mediation mechanism is at work (Sect. 6.3) or whether it is instead the synergetic relationship between the two territorial factors (cultural heritage and identity) that is able to generate economic spillovers (Sect. 6.4). Section 6.5 provides some further remarks on the results and concludes.

6.2 The Territorial Identity-Local Development Nexus in the Existing Literature

European cultural heritage is nowadays considered as an essential and valuable resource for the territories in which it is located. Several spillovers are associated with the local presence of different forms and expressions of cultural heritage. One of the strongest and most recurring associations is the one between cultural heritage and identity. As already discussed in previous chapters, cultural heritage being at once inherited from the past and a legacy for future generations, it is considered as a source of sense of belonging to a place and territorial identity. The association between cultural heritage and identity is commonly presented as socio-cultural in nature expressing its implications on—and being influenced by—society or culture in its broader sense. However, economic implications might result as well from this nexus. In fact, territorial identity and territorial identification give rise to varied feelings such as trust or togetherness but also disaffection or resentment. These elements, in turn, influence the ways in which economic dynamics work, leading to visible consequences for local economic development.

Since identity and territorial identity are multifaceted concepts, difficult to define and measure, it is hard to find a specific stream of the literature dedicated to empirically prove the existence of a cause-effect relationship for economic development. However, representing territorial identity as an integral part of territorial capital, identification and attachment to places strengthen the efficiency of a community through the development of collective and cooperative behaviors stemming from the recognition of a certain correspondence between private and public interests. Furthermore, if the role of cultural heritage as a source of new knowledge and recognition of other cultures is fully appreciated, the presence of multiple territorial identities makes places more flexible, future-oriented, open-minded and capable of change, positively influencing economic dynamics.

As reported by Schneider et al. (2000), Putnam in *Making democracy work* explores the nexus between civic traditions and economic development. The social capital of a specific society can be strengthened by its capacity to communicate and cooperate following nonhierarchical dynamics. People start to trust each other and these positive attitudes, together with consolidation of social capital, influence the economic practices (Guiso et al., 2007). As Putnam et al. (1993) argued, a crucial role is played by the social capital acquired and built by a society through norms, trust and networks in shaping economic behaviors improving, for instance, the efficiency of a society by helping overcome collective issues. Generally speaking, social capital and social bonds support, stimulate and facilitate interactions (Bourdieu, 1983; Coleman, 1990; Putnam et al., 1993). In other words, sets of associations and networks between people contribute to the productivity of a community by facilitating coordination and cooperation fed by the awareness of mutual benefits (Iyer et al., 2005). These elements are strictly linked to the solidarity dimension used in the context of this book to define the categories of territorial identity (see Sect. 4.4).

Territorial identity could be interpreted as a “soft architecture” to emphasize, as highlighted in Staber and Sautter (2011), its intangible nature and the intangible elements that it brings with it such as shared mindsets or common goals. Talking about firms, Staber and Sautter (2011, p. 1350) write: “*collective identity constitutes an asset that firms can use for developing a joint strategy. A common identity gives purpose to the entity with which the members identify. It may also enhance firms' absorptive capacity helping them to acquire new information from the environment, assimilate it, and apply it innovatively.*” The same reasoning can be enlarged and applied to other typologies of groups or political entities such as regions, nations or even the European Union. A shared understanding of rules, norms and behaviors and a mutual awareness of traditions or informal attitudes can become competitive resources and conditions facilitating economic development. Since territorial identities involve specific combinations of similarity and solidarity and internal and/or external reach of the founding networks, they contribute to governing people's interactions therefore supporting economic and social development (Iyer et al., 2005). A higher degree of solidarity, for instance, implies greater levels of trust and civic responsibility. A stronger feeling of EU citizenship might imply higher respect for civic and political liberties and greater willingness to participate or respect governments and institutions.

As argued by Malecki (2012), since innovation is increasingly fundamental in a knowledge economy, territorial production systems need to learn fast and adapt continuously to new circumstances and conditions to remain competitive. Soft elements of territorial capital such as territorial identity or social capital contribute to generate and foster interactive and collective learning processes through the presence of networks, interactions and social proximity, consequently promoting innovativeness and competitiveness. Citing form Malecki (2012, p. 1028) “*Networks provide several benefits: faster access to information and knowledge, lower information and knowledge costs, and increased quantity and quality of information and knowledge.*” Successful examples of the strength of networks and the positive economic spillovers stemming from soft elements such as trust, cooperative behaviors and territorial loyalty are to be found in innovative milieux and industrial districts. A large literature describes the benefits in terms of socio-economic development derived from these specific systems (see for instance Camagni, 2004; Santagata, 2004).

Some limitations and downsides are also to be mentioned as related to the potential link between territorial identity and economic dynamics. First, the nexus with economic growth and development depends on and interacts with many other elements and it is therefore complex to generalize and abstract from the specific characteristics of the corresponding territories (Schneider et al., 2000). Besides, as highlighted in Iyer et al. (2005), multiple simultaneous effects are associated with soft elements such as territorial identity and social capital that are difficult to disentangle. In fact, innovation, happiness, cohesiveness and also health may be related to different types of territorial identity and they all might influence economic development but, at the same time, they are also interlinked and either in conflict or in line with one another. Another potential risk is related to the possibility that territorial identity becomes a rigidity and an obstacle to innovation, openness, change and evolution (see for instance Staber & Sautter, 2011; Malecki, 2012).

What further makes the reasoning more complicated is that, as Prokkola et al. (2012) argue, each place is an arena for multiple identities that often overlap and change. "*Performances of regional identity cannot be understood as separate from people's life experience and ambitions, or from the material conditions which enable them to carry out their projects*" (Prokkola et al., 2012, p. 106).

Undoubtedly, territorial identity and economic dynamics are strictly interlinked. In Chapter 5, an empirical demonstration of the association between cultural heritage and territorial identity has been provided. The following sections will be dedicated to exploring whether these two blocks of relationships (cultural heritage-territorial identity nexus and territorial identity-economic dynamics nexus) can be considered jointly. More specifically, the role of territorial identity in influencing the relationship between the endowment of cultural heritage and economic development and the functioning of this mechanism will be the focus of the next sections. A mediation mechanism will be tested in Sect. 6.3 and a synergetic mechanism will be explored in Sect. 6.4.

6.3 Cultural Heritage, Territorial Identity and Development: The Mediation Mechanism

6.3.1 Territorial Identity as a Mediator Between Cultural Heritage and Economic Development: The Empirical Strategy

This section is aimed at empirically testing the hypothesis that the relationship between tangible elements of cultural heritage and local economic development is *mediated* by territorial identity: the endowment of cultural heritage influences territorial identity which in turn affects local economic development. Besides, the different role of diverse modes of expression of territorial identity as defined and described in Chapter 4 will be explored.

The logic of this mechanism is the same as the one adopted in Chapter 3 in which the mediation role of tourism between the presence of cultural heritage and economic development has been empirically demonstrated: a structural equation model has been used to test the assumption. By using this model, two blocks of equations, reflecting two blocks of relationships, can be jointly analyzed. The first block represents the relationship between cultural heritage and territorial identity and the second one represents the relationship between territorial identity and economic development. Territorial identity is simultaneously a dependent variable (in the first block) and an explanatory variable (in the second block). Multiple relationships can in fact be tested with the adoption of a structural equation model (Nunkoo & Ramkissoon, 2012).

The following system of equations formalizes the model:

$$\Delta \text{GDPpc}_{\text{rt}} = \alpha + \beta_1 \text{territorial identity}_{r,(t-1)} + \beta_2 \text{cultural heritage}_r + \beta_3 X_{r,(t-1)} + \beta_4 \text{time fixed effects} + \beta_5 \text{regional fixed effects} + \varepsilon_{r,t} \quad (6.1)$$

$$\text{Territorial Identity}_{r,(t-1)} = \alpha + \beta_6 \text{cultural heritage}_r + \beta_7 Z_{r,(t-2)} + \beta_8 \text{time fixed effects} + \beta_9 \text{regional fixed effects} + \varepsilon_{r,(t-1)} \quad (6.2)$$

The first equation is referred to as the structural equation, while the second equation is referred to as the sub-equation. All the data are considered at NUTS2 regional level of disaggregation.

In the structural equation, the dependent variable is $\Delta GDPpc_{rt}$ that represents the GDP per capita growth rate in two distinct periods, i.e., 2014–2016, 2016–2018.

In the sub-equation, the dependent variable is $TerritorialIdentity_{r,(t-1)}$ that represents the category of territorial identity that characterizes each NUTS2 region in each period considered. Territorial identity is expressed in four different categories as defined in Sect. 4.4, namely *individualistic localism, parochial localism, place-less cosmopolitanism* and *inclusive cosmopolitanism*. For the sake of clarity, the proposed taxonomy is reported again below (Fig. 6.2).

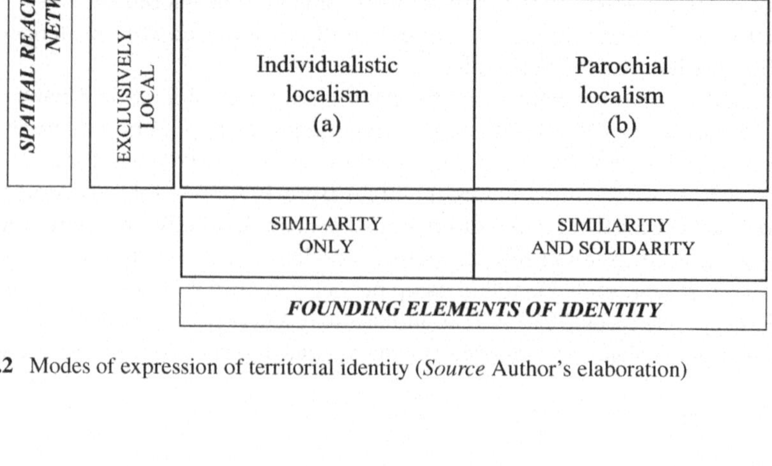

Fig. 6.2 Modes of expression of territorial identity (*Source* Author's elaboration)

The explanatory variable of interest in both the structural equation and the sub-equation is the endowment of cultural heritage. Other variables are included in the two regressions. In the structural equation, the traditional variables used to explain economic growth have been included such as the initial level of per capita GDP, human capital and innovation, population density and accessibility. In the sub-equation, several explanatory variables related to economic, social and political regional conditions have been included (the next Sect. [6.3.2] provides a detailed description of the included variables).

The choice of using a structural equation model stems from the fact that it allows to detect both direct and indirect effects of a variable of interest (in this case the endowment of cultural heritage) on a dependent variable (in this case economic development). More specifically, as explained in Kline (2015), it is presumed that an intervening or mediator variable (in this case territorial identity) transfers some of the causal effects of a prior variable to subsequent variables. In this specific case, territorial identity is assumed to be the mediator variable between cultural heritage and economic development. A heritage-related variable is specified to influence economic growth both directly and indirectly *through* territorial identity.

The following section explains the data used to perform the analysis.

6.3.2 Data

For both the variables related to territorial identity and the endowment of cultural heritage, the data used are the same described in Sect. 4.5 and in Sect. 3.2, respectively. More specifically, following the taxonomy of different modes of expression of territorial identities presented in Fig. 6.2, data gathered through the Eurobarometer surveys have been considered to classify European regions according to their specific type of territorial identity. Two Eurobarometer questions have been selected to represent and measure the dimensions expressed on the horizontal and vertical axes in the matrix for the classification of different typologies of territorial identity, namely the *founding elements of identity* and the *spatial reach of founding networks* (see Chapter 4). As explained in Sect. 4.5, since each Eurobarometer survey includes 1000 interviews per country, four Eurobarometer surveys have been considered jointly in order to have a more representative sample.

The following steps have been undertaken to assign a typology of territorial identity to each European NUTS2 region (as already reported in Sect. 4.5):

1) For each of the selected Eurobarometer questions, the individual answers in four Eurobarometer rounds have been grouped.
2) Each individual answer has been assigned to the corresponding European NUTS2 region according to the information provided by the Eurobarometer surveys.
3) For each NUTS2 region and for each question considered, the average of individual answers in four Eurobarometer rounds has been computed.

4) For each country and for each considered question, the average of individual answers in the same four Eurobarometer rounds has been computed.
5) For each considered question, a class (corresponding to one of the four identified typologies of territorial identity as explained in Fig. 4.1) has been assigned to each NUTS2 region resulting from a comparison between the regional average value and the national average value.

The following figure (Fig. 6.3) graphically shows the method of the territorial identity's categories assignment comparing the regional average values with the national average value.

As per the variable measuring the endowment of cultural heritage, it is the same followed throughout the entire work (see Sect. 3.3).

Going back to Eq. (6.1) and (6.2), the starting point of the analysis is a standard growth regression model (see Barro and Sala i Martin, 2004), the structural equation and the sub-equation include regressors explaining growth (among which territorial identity and cultural heritage) and regressors explaining territorial identity (including cultural heritage).

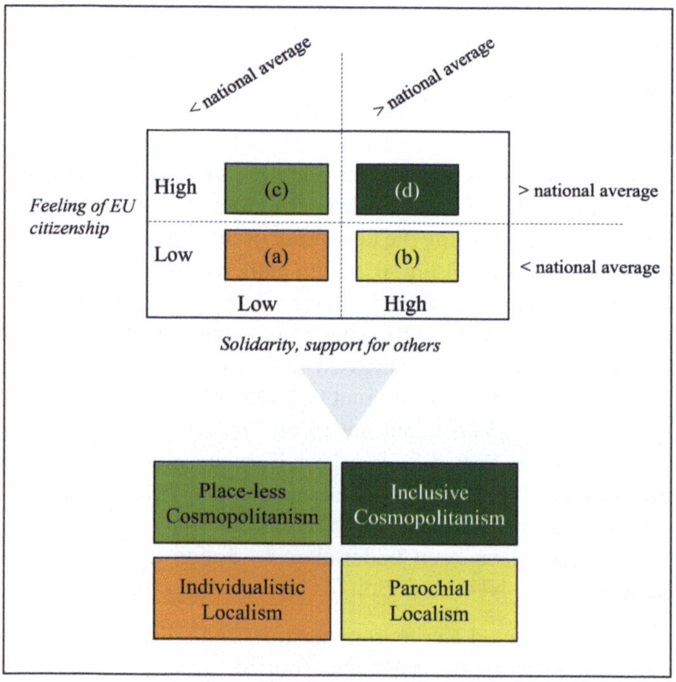

Fig. 6.3 Method of territorial identity categories assignment to European NUTS2 regions

Regarding the structural equation (Eq. [6.1]), other variables have been considered that, according to the literature, explain GDP per capita growth rate. A set of explanatory variables ($X_{r,(t-1)}$) has been added, including the main factors usually included in standard growth regression models and, whenever possible, they have been one year lagged to support the causality direction. The following list summarizes the included explanatory variables:

- the *initial level of per capita GDP*. The variable is included to check for the initial level of wealth and is expected to be associated with a negative coefficient in the presence of a regional convergence process (see for instance Barro and Sala i Martin, 1992; Temple, 1999).
- *Human capital*—measured as the share of graduates over active population—and *Innovation*—measured as the number of patents applications per resident. As well explained in Camagni and Capello (2009) because of the *hypermobility* that currently marks the traditional production factors, i.e., capital and labor, regional development is nowadays highly reliant on other place-specific and more intangible factors such as skills, innovation, cultural elements and, in general terms, knowledge. We therefore included in the structural growth equation a variable proxying human capital accounting for regional accumulation of knowledge and a variable proxying innovation or technological capital (for human capital see, among others, Lucas, 1988; Barro, 2001; for innovation and technological capital see Fagerberg et al., 1997; Rodríguez-Pose & Crescenzi, 2008).
- *Population density* and *accessibility*. The demographic structure of a region together with physical accessibility surely influences regional growth (as per the relationship between population density and growth see for instance Ciccone & Hall, 1996; see Caragliu et al., 2011 for the role of accessibility). However, the casual direction is uncertain: on the one hand urbanization economies and higher endowment of infrastructure allow innovation and knowledge to spread and transmission mechanisms can be fostered (Parr, 2002). On the other hand, congestion and crowding out effects might arise, leading to negative consequences.
- *Quality of Government* controls for the efficient functioning of public institutions.
- *Tourist Attractiveness* has been taken into account to confirm the importance of tourism as a relevant sector for economic development for European regions.
- *Population* is included to control for possible size effects as well as the share of employment in manufacturing to take into account the *industrial structure.*

As per the sub-equation in which territorial identity is the dependent variable, the explanatory variable of interest is the one related to cultural heritage. Other variables have been included ($Z_{r,(t-2)}$) to consider other factors potentially explaining territorial identity. The control variables that have been added are the ones reported in Table 5.2 in Sect. 5.4.2. Since the average regional values of territorial identity are here taken into considerations (and not the individual data as in Chapter 5), all the explanatory variables are expressed as regional values. More specifically, for each considered period, the regional average has been calculated for the variables gathered from the Eurobarometer surveys, originally available at the individual level.

The following table (Table 6.2) summarizes the included variables for both the structural equation and the sub-equation:

Table 6.2 Structural Equation Model (cultural heritage, identity, economic development): List of explanatory variables for the empirical analysis

Variable name	*Description*	*Year(s)*	*Source*
Structural Equation (1)			
GDP per capita growth rate (dependent variable)	Measure of economic growth: average annual GDP per capita growth at constant 2005 prices	2014–2016 2016–2018	EUROSTAT
Territorial identity	Categorical variable declined in four categories corresponding to *individualistic localism, parochial localism, place-less cosmopolitanism* and *inclusive cosmopolitanism*	Avg values between 2012 and 2016; Avg values between 2017 and 2018	Eurobarometer surveys (77.3; 82.3; 84.3; 86.2; 87.3; 88.3; 89.1; 90.3)
Cultural Heritage	Measure of the endowment of tangible forms of cultural heritage: regional number of monuments per square kilometer standardized by country	2003	ESPON
GDP per capita	Measure of regional wealth: GDP per capita at current prices	2013 2015	EUROSTAT
Arrivals per capita	Measure of regional tourism demand: number of arrivals per inhabitant	2013 2015	EUROSTAT
Human Capital	Share of population with tertiary education per active population	2013 2015	EUROSTAT
Population Density	Measure of urbanization/agglomeration economies. Dummy = 1 if at least one metropolitan area is present in the region	2013 2015	EUROSTAT
Innovation	Number of patent applications to the EPO per resident	2010 2012	EUROSTAT
Population	Measure of regional economy size	2013 2015	EUROSTAT
Accessibility	Measure of regional accessibility and infrastructure endowment: composite indicator of regional accessibility integrating different modes of transport (air, road and rail)	2006	ESPON

(continued)

Table 6.2 (continued)

Variable name	*Description*	*Year(s)*	*Source*
Quality of government	Composite indicator including core features of Quality of Government (impartiality, bureaucratic, quality and corruption) as well as measures that are broader (rule of law and transparency)	2010 2017	University of Gothenburg
Capital city	Dummy = 1 if the region includes the country capital city		
Industrial structure	Share of employment in manufacturing over active population	2013 2015	EUROSTAT
Sub-Equation (2)			
Territorial identity (dependent variable)	Categorical variable declined in four categories corresponding to *individualistic localism, parochial localism, place-less cosmopolitanism* and *inclusive cosmopolitanism*	Avg values between 2012 and 2016; Avg values between 2017 and 2018	Eurobarometer surveys (77.3; 82.3; 84.3; 86.2; 87.3; 88.3; 89.1; 90.3)
Cultural Heritage	Measure of the endowment of tangible forms of cultural heritage: regional number of monuments per square kilometer standardized by country	2003	ESPON
Quality of government	Composite indicator including core features of Quality of Government (impartiality, bureaucratic, quality and corruption) as well as measures that are broader (rule of law and transparency)	2010 2017	University of Gothenburg
GDP per capita	Measure of regional wealth: GDP per capita at current	2012 2014	EUROSTAT
Human Capital	Share of population with tertiary education per active population	2012 2014	EUROSTAT

(continued)

Table 6.2 (continued)

Variable name	*Description*	*Year(s)*	*Source*
Population Density	Measure of urbanization/agglomeration economies. Number of metropolitan areas	2012 2014	EUROSTAT
Innovation	Number of patent applications to the EPO per resident	2010 2012	EUROSTAT
Arrivals per capita	Measure of regional tourism demand: number of arrivals per inhabitant	2012 2014	EUROSTAT
Ethnolinguistic Fractionalization	Measure of diversity within each region The index has been calculated as follows: $ELF = 1 - \sum_i s_i^2$ where s_i is the share of the citizenship group i over the total population (see Alesina and La Ferrara, 2005) The available citizenship groups are: European Union foreign countries European foreign countries African countries North American countries Other American countries Asian countries Oceania countries Other countries	2011	Eurostat Census data
Economic expectations at the country level	A scale from 1 to 3 has been created corresponding to the following Eurobarometer question: "*What are your expectations for the next twelve months: will the next twelve months be better, worse or the same, when it comes to the economic situation of your country?*" 1 corresponds to *worse* 2 corresponds to *same* 3 corresponds to *better*	Avg values between 2012 and 2016; Avg values between 2017 and 2018	Eurobarometer

(continued)

Table 6.2 (continued)

Variable name	*Description*	*Year(s)*	*Source*
Occupation	Dummy equal to 1 if the respondent is self-employed Dummy equal to 1 if the respondent is a manager/professional Dummy equal to 1 if the respondent is a white collar Dummy equal to 1 if the respondent is a manual worker Dummy equal to 1 if the respondent is a house person Dummy equal to 1 if the respondent is unemployed Dummy equal to 1 if the respondent is retired Dummy equal to 1 if the respondent is a Student	Avg values between 2012 and 2016; Avg values between 2017 and 2018	Eurobarometer
Job-related personal expectations	A scale from 1 to 3 has been created corresponding to the following Eurobarometer question: "*What are your expectations for the next twelve months: will the next twelve months be better, worse or the same, when it comes to your personal job situation?*" 1 corresponds to *worse* 2 corresponds to *same* 3 corresponds to *better*	Avg values between 2012 and 2016; Avg values between 2017 and 2018	Eurobarometer
Perception of inclusiveness of the EU	Dummy equal to 1 if the respondent indicated *cultural identity* as an answer to the following question: "*What does EU mean to you personally?*"	Avg values between 2012 and 2016; Avg values between 2017 and 2018	Eurobarometer

(continued)

Table 6.2 (continued)

Variable name	*Description*	*Year(s)*	*Source*
Perception of loss of cultural identity due to EU	Dummy equal to 1 if the respondent indicated *loss of cultural identity* as an answer to the following question: "*What does EU mean to you personally?*"	Avg values between 2012 and 2016; Avg values between 2017 and 2018	Eurobarometer
Trust in political parties	Dummy variable equal to 1 if the respondent answered *tend to trust* to the following question: "*I would like to ask you a question about how much trust you have in certain institutions. Please tell me if you tend to trust or tend not to trust political parties*"	Avg values between 2012 and 2016; Avg values between 2017 and 2018	Eurobarometer
Solidarity with poorer regions	Dummy equal to 1 if the respondent indicated *Solidarity with poorer region* as an answer to the following question: "*In your opinion among the following issues, which are those that most create a feeling of community among European citizens?*"	Avg values between 2012 and 2016; Avg values between 2017 and 2018	Eurobarometer
Satisfaction with the national democracy	A scale from 1 to 4 has been created corresponding to the following Eurobarometer question: "*On the whole, are you very satisfied, fairly satisfied, not very satisfied or not at all satisfied with the way democracy work in your country?*" 1 corresponds to *not at all satisfied* 2 corresponds to *not very satisfied* 3 corresponds to *fairly satisfied* 4 corresponds to *very satisfied*	Avg values between 2012 and 2016; Avg values between 2017 and 2018	Eurobarometer

(continued)

Table 6.2 (continued)

Variable name	*Description*	*Year(s)*	*Source*
Satisfaction with the EU democracy	A scale from 1 to 4 has been created corresponding to the following Eurobarometer question: "*On the whole, are you very satisfied, fairly satisfied, not very satisfied or not at all satisfied with the way democracy work in the EU?*" 1 corresponds to *not at all satisfied* 2 corresponds to *not very satisfied* 3 corresponds to *fairly satisfied* 4 corresponds to *very satisfied*	Avg values between 2012 and 2016; Avg values between 2017 and 2018	Eurobarometer
Political self-placement	A scale from 1 to 10 has been created corresponding to the following question: "*In political matters people talk of "the left" and "the right". How would you place your views on this scale?*" where 1 indicates extreme left and 10 indicates extreme right	Avg values between 2012 and 2016; Avg values between 2017 and 2018	Eurobarometer
Perception of personal political relevance in EU matters	A scale from 1 to 4 has been created corresponding to the following question: "*Please tell me to what extent you agree or disagree with the following statement: my voice counts in the EU: totally agree, tend to agree, tend to disagree, totally disagree*" 1 corresponds to *totally disagree* 2 corresponds to *tend to disagree* 3 corresponds to *tend to agree* 4 corresponds to *totally agree*	Avg values between 2012 and 2016; Avg values between 2017 and 2018	Eurobarometer

(continued)

Table 6.2 (continued)

Variable name	*Description*	*Year(s)*	*Source*
Age	Age of the respondent	Avg values between 2012 and 2016; Avg values between 2017 and 2018	Eurobarometer
Gender: Female	Dummy equal to 1 if the respondent is a woman	Avg values between 2012 and 2016; Avg values between 2017 and 2018	Eurobarometer
Rural Area	Dummy equal to 1 if the respondent declares to leave in a rural area or village	Avg values between 2012 and 2016; Avg values between 2017 and 2018	Eurobarometer

The following section reports the results of the empirical analysis.

6.3.3 Empirical Results

The empirical results are presented in a synthetic graphical way focusing on the main variables of interest (endowment of cultural heritage, territorial identity and economic development). Consistently with Chapter 5, the baseline category of territorial identity is *individualistic localism.* The structural equation model is applied to 260 European NUTS2 regions in two periods of time. The parameters indicated in Eq. (6.1) and (6.2) are estimated through a linear maximum likelihood estimation. The following figure (Fig. 6.4) schematically reports the results of the model:

As evident from the reported results, the assumption related to the potential mediating role of territorial identity between cultural heritage and local economic growth is not empirically validated. The only statistically significant relationship in the one between tangible elements of cultural heritage and place-less cosmopolitanism type of identity, with respect to individualistic localism. This result confirms the one obtained in Chapter 5. The endowment of cultural heritage influences the dimension of *spatial reach of founding networks* but, the sheer presence of heritage sites is not sufficient to stimulate solidarity. In fact, the endowment of cultural heritage does not show any statistically significant relationship with *parochial localism* and *inclusive cosmopolitanism* with respect to *individualistic localism.* Furthermore, neither a

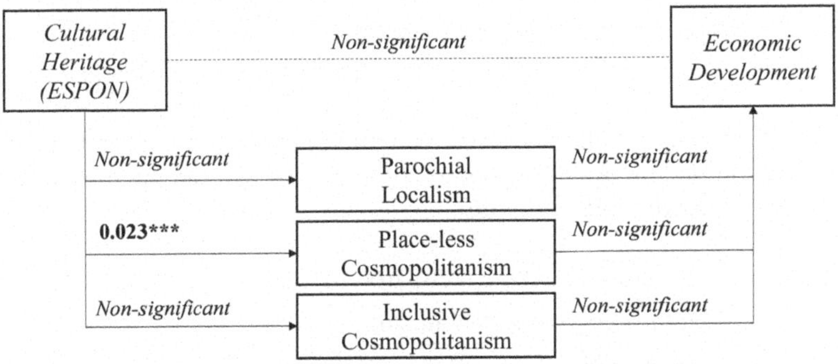

Fig. 6.4 The mediation role of territorial identity between cultural heritage and economic development: the standardized coefficients

direct effect between the presence of cultural heritage and regional economic development nor a causality nexus between the typologies of territorial identity and economic development have been detected.

It can be therefore argued that territorial identity does not function as a mediator element between the endowment of cultural heritage and local economic development. The following section will be devoted at exploring the validity of an alternative hypothesis about the role of territorial identity: a synergy mechanism with other context variables at work.

6.4 Cultural Heritage, Territorial Identity and Economic Development: The Synergy Logical Mechanism

6.4.1 The Empirical Strategy and Data

Having empirically rejected the assumption of a mediation role for territorial identity in the relationship between the endowment of cultural heritage and economic development, this section is aimed at empirically testing the functioning of a synergy role. More specifically, two hypotheses will be tested:

1) tangible elements of cultural heritage are able to influence economic development across European regions;
2) this role played by cultural heritage is influenced by the typology of territorial identity that characterizes the region in which heritage sites are located.

More specifically a traditional growth model will be used here, augmented by heritage-related and territorial-identity-related variables and, most importantly, by their interactions. A standard growth regression model (see for instance Barro and Sala i Martin, 2004) has been applied to 260 European NUTS2 regions in two periods of time (the same described in Sect. 6.3). The empirical model used to test the first assumption takes the following form:

$$\Delta\mathrm{GDP}_{\mathrm{pc}_{\mathrm{rt}}} = \alpha + \beta_1 \text{cultural heritage}_{\mathrm{r}} + \beta_2 \mathrm{X}_{\mathrm{r},(\mathrm{t}-1)} + \beta_3 \text{time fixed effects} + \beta_4 \text{regional fixed effects} + \varepsilon_{\mathrm{rt}} \quad (6.3)$$

To test the second hypothesis interaction terms between heritage endowment and the various identified modes of expression of territorial identity have been included and the model takes the following form:

$$\begin{aligned}\Delta\mathrm{GDP}_{\mathrm{pc}_{\mathrm{rt}}} = {} & \alpha + \beta_1 \text{cultural heritage}_{\mathrm{r}} + \beta_2 \text{parochial localism}_{\mathrm{r}(\mathrm{t}-1)} \\ & + \beta_3 \text{placeless cosmopolitanism}_{\mathrm{r}(\mathrm{t}-1)} \\ & + \beta_4 \text{inclusive cosmopolitanism}_{\mathrm{r}(\mathrm{t}-1)} \\ & + \beta_5 \text{parochial localism}_{\mathrm{r}(\mathrm{t}-1)} * \text{cultural heritage}_{\mathrm{r}} \\ & + \beta_6 \text{placeless cosmopolitanism}_{\mathrm{r}(\mathrm{t}-1)} * \text{cultural heritage}_{\mathrm{r}} \\ & + \beta_7 \text{inclusive cosmopolitanism}_{\mathrm{r}(\mathrm{t}-1)} * \text{cultural heritage}_{\mathrm{r}} + \beta_8 \mathrm{X}_{\mathrm{r},(\mathrm{t}-1)} \\ & + \beta_9 \text{time fixed effects} + \beta_{10} \text{regional fixed effects} + \varepsilon_{\mathrm{rt}} \quad (6.4)\end{aligned}$$

where $\Delta GDPpc_{rt}$ is the regional GDP per capita growth rate in two different periods i.e., 2014–2016, 2016–2018. A set of explanatory variables ($X_{r,(t-1)}$) is added to the model in order to include the standard regressors for growth together with time and regional fixed effects (see for instance Temple, 1999 and Barro, 1997). All the explanatory variables (whenever possible and when not time-fixed) have been one-year lagged with respect to the first year of each growth period.

The independent variables of interest are the ones related to cultural heritage endowment and the interactions between the heritage variable and the modes of existence of territorial identity, taking *individualistic localism* as the category of reference. Since the variable of interest is time invariant the adopted model is a random-effects model and regional fixed effects at Nuts1 level have been included[1] together with time fixed effects.

Following the literature aimed at explaining regional growth, other categories of explanatory variables have been added to the equations. As argued by Camagni and Capello (2009), traditional factors such as labor and capital are no longer the only and most fundamental ones and nowadays are highly mobile. Other place-based resources are instead relevant within the context of modern regional development models such as innovation capacity, competencies and knowledge. Therefore, different typologies of regressors have been included in the empirical analysis such as the initial level of per capita GDP (to check for possible cumulative effects); human capital and innovation (in order to take into account intangible factors such as skills, cultural elements and, in general terms, knowledge); population density and accessibility; quality of government (to consider the efficiency of regional public institutions); tourist attractiveness (consistently with the rest of the book); the industrial structure of the region, the presence of the capital city in the region, and population (to control

[1] The results are consistent using a pooled OLS with regional fixed effects at Nuts1 level.

for size effects). The included regressors are the same as the ones used in the structural equation and presented in Sect. 6.3.

6.4.2 Empirical Results

The following table (Table 6.3) reports the results of the empirical analysis.

Model (1) includes the factors that are traditionally and usually considered as determinants of regional growth together with the variable measuring cultural heritage. As expected, the higher the degree of human capital, the greater the regional economic growth. The initial level of GDP per capita is instead negatively associated with regional growth of GDP per capita indicating that, on average, there is a catching up process by less wealthy regions. Population density is also negatively associated with GDP per capita growth rate indicating that less agglomerated areas grow more than others. Interestingly the coefficient associated with cultural heritage is positive and significant meaning that higher amount of cultural heritage corresponds to greater regional economic growth.

Model (2) adds the variable measuring tourism attractiveness in terms of number of tourist arrivals per capita. By introducing this variable, the coefficient associated with cultural heritage is no longer statistically significant and, on the contrary, the coefficient associated with the number of tourist arrivals is positive and statistically significant. This means that, in the previous specification, the positive and significant effect of the coefficient associated with the endowment of tangible forms of heritage was mainly driven by the touristic attractiveness stemming from the presence of cultural heritage. Therefore, the first hypothesis according to which cultural heritage per se plays a role in regional economic development is rejected. The positive economic effect of the presence of cultural heritage passes through the channel of tourism attractiveness which is confirmed as the main mechanism at work.

Models (3), (4) and (5) introduce the interaction terms between cultural heritage and the typologies of territorial identity in order to test the second hypothesis.

Model (3) introduces both the alternative modes of expression of territorial identity and their interactions with tangible forms of cultural heritage. The category *individualistic localism* is taken as a reference. As evident from the results, none of the typologies of territorial identity is statistically significant per se nor the heritage-related variable. The interactions between cultural heritage and *parochial localism, place-less cosmopolitanism* and *inclusive-cosmopolitanism* typologies are instead positive and significant. This result seems to suggest that cultural heritage is beneficial for regional economic growth if activated by all these three modes of expression of territorial identity with respect to *individualistic localism*. However, in order to interpret the coefficients correctly, marginal effects should be calculated. The following table (Table 6.4) reports the marginal effects of cultural heritage on regional GDP growth in the four typologies of territorial identity:

As evident from the table, cultural heritage expresses its positive impact on regional economic growth only in contexts characterized by cosmopolitan types of

Table 6.3 The synergy logical mechanism: Regression results

	(1)	(2)	(3)	(4)	(5)
VARIABLES					
GDP per capita	−0.689*** (0.259)	−0.833*** (0.252)	−0.828*** (0.261)	−0.780*** (0.270)	−0.782*** (0.270)
Human capital	0.326*** (0.113)	0.352*** (0.112)	0.297** (0.122)	0.286** (0.122)	0.289** (0.124)
Innovation	0.011 (0.042)	0.063 (0.045)	0.077* (0.045)	0.050 (0.043)	0.048 (0.044)
Multimodal Accessibility	0.102 (0.083)	0.151* (0.087)	0.172* (0.088)	0.144* (0.087)	0.145 (0.089)
Population Density	−0.118* (0.070)	−0.100 (0.079)	−0.118 (0.076)	−0.134* (0.077)	−0.131* (0.078)
Population	0.004 (0.037)	0.041 (0.036)	0.036 (0.037)	−0.097 (0.063)	−0.102 (0.067)
Cultural Heritage (Monuments)	0.020*** (0.006)	0.009 (0.007)	−0.026 (0.017)	−0.024 (0.017)	−0.024 (0.017)
Capital City	−0.115 (0.203)	−0.126 (0.197)	−0.182 (0.201)	−0.194 (0.200)	−0.186 (0.204)
Number of tourist arrivals per capita		0.156*** (0.049)	0.153*** (0.050)		
2._Parochial Localism			−0.072 (0.105)	−0.075 (0.105)	−0.073 (0.106)
3._Place-less Cosmopolitanism			−0.077 (0.100)	−0.081 (0.102)	−0.082 (0.103)
4._Inclusive Cosmopolitanism			0.003 (0.116)	0.003 (0.121)	0.003 (0.124)
2._Parochial Localism*Cultural Heritage			0.066* (0.037)	0.066* (0.035)	0.065* (0.037)
3._Place-less Cosmopolitanism*Cultural Heritage			0.043** (0.018)	0.043** (0.018)	0.044** (0.018)
4._Inclusive Cosmopolitanism*Cultural Heritage			0.077** (0.033)	0.075** (0.034)	0.073** (0.035)
Tourist Arrivals				0.250* (0.144)	0.260* (0.149)
Tourist Arrivals Squared				−0.156 (0.147)	−0.163 (0.150)
Quality of government					−0.006 (0.125)
Industrial Structure					0.015 (0.064)

(continued)

Table 6.3 (continued)

	(1)	(2)	(3)	(4)	(5)
Regional Fixed Effects	Yes	Yes	Yes	Yes	Yes
Time Fixed Effects	Yes	Yes	Yes	Yes	Yes
Constant	−0.220 (0.151)	−0.239 (0.175)	−0.227 (0.179)	−0.210 (0.169)	−0.207 (0.190)
Observations	520	520	510[2]	510	510
Number of nuts2_code	260	260	255	255	255
R-sq between	0.84	0.85	0.85	0.84	0.84
Robust standard errors in parentheses					
**** p < 0.01, ** p < 0.05, * p < 0.1*					

Table 6.4 Marginal Effects of tangible forms of cultural heritage on GDP per capita growth rate in the four typologies of territorial identity from speficiation (3)

	Model (3)
Individualistic Localism	−0.026 (0.017)
Parochial Localism	0.041 (0.033)
Place-less Cosmopolitanism	0.017** (0.007)
Inclusive Cosmopolitanism	0.051* (0.027)
Robust standard errors in parentheses; *** p < 0.01, ** p < 0.05, * p < 0.1	

territorial identity both place-less and inclusive. This result is highly interesting because it empirically confirms that cultural heritage and territorial identity do interact and generate synergies which are beneficial for regional economic development. The relationship between tangible forms of cultural heritage and local economic dynamics is not neutral to the typology of territorial identity: in fact, a *cosmopolitan* type of territorial identity is needed to trigger the role of built heritage as a catalyst for economic development. Places characterized by open mindsets, international habits and curiosity beyond the borders are more capable to valorize cultural heritage as an engine for growth, particularly when these attitudes are accompanied by solidarity sentiments (in fact the magnitude of the coefficient associated with cultural heritage in inclusive cosmopolitan regions is higher than the one in place-less cosmopolitan regions). On the other hand, territories characterized by individual localism and parochial localism seem to lack the ability to enjoy the full potentialities of their cultural heritage. The simultaneous presence of a wider spatial reach of founding network and high levels of solidarity represents the best condition for

[2] Note that Eurobarometer data related to territorial identity as measured through the taxonomy are not available for the following NUTS2 codes: EL41, EL42, EL62, FI20, FR83, PT20, PT30.

cultural heritage to be valued as an effective economic resource. Open-minded and inclusive attitudes might reflect higher attractiveness and forward-looking strategies, and solidarity could generate a deeply rooted acknowledgment of cultural heritage as a common good. All this may contribute to generate an environment in which inhabitants are supportive to valorization and conservation strategies reducing free riding risks usually associated with common goods. All the sectors related to the value-chain activated by the presence of cultural heritage (such as, for instance, archaeology, architecture, real estate and construction) function in a more effective way if embedded in environments characterized by cosmopolitan mindsets that valorize cultural heritage in a way that is beneficial also for the local economic conditions. By caring, respecting and managing cultural heritage through constructive, effective and forward-looking practices, the positive economic consequences of all the economic activities associated with the presence of cultural heritage are well-exploited.

In Model (4), the variable accounting for tourism is substituted by the absolute number of tourist arrivals and the squared value of this variable is also included. By introducing these variables, the coefficient associated with cultural heritage is no longer statistically significant (as in Model (1)) and, on the contrary, the coefficient associated with the number of tourist arrivals is positive and statistically significant. It is worth here noting that the number of tourist arrivals might not have a linear relationship with economic growth: even though not statistically significant, the coefficient associated with the squared number of arrivals is negative. This seems to suggest that up to a certain level the arrival of tourists is beneficial for local economies but, once a certain threshold is exceeded, the effect could no longer be positive. Some further dedicated research is needed to explore this issue.

Model (5) further adds some other control variables in order to check for the stability of the results: the quality of government and the industrial structure are included as regressors.

Both Model (4) and Model (5) confirm the results obtained in Model (3) with respect to the synergies between cultural heritage and modes of expression of territorial identity. The following table (Table 6.5) reports the marginal effects of cultural

Table 6.5 Marginal Effects of tangible forms of cultural heritage on GDP per capita growth rate in the four typologies of territorial identity from specification (4) and (5)

	Model (4)	*Model (5)*
Individualistic Localism	−0.024 (0.017)	−0.024 (0.017)
Parochial Localism	0.042 (0.032)	0.041 (0.033)
Place-less Cosmopolitanism	0.021** (0.008)	0.021*** (0.008)
Inclusive Cosmopolitanism	0.051* (0.029)	0.051* (0.031)

Robust standard errors in parentheses; *** $p < 0.01$, ** $p < 0.05$, * $p < 0.1$

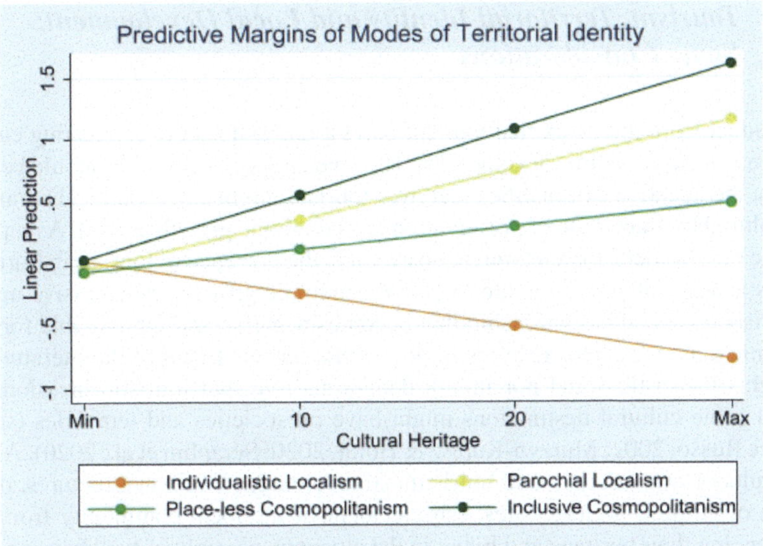

Fig. 6.5 Marginal Effects of tangible forms of cultural heritage on GDP per capita growth rate in the four typologies of territorial identity

heritage on regional GDP growth in different identitarian contexts as obtained in Model (4) and (5).

The following Figure (Fig. 6.5) graphically represents the results by showing the relationship between tangible cultural heritage and regional economic growth predicted by the model in the four typologies of territorial identities. As evident, individualistic localism does not enable cultural heritage as a catalyst for local economic growth. The marginal effects associated with cultural heritage in areas characterized by individualistic localism are negative. However, no statistical significance is associated with this coefficient. Even though the marginal effects of cultural heritage when embedded in areas characterized by parochial localism is positive, also in this case it is not statistically significant. On the contrary, the marginal effects of cultural heritage on GDP per capita growth rate are positive and statistically significant both in areas characterized by place-less and inclusive cosmopolitanism. Furthermore, these positive relationships increase as the endowment of tangible heritage increases.

As evident from Fig. 6.5, the effects are much higher in inclusive cosmopolitan areas which are the ones that best valorize their cultural heritage as an engine for local development.

It has to be noted that an effective step forward for further improve the empirical analysis might be the use of a multi-level model so that potential endogeneity issues would be better controlled by separating the effects stemming from the nature, essence and inclination of regions and the ones deriving from territorial identity.

6.4.3 Tourism, Territorial Identity and Local Development: Some Considerations

It is evident from this work that tourism plays a relevant role in connecting cultural heritage to local economic development. However, a special attention should be dedicated at the negative externalities that over-tourism might cause on local communities, cultural heritage state of preservation and economic growth as well. As reported in Table 6.3 (Model 2), even though, on average, the presence of tourists in European regions is associated with greater regional economic growth, an excessive number of tourists reverse the relationship that becomes negative and unfavorable for local economic dynamics. This result is in line with a recent stream of the literature that highlights the critical and potentially dangerous role that touristic invasions that interest some cultural destinations might have on societies and territories (see for instance Russo, 2002; Murzyn-Kupisz & Holuj, 2020; Séraphin et al., 2020). Among the results of over-tourism and touristification, changes in urban structures, deterioration of cultural heritage sites, estrangement of the local community from both experiencing their heritage and living in the city centers might as well have negative consequences on economic development (see Chapter 2).

As mentioned both in Chapters 2, 4 and 5, experiences of massive tourism might contribute to attitudes and feelings of the residents pushing them towards psychological closure and more individualistic behaviors. Feeling of solidarity, openness and cosmopolitanism might be undermined by over-tourism phenomena that instead could favor inward-looking and reluctant psychological attitudes towards welcoming and trust the others. Among the identified four typologies of territorial identity, *individualistic localism* does not present positive synergies with cultural heritage that benefit local economic dynamics and, at the same time, it is quite impacted by the presence of tourists. As highlighted in Kebir and Crevoisier (2008, p. 1203), on the one hand cultural resources and heritage can represent relevant economic stimuli; however, the excessive exploitation of these assets as touristic attractions might transform them into "*folkloric spectacle*". Dysneyfication and commodification phenomena could cause the loss and damage of that very same cultural heritage and cultural legacy.

Therefore, even though it is not strictly related to the objectives of this work, the potential negative effects of mass cultural tourism both on economic development and territorial identity should be taken into account and further examined.

6.5 Conclusions

This chapter was aimed at conceptually and empirically exploring the idea that the socio-cultural relationships that tie cultural heritage and territorial identity do not end up influencing social and cultural domains only. In fact, positive spillovers can also appear on the economic sphere.

The empirical analysis did not support a first hypothesis that identitarian elements might play a mediation role between (tangible) cultural heritage and local development but has fully supported the alternative hypothesis that these identitarian context elements synergistically reinforce the role of cultural heritage in promoting growth. Different typologies of local identity lead to different outcomes, though if cultural heritage is located in a territory characterized by forms of cosmopolitanism, its role as an engine for local economic development is fully recognized, validated and effectively functioning. This effect is particularly present in the last typology of territorial identity, namely inclusive cosmopolitanism. Awareness of a certain coincidence between individual and collective interests together with a stronger feeling of European citizenship represent the most favorable conditions for a valorization of local cultural heritage.

At evidence, merging cosmopolitanism and solidarity may generate positive preconditions for local attractiveness and the appropriate mentalities and capabilities for the conservation and valorization of cultural heritage. In this sense, it can follow that tangible elements of cultural heritage need to be "activated" through effective management, conservation and valorization activities to achieve both socio-cultural and economic results. Local economic development can be fostered by the presence of cultural heritage in those places where local stakeholders and the local community get involved and open-minded and flexible attitudes prevail.

References

Backman, M., & Nilsson P. (2018). The role of cultural heritage in attracting skilled individuals. *Journal of Cultural Economics, 42*, 111–138.

Barro, R. J. (Ed.). (1997). *Determinants of economic growth: A cross-country empirical study*. The MIT Press.

Barro, R. J. (2001). Human capital and growth. *American Economic Review, 91*(2), 12–17.

Barro R. J., & Sala i Martin X. (1992). Convergence. *Journal of Political Economy, 100*(2), 223–251.

Barro R. J., & Sala i Martin X. (Eds.) (2004). Economic growth. The MIT Press.

Bourdieu P. (1983). Ökonomisches Kapital, kulturelles Kapital, soziales Kapital. In Kreckel (Ed.), *Soziale Ungleichheiten*. Soziale Welt, Sonderband 2.

Bowitz E., & Ibenholdt K. (2009). Economic impacts of cultural heritage – research and perspectives. *Journal of Cultural Heritage, 10*, 1–8.

Camagni R. (2004). Uncertainty, social capital and community governance: The city as a milieu. *Contributions to Economic Analysis, 266*, 121–149.

Camagni, R. (2019). Territorial capital and regional development: Theoretical insights and appropriate policies. In R. Capello & P. Nijkamp (Eds.), *Handbook of regional growth and development theories – Revised and extended* (2nd ed., pp. 124–148). Edward Elgar.

Camagni, R., & Capello, R. (2009). Knowledge-based economy and knowledge creation: The role of space. In U. Fratesi & L. Senn (Eds.), *Growth and innovation of competitive regions* (pp. 145–165). Springer.

Capello, R., & Perucca, G. (2017). Cultural capital and local development nexus: Does the local environment matter? In H. Shibusawa, K. Sakurai, T. Mizunoya, & S. Uchida (Eds.), *Socioeconomic environmental policies and evaluations in regional science – Essays in Honor of Yoshiro Higano* (pp. 103–124). Springer.

Caragliu, A., Del Bo, C., & Nijkamp, P. (2011). Smart cities in Europe. *Journal of Urban Technology, 18*(2), 65–82.
Cerisola, S. (2019a). A new perspective on the cultural heritage-development nexus: The role of creativity. *Journal of Cultural Economics, 43*(1), 21–56.
Cerisola, S. (2019b). *Cultural heritage*. Edward Elgar Publishing Limited.
Ciccone, A., & Hall, R. (1996). Productivity and the density of economic activity. *American Economic Review, 86*(1), 54–70.
Coleman, J. S. (1990). *Foundations of social theory*. The Belknap Press.
Fagerberg, J., Verspagen, B., & Caniëls, M. (1997). Technology, growth and unemployment across European regions. *Regional Studies, 31*(5), 457–466.
Guiso L, Sapienza P., & Zingales L. (2007). Social capital as good culture. *Journal of the European Economic Association, 6*(2–3), 295–320.
Iyer, S., Kitson, M., & Toh, B. (2005). Social capital, economic growth and regional development. *Regional Studies, 39*(8), 1015–1040.
Kebir, L., & Crevoisier, O. (2008). Cultural resources and regional development: The case of the cultural legacy of watchmaking. *European Planning Studies, 16*(9), 1189–1205.
Kline, R. B. (Ed.). (2015). *Principles and practice of structural equation modeling* (4th ed.). The Guilford Press.
Lazrak F., Nijkamp P., Rietveld P., & Rouwendal J. (2014). The market value of cultural heritage in urban areas: an application of spatial hedonic pricing. *Journal of Geographical Systems, 16*, 89–114.
Lucas, R., Jr. (1988). On the mechanics of economic development. *Journal of Monetary Economics, 22*(1), 3–42.
Malecki, E. J. (2012). Regional social capital: Why it matters. *Regional Studies, 46*(8), 1023–1039.
Murzyn-Kupisz M., & Holuj D. (2020). Museums and coping with overtourism. *Sustainability, 12*, 2054.
Nunkoo, R., & Ramkissoon, H. (2012). Structural equation modelling and regression analysis in tourism research. *Current Issues in Tourism, 15*(8), 777–802.
Parr, J. B. (2002). Agglomeration economies: Ambiguities and confusions. *Environment and Planning a: Economy and Space, 34*(4), 717–731.
Patuelli, R., Mussoni, M., & Candela, G. (2013). The effects of World Heritage Sites on domestic tourism: A spatial interaction model for Italy. *Journal of Geographical Systems, 15*(3), 369–402.
Prokkola, E., Zimmerbauer, K., & Jakola, F. (2012). Performance of regional identity in the implementation of European cross-border initiatives. *European Urban and Regional Studies, 22*(1), 104–117.
Putnam, R. D., Leonardi, R., & Nanetti, R. Y. (Eds.). (1993). *Making democracy work: Civic traditions in modern Italy*. Princeton University Press.
Rodríguez-Pose, A., & Crescenzi, R. (2008). Research and development, spillovers, innovation systems, and the genesis of regional growth in Europe. *Regional Studies, 42*(1), 51–67.
Russo, A. P. (2002). The "vicious cycle" of tourism development in heritage cities. *Annals of Tourism Research, 29*(1), 165–182.
Santagata W. (2004). Cultural Districts and Economic Development, Working Paper No. 01/2004, Dipartimento di Economia "S. Cognetti de Martiis" - International Centre for Research on the Economics of Culture, Institutions, and Creativity (EBLA).
Schneider, G., Plumper, T., & Baumann, S. (2000). Bringing Putnam to the European regions – On the relevance of social capital for economic growth. *European Urban and Regional Studies, 7*(4), 307–317.
Sèraphin H., Gladkikh T., & Thanh T.V. (Eds.) (2020). Overtourism. *Causes, Implications and Solutions*. Springer Nature.
Staber, U., & Sautter, B. (2011). Who are we, and do we need to change? Cluster identity and life cycle. *Regional Studies, 45*(10), 1349–1361.
Temple, J. (1999). The new growth evidence. *Journal of Economic Literature, 37*(1), 112–156.

Chapter 7
Conclusions and Policy Considerations

7.1 The Link Cultural Heritage-Development and the Role of Traditional and Innovative Channels: Some Conclusive Remarks

The unique and extraordinary cultural heritage which European regions are endowed with represents a special and exceptional resource for societies, communities and inhabitants. Without neglecting or denying the intrinsic value that heritage carries per se with its mere presence, this work aimed at understanding and deepening the functioning of some of the channels through which the endowment of cultural heritage plays a role as an engine for local economic development. In fact, by acknowledging, respecting and appreciating the actual contribution that heritage provides as a catalyst and enhancer for local development, its conservation, preservation and valorization become more than a moral duty. Testing and demonstrating that the presence of cultural heritage acts as a generator of concrete socio-economic benefits for the local communities in which heritage is located grant a further chance for cultural heritage protection, maintenance and renovation to obtain the proper political attention and subsequent allocation of adequate dedicated resources.

To fulfill this aim, two different channels through which the endowment of cultural heritage influences local socio-economic dynamics in European regions have been analyzed adopting an economic perspective and methodology:

- directly through tourism;
- indirectly through the effects on local identitarian values.

The first channel, which is deepened and discussed in Part A of this work, is represented by tourism attractiveness. The choice of focusing on tourism demand as a channel of transmission between the presence of cultural heritage and local economic development stems from the predominant role that the economic literature has dedicated to the tourism discourse in analyzing the economic implications of cultural heritage. Even though many sectors can be related to the presence of heritage sites (such as, among others, construction, real estate, archaeology, information and

E. Panzera, *Cultural Heritage and Territorial Identity*, Advances in Spatial Science,
https://doi.org/10.1007/978-3-030-94468-1_7

communication), tourism is the most studied one and it is the only one that received autonomous relevance within the literature aimed at studying economic effects of cultural heritage. Citing from the report Cultural Heritage Counts for Europe "*Cultural heritage provides European countries and regions with a unique identity that creates compelling city narratives providing the basis for effective marketing strategies aimed at developing cultural tourism and attracting investment*" (CHCfE Consortium, 2015, p. 20) and citing from the 2018 UNWTO report titled Tourism and Culture Synergies, p. 8 "*Europe is a key cultural tourism destination thanks to its incomparable cultural heritage that includes museums, theatres, archaeological sites, historical cities and industrial sites, as well as music and gastronomy. Europe's cultural heritage enriches our lives and provides inspiration for our cultural and creative industries. By making Europe a top tourist destination, it helps generate economic growth, employment and social cohesion. The combination of culture and tourism can be a powerful driver of economic activity*" (World Tourism Organization, 2018). A work dedicated at exploring the role of cultural heritage in fostering local development cannot neglect to analyze this channel. Furthermore, the literature has not yet reached a clear position on the power of cultural heritage as an attractor of tourists and the nexus cultural heritage-tourism-economic development has been analyzed in a fragmented and disjointed way. In fact, either the role of heritage in fostering tourism demand or the economic relevance of the tourism sector have been independently explored by the economic literature. This book aimed instead at jointly analyze these relationships closing a reasoning which has been left open by the literature trying to prove that cultural heritage represents a beneficial element for tourism attractiveness which, in turn, stimulates local economic development.

A second more innovative channel, intangible and socio-cultural in nature, has been explored in Part B of this work, namely territorial identity enhancement. The theoretical assumption that has been empirically tested is that the endowment of cultural heritage reveals its effects on local economic dynamics also through socio-cultural territorial elements directly linked to the presence of heritage. More specifically, cultural heritage, because of its values, interacts with local communities shaping cultural, social and psychological attitudes of both individuals and communities, enhancing identitarian capital, creativity and, more generally, immaterial capital. All these aspects, in turn, influence and determine local potentialities of development and competitiveness. The relationship between cultural heritage and the place in which it is embedded gives rise to different schemes of development. The idea to test this assumption stems from the fact that both the literature and public institutions propose the concept that cultural heritage is a powerful engine of individual, social and political identity, of community cohesiveness and sense of place and belonging. However, these relationships are treated as exclusively socio-cultural without considering their potential economic spillovers and externalities. By the same token, when the local economic impact of the presence of cultural heritage is explored, the role of socio-cultural and immaterial characteristics is never considered in the analysis. The main idea proposed in this work is that economic effects might derive from peculiarities and traits of societies such as community participation, social cohesion and territorial identity. These territorial elements are influenced by the presence of

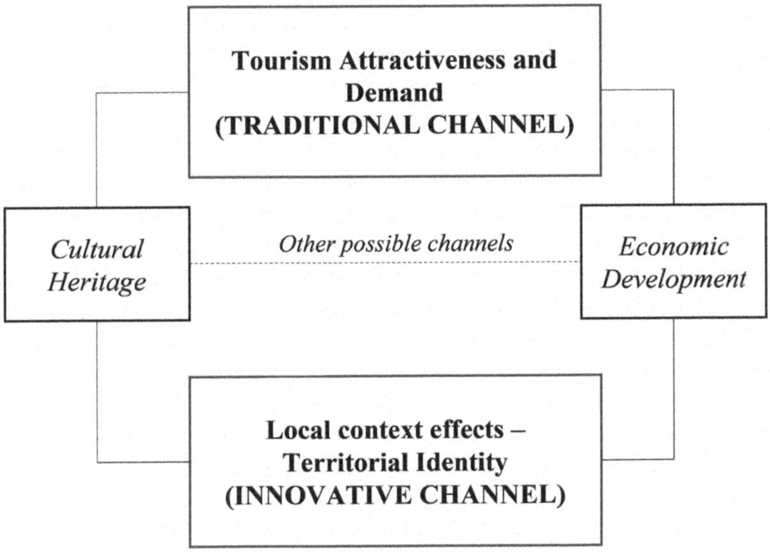

Fig. 7.1 Cultural heritage-economic development link: the proposed conceptual framework

cultural heritage and, in turn, the combination between these context socio-cultural elements and the endowment of cultural heritage affects local economic development.

The following figure (Fig. 7.1) reviews the conceptual framework proposed in the book and it is followed by a summary of the obtained results:

In Part A, Chapters 2 and 3 of this work have been dedicated at exploring the link between the endowment of cultural heritage and local economic development through a traditional channel represented by tourism attractiveness. The main aims, themes and findings of these chapters can be summarized as follows:

a. Chapter 2 is dedicated at performing a comprehensive review of the literature divided into two parts: the first section describes the literature aimed at exploring the relationship between the presence of cultural heritage and tourism attractiveness; the second section analyzes the literature that investigates the link between tourism and economic development. Besides illustrating the progresses and results obtained by these two strands of the literature, the main aim of these sections is highlighting the potential research gaps to be filled. Furthermore, Chapter 2 focuses on two recent issues directly related with tourism and cultural tourism, namely overtourism and the COVID-19 crisis which severely hit the sector.
b. Chapter 3 investigates the impact that the relationship between cultural heritage and tourism attractiveness has on local economic development. By performing a conjoint analysis of cultural heritage, tourism attractiveness and economic development (through a structural equation model methodology), it has been possible to overcome the fragmented approach proposed by the literature so far. More specifically, the results of the analysis support the logic according

to which cultural heritage attracts tourists and, in turn, this increased tourism demand positively affects local economies.

Therefore, cultural heritage plays its role in local economic development indirectly through the tourism demand channel which *mediates* the relationship between the endowment of heritage and local economic growth. Overall, being the scope of the analysis the European Union regions, it is possible to generalize the results and therefore identifying a functioning mechanism.

Part B of this work (Chapters 4, 5 and 6) has been instead dedicated at deepening the relationship between the endowment of cultural heritage and local economic dynamics through a more intangible, socio-cultural and context-related channel, namely territorial identity. Territorial identity, as an integral element of territorial capital, originates by the shared consciousness of the presence of localized specificities and values, determining at the same time the character of local communities, their sense of belonging, their pride and demand for recognition. Identification mechanisms, perceptions of common cultural or historical grounds, recognition of political institutions acquire different meanings when associated with different territorial levels. Multiple territorial identities exist, coexist and are nested within each other. Territorial identity is conceived as a potential asset of economic development, leading, as almost all immaterial elements of territorial capital, to an increase in the efficiency of traditional, material production factors. The main findings of these chapters can be summarized as follows.

c. A first innovative contribution of this Part of the work, presented in Chapter 4, is the proposal of an original taxonomy of territorial identity. More specifically, territorial identity has been interpreted as the perception of sameness felt and experienced by the inhabitants of a specific territory. In other words, all the people living in a same territory share a similarity condition that constitutes the basic requirement for territorial identity. This sameness condition can be then declined according to two main dimensions: a behavioral and a geographical dimension. The perception of being similar to a certain group can be associated with a feeling of solidarity which is present whenever a certain correspondence between private and common interests is recognized by the participating individuals. Furthermore, the fundamental feeling of sameness can be felt and experienced towards different geographical levels (e.g., the neighborhood, the city, the region, the nation, the European Union) either exclusively or simultaneously.

A classification has therefore been conceived as a consequence of different combinations of these aspects. Four typologies of territorial identities have been identified: *individualistic localism* (exclusively local territorial identity with scarce solidarity); *parochial localism (*exclusively local territorial identity with solidarity behaviors); *place-less cosmopolitanism* (simultaneously local and supra-local with scarce solidarity); *inclusive cosmopolitanism* (simultaneously local and supra-local with solidarity behaviors).

A subsequent attempt of measuring territorial identity has been carried out together with the investigation of how the four different identified typologies of territorial identity are spread across the European Union and its regions.

Eurobarometer data have been exploited and each region has been assigned with a specific typology of territorial identity. Furthermore, two timespans have been taken into consideration: the first one refers to a partial recovery from 2008 financial crisis (2012–2016) and the second one to a full recovery (2017–2018).

From the comparison of the changes in the typology of territorial identity showed by the European regions between the two periods, some interesting considerations can be made:

- overall, there is a relevant stability over time across European regions in terms of their identitarian characterization;
- a clear identitarian separation exists between localism and cosmopolitanism, and the juxtaposition between the two typologies of territorial identity represents a quasi-structural element in the identitarian realm of European regions;
- the element regarding solidarity is instead more linked to a political dimension and appears to be more precarious and more easily influenced;
- a prevalence of movements in the direction of selfish and individualistic conditions can be detected with time.

d. Chapter 5 has been dedicated at deepening the nexus between cultural heritage and territorial identity. These two elements can be easily associated being their connections and synergies tight, strong, and solid. Thanks to its symbolic power cultural heritage is a herald and a source of values that shapes and influences specific typologies of territorial identities. With its historic nature, cultural heritage represents and embodies a common past of a community and with its authenticity and social values, it witnesses and transfers common interpretations of the reality, shared wisdom, experiences and meanings. In other words, cultural heritage with its multiple and multifaceted values and peculiarities can inspire sense of belonging, attachment, affection and connection to a territory.

Chapter 5 deepens the nexus between cultural heritage and territorial identity and, more specifically, the relationship with the four identified typologies of territorial identity (*individualistic localism, parochial localism, place-less cosmopolitanism* and *inclusive cosmopolitanism*). Furthermore, by using the data gathered from Eurobarometer surveys, an econometric analysis has been performed to investigate the relationship between the endowment of cultural heritage and the four identified typologies of territorial identity. The findings indicate that:

- the presence of cultural heritage is associated with a *place-less cosmopolitan* type of territorial identity. In other words, cultural heritage can inspire sense of belonging to a wider community and generate a multicultural, flexible and cosmopolitan atmosphere;
- on the contrary, the solidarity dimension of territorial identity does not seem to be particularly influenced by the presence of tangible forms of cultural heritage. This is reasonable in the sense that cultural heritage needs to be activated to create a supportive and integrated community. Therefore, on the

one hand, the presence of heritage, through its educational, historic, symbolic and aesthetic values, instills a cosmopolitan type of attitude. On the other hand, the active use of heritage that takes place, for instance, in museums activities or in culture-led regeneration projects, is likely to be needed to animate solidarity and cooperative behaviors;

- a further interesting finding is related to the influence of cultural tourism on the four typologies of territorial identities. When the number of tourists visiting cultural heritage increases and become excessive, congestion and discomfort problems arise causing stress for local communities. The uncontrolled overtourism of cultural heritage disturbs local inhabitants forcing people to shift towards more individualistic and closed attitudes.

e. Chapter 6 deepens the analysis of the economic spillovers potentially derived from synergies between heritage and territorial identity. An empirical analysis has been performed to test the role of territorial identity in influencing the relationship between the endowment of cultural heritage and local economic development. More specifically, two different alternative logical mechanisms have been tested namely, a *mediation mechanism* and a *synergy mechanism.*

According to the *mediation mechanism,* cultural heritage generates, shapes or enhances specific typologies of territorial identity which, in turn, generates local economic development. According to a *synergy mechanism*, all the channels through which cultural heritage may affect economic development are encompassed in the analysis. The role of territorial identity is interpreted as a context element able to foster, enhance and strengthen the economic consequences stemming from the presence of cultural heritage. In other words, territorial identity, according to its specificities and peculiarities, represents a context externality able to influence the impact that cultural heritage has on local development.

The findings fully supported the functioning of a *synergy mechanism* according to which identitarian context elements synergistically reinforce the role of cultural heritage in promoting growth. Different typologies of local identity lead to different outcomes: if cultural heritage is located in a territory characterized by forms of cosmopolitanism, its role as an engine for local economic development is fully recognized, validated and effectively functioning. This effect is particularly present in the last typology of territorial identity, namely inclusive cosmopolitanism. Awareness of a certain coincidence between individual and collective interests together with a stronger feeling of European citizenship represent the most favorable conditions for a valorization of local cultural heritage. At evidence, merging cosmopolitanism and solidarity may generate positive preconditions for local attractiveness and the appropriate mentalities and capabilities for the conservation and valorization of cultural heritage.

Considering these findings, the following section is dedicated at expressing some policy issues related to conservation, preservation and valorization of cultural heritage.

7.2 The Economic Relevance of Cultural Heritage for Europe: Some Policy Considerations

7.2.1 The Relevance of Conservation, Preservation and Valorization Programs

The acknowledged relevance of cultural heritage for European citizens in terms of cultural, social, economic and environmental aspects supports the need for appropriate strategies and actions of conservation, preservation and valorization of cultural heritage. By adopting an economic perspective, this book demonstrated the economic importance of cultural heritage as an integral and essential component of the territories in which it is located, where the term *territory* is intended in its broader and comprehensive sense encompassing material and immaterial resources, systems of relationships and networks, institutions and systems of values.

In this sense, conservation, preservation and valorization activities show positive externalities and synergies with the economic territorial fabric. As highlighted by Della Torre (2010a), conservation activities inspire the ability to doubt, to learn and to innovate. In other words, the focus is shifted from the heritage as an asset to conservation activities as opportunities to increase the territorial intellectual capital. By demonstrating that cultural heritage does play a role in fostering local economic development, the relevance of preservation strategies passes from being a mere moral duty to become a forward-looking, cardinal and vital strategy for local economies. Since conservation and valorization activities of cultural heritage present high fixed costs and investments, it becomes crucial to appreciate whether these activities generate values also aside from fruition of heritage. In this sense, the findings of this book, especially the ones obtained in Part B and related to the relationships between the endowment of cultural heritage, territorial identity and local economic development, focus on cultural heritage as an endogenous competitiveness factor interacting and creating synergies with other context elements, being both a distinctive resource and a generator of development.

Because of the socio-economic relevance of cultural heritage for societies, conservation and preservation activities deserve increased attention, political priority and strategic attitudes and visions. Della Torre (2010b) talks about programmed conservation to address at a set of planned actions and activities that, in the long run, aim at preserving cultural heritage and at the same time focus on the positive externalities of the conservation process on local communities and local economies. Within the context of programmed conservation, conservation itself, rather than being just related to punctual restoration activities, it is considered and recognized as a long run means for generating values, catalyzing networking, fostering cognitive innovation and enhancing territorial identity. And, as highlighted by the results of this book, the synergies between the endowment of cultural heritage and specific territorial, context or atmosphere characteristics are fundamental for the role and relevance of cultural heritage in local economies. By adopting a programmed approach to conservation, according to which both large-scale risks mitigation and daily-care activities related to cultural heritage are simultaneously performed and planned, a greater focus on positive externalities stemming from these conservation activities is reached. By increasing quality, rewarding competences, by associating education and participation projects to conservation activities, by developing networks between firms, research centers and territories, programmed conservation allows to fully appreciate and realize both the main objective of conservation and its externalities. Furthermore, as highlighted in Amoeda et al. (2018), it has to be noted that the context surrounding the heritage site is a fundamental component of its conservation strategy and, therefore, deserves full consideration.

It has to be remarked that high costs are associated to these conservation-related activities and a still scarce actual political priority characterizes cultural heritage. At the same time, the acknowledged importance of cultural heritage in both cultural, social, economic and environmental domains calls for the need to preserve and valorize this resource. Citing from Boniotti (2016, p. 9), "*given that the public financing is not sufficient to support conservation costs, the general objective is addressed to reflect upon the different and innovative ways to perform the preservation and enhancement of built heritage and to focus upon other possible solutions, connecting conservation to valorization*". Possible proposed solutions refer, for instance, to the adoption of new business models in which the private sector is involved in conservation and valorization activities through Public–Private Partnerships. As suggested by the European Commission in 2015, *the private sector should be incentivized to get involved through instruments such as tax breaks, differentiated VAT rates, well designed grant or loan programmes, public private partnerships (PPP) schemes, rights releases,* etc. *It should generally create more of an environment encouraging the private sector to invest in cultural heritage*" (European Commission, 2015, p. 8). However, the risk that private actors are focused on the short time for payback is real and needs to be prevented.

Stemming from the Horizon 2020 project named "*CLIC – Circular models Leveraging Investments in Cultural heritage adaptive reuse*" (Clic Consortium, 2020) a Taskforce on circular models for cultural heritage adaptive reuse in cities and regions has been established with the aim of creating a trans-disciplinary community of researchers and professionals that identifies, explores and analyzes innovative circular business and financial models *"to place cultural heritage adaptive reuse at the forefront for the implementation of a European model of circular economy and circular city-region centered on the adaptive reuse and regeneration of cultural and natural capital"* (https://www.clicproject.eu/taskforce/). Both the results of this book and these new initiatives confirm the relevance of cultural heritage as a founding element of territorial and community identity and as an engine for development which is local in the resources, global in the relations and self-sustainable in the modalities (circular economy, circular city-region and adaptive reuse). As highlighted in Fusco Girard and Gravagnuolo (2017), synergies in the business/financial sectors, in the cultural, institutional and social domains are the basis of a circular economy model and can be supported and achieved through innovative public–private partnerships specifically meant for the management of public goods. The implementation of this model requires actions at different levels, namely a macro level (which refers to governmental actions), a micro level (which refers to single actors involved in the model) and a meso level (which refers to the relationships and synergies between territorial actors). Besides, new and innovative tools should be used to support conservation and valorization processes such as digital surveying (see for instance Amoeda et al., 2018).

Therefore, the governance of cultural heritage involves both public and private actors as well as both national and supranational institutions. Besides, international institutions and civil society are considered as central actors in cultural heritage governance. Since the analyses performed in this book have encompassed the whole European Union, the following section is dedicated at providing an overview of the policies that the EU has carried out regarding heritage conservation and valorization.

7.2.2 Cultural Heritage Policies at the European Union Level

Even though culture and cultural heritage are competencies that lie with the 28 (now 27) member states, the European Union acts as a supporting supranational actor. According to the Treaty of Functioning of the European Union (TFEU—Article 6c), the EU has the power to support, coordinate and complement national actions. As well explained by Lähdesmäki (2016), the key political actors involved in the governance of cultural heritage are the European Commission, the European Parliament, the Council of the European Union and the Committee of Regions. In particular, the Council of Europe adopted three fundamental Conventions: the European Cultural Convention in 1954, which states in page 1 that "*Each Contracting Party shall take appropriate measures to safeguard and to encourage the development of its national contribution to the common cultural heritage of Europe*" (Council of Europe, 1954), the European Convention on Landscape which aim was to create an obligation to protect, plan and manage landscape and the Framework Convention on the Value of Cultural Heritage for Society (Faro Convention) which clearly speaks about a common heritage of Europe and encourages the States to "*recognize the value of cultural heritage situated on territories under their jurisdiction, regardless of its origin*" (Council of Europe, 2005, Article 5). Furthermore, the Faro Convention supports the idea of an individual and common responsibility in heritage conservation, preservation and valorization and the need to involve multiple actors in the decision-making processes, especially the local community. More recently, following the initiative of the European Year of Cultural Heritage launched in 2018, the Council of the European Union wrote the Work Plan for Culture 2019–2022 (Council of the European Union, 2018; European Commission, 2018) and the European Commission introduced a set of 60 actions in the European Framework for Action on Cultural Heritage (for a comprehensive overview of the multi-level governance of cultural heritage see Garzillo et al., 2018). As argued in Lähdesmäki (2016), the policies put in place by the European Union are also largely devoted at granting rewarding labels and awards to sites (for instance through the European Heritage Days, the European

Capital of Culture program, the European Heritage Label, the EU Heritage Prize, the EU Prize for Contemporary Architecture or Mies van der Rohe Award).

It can be noted that the main objective behind official documents, conventions, awards and, in general, European policies dedicated at cultural heritage are the recognition, appreciation and promotion of a common and shared European cultural heritage. More specifically, as highlighted by both Lähdesmäki (2016) and Sassatelli (2002), by promoting a collective European heritage, the EU treats it as a powerful symbol able to create and foster a European identity not only based on bureaucratic or economic legitimizing elements but also, and especially, on culture, shared past and common memories and values. Citing from Sassatelli (2002, p. 436), "*European cultural policy is conceived, even more self-consciously than at other levels, as an instrument to build a cultural identity for the Europe of the European Union. [...] The Europe referred to by the EU can be envisaged as an imagined community in the making*". The European Union recognizes the potentialities of cultural heritage to develop and shape a thick territorial identity rather than a thin one. Apart from the identitarian role of cultural heritage, other benefits stemming from its endowment are acknowledged by the European Union such as its role in fostering inclusiveness, cohesiveness, distinctiveness and development of European Union's territories. As proposed by Thatcher (2019, pp. 585–586) and as reported by the European Commission, cultural heritage is recognized to have "*a dual nature, being on the one hand an economic good that offers important opportunities for the creation of wealth and employment, and, on the other, a vehicle of identities, values and meanings that mirror and shape our societies*" (European Commission, 2014, paragraph 72).

However, as highlighted throughout the book and as confirmed by the empirical results, the synergies and interrelations between the endowment of cultural heritage and territorial identity do have economic effects that need to be considered when dealing with policies related to cultural heritage. This dual nature of heritage should be overtaken to allow and support cultural heritage to express all its potentialities.

Because cultural heritage is a common and public good that suffers from market failure problems and because of its fundamental values for different domains (cultural, social, environmental and economic), it needs to be safeguarded and promoted through systems of governance that allow the dialogue among diverse actors, starting from local communities, passing through national states and the European Union, arriving to international organizations. It is not to be taken for granted that the benefits stemming from the presence of cultural heritage and the mechanisms that allow the functioning of a relationship between the endowment of heritage and local development do not interfere with each other. Considering the findings of this book, cultural heritage plays a role on local development both by attracting more tourists and presenting synergies with different typologies of territorial identity. The following section will be dedicated at deepening some potential interferences of the uncontrolled interactions between the two channels.

7.2.3 *Tourism and Territorial Identity: Synergy But also Contradiction*

The roles that tourism and territorial identity have in mediating and enhancing the potential economic implications of the endowment of cultural heritage have been separately discussed throughout the book. However, some considerations are due on the likely interrelations between tourism attractiveness and territorial identity.

Special attention must be paid to the potentially dangerous downsides and consequences of mass tourism for both heritage conservation and local communities well-being and sense of belonging. Citing from the OECD report on Tourism Trends and Policies 2020 "*Continued [tourism] growth is causing pressure on infrastructure, the environment, local communities, other economic sectors, and wider society. When unchecked, this growth can lead to significant impacts on sensitive cultural heritage and environmental sites, as well as the day-to-day lives of residents, often resulting in negative perceptions or even resentment towards tourists and tourism more broadly*" (OECD, 2020a, p. 90).

As highlighted in Pasquinelli and Trunfio (2020), three main issues have been identified since the 1970s related to overtourism, namely growing visitor numbers and temporal and spatial concentration; tourist behavior which impacts destination quality of life; and changes to the physical environment (e.g., exploitation of natural resources, touristification). In more recent years, the displacement of residents from the urban residential areas caused by rental platforms has as well emerged as a consequence of mass tourism. Undeniably, tourism carries potentialities and opportunities for destinations. However, neglecting to recognize the risks of overexploitation might neutralize the advantages leading to a "vicious cycle" especially if we are dealing with cultural tourism. As highlighted in Russo (2002, p. 168) "*the quality of the experience enjoyed [...] deteriorates with the physical stress imposed by tourism, with declining quality of environment where the act of consumption takes place, and with the quality of the auxiliary facilities*". Several indications have been proposed to guarantee tourism sustainability such as supporting evidence-based decision making, strengthening sustainability policies and partnerships, diversifying to sustainable products and services, creating and marketing alternative tourism products, improving infrastructures (OECD, 2020a; Pasquinelli & Trunfio, 2020).

Being aware of whether or not the endowment of tangible forms of cultural heritage is a relevant determinant of tourism attractiveness plays a fundamental role in the subsequent definition of policies and strategies aimed at planning and controlling both cultural tourism and conservation and valorization interventions. At the same time, as explained in Pracchi (2017), being aware that culture includes artefacts, goods, technical processes, ideas, habits and values that are socially passed down and therefore part of social heritage, should prevent from exploiting heritage as an exclusively touristic good.

As highlighted by the Franceschini Commission, the concept of "*culturally relevant good*" includes those heritage sites and resources that are able to represent and embody the heritage of a community rather than an important artistic expression or an object with a specific archaeological value. In this sense, the most relevant attribute of cultural heritage is not its value per se but its relationship with the community and with the sense that the community attributes to it (Pracchi, 2017).

It is also relevant to mention that the chosen narrative keys associated with heritage reflect the messages that are considered worth to pass down. The way in which cultural heritage is communicated should be linked to and aimed at transferring relevant messages in a conceptual framework such as the visitor can acknowledge and internalize. In this sense, special attention must be paid to the relationship between tourism and territorial identity when policies aimed at regulating and fostering touristic activities are put in place. On the one hand, an increased flow of tourists linked with cultural heritage might be beneficial to the local community by supporting the local economy and by fostering a sense of pride. On the other hand, overtourism phenomena might disturb the local inhabitants that may be forced to move out from their places of living. In this case, the meaning attributed to heritage does also change resulting in a touristification or dysneyfication effect. Citing from Fainstein (2007, p. 8) "*Most tourist-historic cities have engaged in very conscious marketing, in order to attract visitors and have changed the nature of their attraction*".

Both national, European and international policies should be devoted at assuring the right balance between usage and conservation of heritage and between tourism attractiveness and respect for local territorial identities and communities.

7.3 Perspectives for Further Research

Cultural heritage represents a complex and multifaceted resource that, with its multiple values, attributes, meanings and interpretations gives rise to endless benefits and impacts for societies, communities and individuals. Studying and exploring the field of cultural heritage is a surprisingly vast and extensive endeavor even when the perspective is limited to the economic one. In fact, several research possibilities stem from the results obtained in this book. Starting from the faith and confidence that future research will be supported by more comprehensive, detailed and accurate data related to the field of cultural heritage, considering the role that intangible forms of cultural heritage have on economic development, and discovering which mechanisms make this relationship work, is a first potential line of future research.

Another interesting research idea is linked to the investigation and exploration of other intangible, context elements that might catalyze the relationship between cultural heritage and local development. It would be extremely interesting, for instance, to find out which is the role that cultural participation or continuity of cultural life have on economic development. Another interesting aspect is related to the different effects that derive from diverse typologies of cultural heritage. It would be for instance interesting to empirically test how differently heritage sites, museums, cultural events or cultural-led regeneration projects affect economic dynamics and through which specific mechanism.

Even though diverse lines of future research are desirable and stimulating, one of the main problems related to quantitative and empirical analysis on cultural heritage is the lack of comprehensive, reliable and coherent data at fine disaggregation levels and comparable across country. More effort, research and political interest should be devoted at facing this issue to come up with a complete and exhaustive cultural database.

By the time of accomplishing this book, the European countries, together with the whole world, are facing the second wave of the Covid-19 pandemic which is drastically changing dynamics, habits and certainties of our systems. The cultural heritage sector has been hardly hit by this crisis that led societies to an unprecedented lockdown of people, activities and economies. In this context, heritage sites have been completely shut down and investments directed to cultural heritage have been postponed. Cultural tourism has also been strongly impacted by the outbreak of the pandemic and millions of cultural professionals have been threatened. However, as highlighted by the UNWTO, tourism and culture sectors can transform the crisis in an opportunity to create new partnerships and collaborations, innovative ways of fruition (mainly linked to digital advancements, new technologies and media) and develop new skills. In this sense several initiatives are proposed that goes toward this direction namely, improve information and data exchange between sectors, launch innovative alliances, inspire a more sustainable future for both culture, cultural heritage and cultural tourism, form a more resilient tourism and culture workforce, strengthen governance structure for better coordination and information sharing and attract new audience (https://www.unwto.org/cultural-tourism-covid-19).

As highlighted in the 2020 OECD report "Culture shock: COVID-19 and the cultural and creative sectors", cities and regions can benefit from the creative potential of culture to recover from the COVID-19 crisis. Citing from the report, "*…cities and regions may consider cultural and creative sectors as well as cultural participation as a driver of social impact in its own right and throughout the economy. The sector is already an economic driver and source of innovation. In many cities and regions, specialization in the cultural and creative sectors are evolving and being used to tackle competitive and societal challenges from new angles, favoring resilience, skills creation and prosocial behavioral changes. In the recovery, there is an opportunity […] to reconsider growth models moving away from culture-based large-scale tourism towards models fostering cross-innovation between cultural and creative sectors and traditional manufacturing and services that can be incorporated into creative tourism programmes. […] The contribution of culture can also be important in other areas of local development, from rebuilding public trust to contributing to post-pandemic urban design adapted to social distancing rules*" (OECD, 2020b, p. 4).

Now more than ever cultural heritage should perform a fundamental role and should be put at the center of recovery strategies catching up all its essential values for communities, nations, regions and inhabitants and exploiting all its potentialities for local reconstruction and development.

References

Amoeda, R, Lira, S., Pinheiro, C., Santiago Zaragoza, J. M., Calvo Serrano, J., & Garcia Carrillo F. (Eds.). (2018), *Heritage 2018—Proceedings of the* 6th *International Conference on Heritage and Sustainable Development—10*th *Anniversary Edition—Volume 2*, Granada and Barcelos: Editorial Universidad de Granada and Green Lines Institute for Sustainable Development.

Boniotti, C. (2016). *Innovative Funding and Management Models for a Sustainable Development of Public Cultural Heritage.* In J. Železná, P. Hájek, J. Tywoniak, A. Lupíšek & K. Sojková (Eds.), *YRSB16—iiSBE forum of young researchers in sustainable building 2016*. Czech Technical University in Prague.

CHCfE Consortium. (2015). *Cultural heritage counts for Europe.* http://blogs.encatc.org/culturalheritagecountsforeurope//wp-content/uploads/2015/06/CHCfE_FULL-REPORT_v2.pdf, [29/10/2020].

Clic Consortium. (2020). *Clic project—Circular models leveraging investments in cultural heritage adaptive reuse.* https://www.clicproject.eu/

Council of Europe. (1954). *European cultural convention* (Paris 1954). https://rm.coe.int/CoERMPublicCommonSearchServices/DisplayDCTMContent?documentId=090000168006457e, [26/11/2020].

Council of Europe. (2005). *Council of Europe framework convention on the value of cultural heritage for society.* https://rm.coe.int/CoERMPublicCommonSearchServices/DisplayDCTMContent?documentId=0900001680083746, [29/10/2020].

Council of the European Union. (2018). *Council conclusions on the work plan for culture 2019–2022.* https://eur-lex.europa.eu/legal-content/EN/TXT/PDF/?uri=CELEX:52018XG1221%2801%29, [26/11/2020].

Della Torre, S. (2010a). *Conservazione programmata: i risvolti economici di un cambio di paradigm. Il capitale culturale, I*, 47–55.

Della Torre, S. (2010b). *Economics of planned conservation.* In M. Malkki & K. Schmidt-Thome (Eds.), *Integrating aims—Built heritage in social and economic development* (pp. 143–157). Centre for Urban and Regional Studies Publications.

European Commission. (2014). *Communication towards and integrated approach to cultural heritage for Europe.* Brussels: COM (2014) 477 final.

European Commission. (2015). *Getting cultural heritage to work for Europe.* https://op.europa.eu/en/publication-detail/-/publication/b01a0d0a-2a4f-4de0-88f7-85bf2dc6e004, [29/10/2020].

European Commission. (2018). *A new European agenda for culture*, [22/10/2021].

Fainstein, S. S. (2007). *Tourism and the commodification of urban culture. The Urban Reinventors, 2*, 1–20.

Fusco Girard, L., & Gravagnuolo, A. (2017). *Circular economy and cultural heritage/landscape regeneration. Circular business, financing and governance governance models for a competitive Europe. BDC—Bollettino del Centro Calza Bini—Università degli Studi di Napoli Federico II, 17*(1), 35–53.

Garzillo, C., Gravagnuolo, A., & Ragozino, S. (2018). Circular governance models for cultural heritage adaptive reuse: the experimentation of Heritage Innovation Partnerships. *Urbanistica Informazioni*, special issue.

Lähdesmäki, T. (2016). Politics of tangibility, intangibility, and place in the making of a European cultural heritage in EU heritage policy. *International Journal of Heritage Studies, 22*(10), 766–780.

OECD. (2020a). *OECD tourism trends and policies 2020.* https://www.oecd.org/cfe/tourism/oecd-tourism-trends-and-policies-20767773.htm, [20/11/2020].

OECD. (2020b). *Culture shock: COVID-19and the cultural and creative sectors.* https://read.oecd-ilibrary.org/view/?ref=135_135961-nenh9f2w7a&title=Culture-shock-COVID-19-and-the-cultural-and-creative-sectors, [26/11/2020].

Pasquinelli, C., & Trunfio, M. (2020). Overtouristified cities: An online news media narrative analysis. *Journal of Sustainable Tourism, 28*(11), 1805–1824.

Pracchi, V. N. (2017). *La 'domanda' o il 'bisogno' di fruizione dei beni culturali*. In D. Fiorani (Ed.), *RICerca/REStauro. Sezione 4. Valorizzazione e gestione delle informazioni*. A cura di Renata Prescia (pp. 857–865). Edizioni Quasar.

Russo A. P. (2002). *The "vicious cycle" of tourism development in heritage cities*. *Annals of Tourism Research, 29*(1),165–182.

Sassatelli, M. (2002). Imagined Europe—The shaping of a European cultural identity through EU cultural policy. *European Journal of Social Theory, 5*(4), 435–451.

Thatcher, M. (2019). *Direct and market governance paths for the creation of an EU political identity: cultural heritage policy*. *Comparative European Politics, 17*, 585–602.

World Tourism Organization. (2018). *Tourism and culture synergies*. https://www.e-unwto.org/doi/book/10.18111/9789284418978, [20/11/2020].

The manufacturer's authorised representative in the EU is Springer Nature Customer Service Centre GmbH, Europaplatz 3, 69115 Heidelberg, Germany. If you have any concerns regarding our products, please contact ProductSafety@springernature.com

Printed and bound by CPI Group (UK) Ltd, Croydon, CR0 4YY
22/09/2026
02221055-0001